John Cornwell

Powers of Darkness
Powers of Light

Travels in Search of the
Miraculous and the Demonic

VIKING

VIKING

Published by the Penguin Group
Penguin Books Ltd, 27 Wrights Lane, London W8 5TZ, England
Penguin Books USA Inc., 375 Hudson Street, New York, New York, 10014, USA
Penguin Books Australia Ltd, Ringwood, Victoria, Australia
Penguin Books Canada Ltd, 10 Alcorn Avenue, Toronto, Ontario, Canada M4V 3B2
Penguin Books (NZ) Ltd, 182–190 Wairau Road, Auckland 10, New Zealand

Penguin Books Ltd, Registered Offices: Harmondsworth, Middlesex, England

First published 1991
1 3 5 7 9 10 8 6 4 2

The extract from *The Dream of the Rood* on pp. 282–3
is taken from *The Norton Anthology of English
Literature*, vol.1, W. W. Norton & Co., Inc., New York.
Grateful acknowledgement is made to the publishers.

Filmset in 12/14½ pt Lasercomp Sabon
Printed in England by Clays Ltd, St Ives plc

A CIP catalogue record for this book is available from the British Library

ISBN 0–670–82103–9

for
Tobias Wolff

CONTENTS

Contents

Contents

List of Illustrations

List of Illustrations

Every effort has been made to contact all copyright holders. The publisher would be interested to hear from any copyright holder not here fully acknowledged.

Acknowledgements

I owe special thanks to Dan Grisewood and Philip Caraman, who encouraged me to write this book from the outset. My debt to the many people who helped me on my journey will be apparent in the text, and I thank them all.

For their willingness to talk around the topic, I am grateful to Aelred Burrows, Tim Bliss, Audrey Charlton, Bryan Chestle, Don Cupitt, Dr St John Dowling, Eamonn Duffy, Jack Finnegan, Charlie Glass, John Heilpern, Dennis Hickley, Jo Klein, Emma Loveridge, Gerald O'Collins, Chris Rowland, Janet Martin Soskice, Frank Sullivan, Michael Walsh and John Wilkins.

Cyprian Smith's *The Way of Paradox* and Nicholas Lash's *Easter in Ordinary* were crucial sources of inspiration.

My mother, Kathleen Cornwell, gave invaluable moral support, as did my wife Gabrielle, my daughter Johanna and my son Jonathan. Thanks are also due to John Harvey, who read the manuscript, and to Clare Bayley and Matthew Lohn, who gave practical assistance.

I am grateful to the rector and staff of the Venerable English College in Rome for hospitality and conversation.

I completed the book in ideal circumstances at Jesus College, Cambridge, under its professional fellow-commoner scheme; I wish to thank the Fellows of Jesus for their kindness and generosity.

Finally, I must thank Bob Lescher, Carol Smith, Susan Suffes, Judith Flanders, John Guest and Peter Carson.

Then my delivered soul herself shall learn
A darker knowledge and in hatred turn
From every thought of God mankind has had.
Thought is a garment and the soul's a bride
That cannot in that trash and tinsel hide:
Hatred of God may bring the soul to God.

W. B. Yeats

Graham Greene's Time-gap Mystery

A year or so before his death, I was sent by a newspaper to Antibes to interview Graham Greene.

He greeted me at the door of his apartment with a mischievous smile of anticipation. We had agreed to talk about religious belief.

His living room was modest: just enough space for a cane sofa and matching armchairs; a table covered with a simple cloth served as a desk. There were shelves with rows of meticulously displayed books, many of them theological – among them, the distinctive covers of the works of Father Hans Küng.

Our conversation was to range over a number of religious issues. Greene had often been at variance with his Church on matters such as birth-control, Papal infallibility and liberation theology; but the longer we talked, the more he surprised me by proving himself a free thinker on every subject that was raised.

At one point we were talking about sin.

'I've always rather disliked the word sin,' he said. 'It's got a kind of professional, a dogmatic ring about it.'

'Do you believe in Satan?' I asked him.

He smiled wanly. 'No, I don't think so.'

'Do you believe in angels?'

A chuckle. 'No, I don't really.'

1

This led to the obvious question: 'So, what about a future life?'

He paused. He was gazing at me; his bright, cornflower-blue eyes were disconcerting in the light of the morning sun.

'I would love to believe in it,' he said. 'And one would like to let it be more than this world.'

'Do you believe in hell?'

'I don't believe in hell. I never have believed in hell. I think it's contradictory. They say that God is mercy, so it's contradictory. I think there may be nullity, and for others something that is conscious. But I don't believe in hell and I feel that purgatory may happen in this life, not in a future life.'

'And heaven?'

'I can't conceive what heaven could be. If it exists it's an entity I can't visualize in any way. My idea of heaven would be that it would be something active, rather than happiness with people one had loved, a form of activity in which we could influence life on earth . . . perhaps one's prayers in that state could influence somebody on earth.'

'What about God?' I said.

He fell silent. He just sat there, his eyes looking strange, shifty, haunted.

'Do you contemplate God in a pure, disembodied way?' I asked.

'I'm afraid I don't,' he said flatly.

We moved on, eventually to skirt around the question of rational basis for belief or unbelief.

For a brief moment Greene looked down unsmilingly into his lap. Then he began to chuckle breathily with raised shoulders. 'That reminds me of Freddy Ayer,' he said. 'You know, the atheistic philosopher. He always said that given just half an hour he would convince me that there was absolutely nothing.'

'Did you ever take him up on that?'

'No. It would have bored me,' he said with some feeling.

'Your faith,' I said at last, 'is nevertheless tenuous.'

'One is attracted to the faith,' he said. 'Believing is the problem. But in a curious way I've always believed that doubt was a more important thing for human beings. It's human to doubt.'

'So what is it that keeps you within the fold of belief?'

He turned, fixing me with a look that announced an imminent ace.

'I suppose,' he chuckled, 'that I've been lucky enough to doubt my disbelief.'

Just as I was wondering where we could go from there, he said, 'I am able to doubt my disbelief because I once had a very slight mystical experience. In 1949 I travelled out to Italy to see a famous mystic known as Padre Pio. He lived in a remote monastery in the Gargano Peninsula at a place called San Giovanni Rotondo. He had the stigmata, displaying the wounds of Christ in his hands, feet and side. At this time my belief in God had been on the ebb; I think I was losing my faith. I went out of curiosity. I was wondering whether this man, whom I had heard so much of, would impress me. I stopped in Rome on the way and a monsignor from the Vatican came to have a drink with me. "Oh!" he said, "that holy fraud! You're wasting your time. He's bogus."' Greene looked up at me challengingly.

'But Padre Pio had been examined by doctors of every faith and no faith,' he went on. 'He'd been examined by Jewish, Protestant, Catholic and atheist specialists, and baffled them all. He had these wounds on his hands and feet, the size of twenty-pence pieces, and because he was not allowed to wear gloves saying Mass he pulled his sleeves down to try and hide them. He'd got a very nice, peasant-like face, a little bit on the heavy side. I was warned that his was a very long Mass; so I went with my woman friend of that period to the Mass at 5.30 in the morning. He said it in Latin, and I thought that thirty-five minutes had passed. Then when I got outside the church I looked at my watch and it had been two hours .'

Greene stopped for a moment as if to gauge my reaction.

'I couldn't work out where the lost time had gone,' he went on. 'And this is where I came to a small faith in a mystery. Because that *did* seem an extraordinary thing.'

He sat for a while in reverie. Then he took a well-worn wallet from his trouser pocket and fished out two small photographs. They were sepia, dog-eared. As he handed them over I detected a faint air of self-consciousness; as if, English gentleman that he was, he had been caught out in a gesture of Latin superstition. One depicted Padre Pio in his habit, smiling. The other showed the monk gazing adoringly at the host during Mass. The possession of the pictures, the gesture of sharing them, seemed a declaration of loyalty to faith.

'Why do you keep them in your wallet like that?' I asked.

'I don't know why I put them in my pocket,' he said. He looked a trifle haunted. 'I just put them in, and I've never taken them out.'

I decided to press him a little further. 'If you hadn't had your mysterious experience with Padre Pio might you possibly have lost your faith?'

'I don't think my belief is very strong; but, yes, perhaps I would have lost it altogether . . .'

'So what, in the final analysis,' I said, 'does religion mean to you?'

Greene looked at me directly, wonderingly. He seemed at that moment ageless; there was an impression about him of extraordinary tolerance, ripeness.

'I think . . . it's a mystery,' he said slowly and with some

4

feeling. 'There *is* a mystery. There is something inexplicable in life. And it's important because people are not going to believe in all the explanations given by science or even the Churches . . . It's a mystery which can't be destroyed . . .'

There was a time when Greene's remarks might have struck me as superficial, characteristic of a tendency to settle for a 'God of the gaps', a God of missing explanations. For how could anybody propose that a meaningful religious faith could be based on anything so shallow, so haphazardly procurable and ephemeral as a sense of time contraction?

As it was I found the story of his 'small faith in a mystery' both moving and deeply significant, and not a little coincidental, for at the time of our meeting I had been travelling for a year in search of the scope and meaning of the paranormal element in religion. In the course of my journey I had traversed a varied landscape of alleged prodigies, miracles, mysteries, signs and wonders, and encountered many people on the way who had tasted the mysterious in their struggles with belief and unbelief, including, even, the atheist philosopher A. J. Ayer and the remarkable, if by then ghostly, Padre Pio.

By the time I met Greene I had learnt enough to understand that a 'small faith in a mystery' is not the culminating discovery of religious conviction so much as an unexpected trigger for the tussle between doubt and 'doubt of doubt', which often runs its course only to return to its starting point. Who could doubt that Graham Greene of all people was familiar with the restless, circular nature of such a struggle?

In this sense my interview with Greene was both a suitable end to my geographical journey and a fitting prelude to this book, which tells the story of a quest for faith that is both a process of discovery and a returning.

PART ONE

Small Mysteries

1   An American Dream

Several years ago, while travelling in the United States, I experienced a small mystery in the form of a religious dream that was fulfilled within a few days in waking reality. Although this event was unnerving, like having someone else's hand thrust in one's pocket, I now realize that there was nothing unique about it. The unusual aspect is that I was an unbeliever as far as religion was concerned, although twenty-five years earlier I had abandoned, after seven years' study, a vocation to the Catholic priesthood.

So when I decided as a result of that dream to explore the incidence and the significance of the wider realms of paranormal religious phenomena of this sort, I was able to approach the subject from the standpoint of an agnostic investigator who had once been on intimate terms with a religion rich in supernatural and mystical lore.

Throughout my working life as a newspaper executive, which had involved periods as a foreign correspondent and foreign editor, I had frequently reflected that religion lent legitimacy to much of the world's violence and misery. It seemed to me that religion would have something to recommend it if only humanity could act upon the belief that we are all equal in the sight of God; but I saw no evidence that religionists *en masse* were capable of putting this crucial profession of faith into practice. I was a cynic, with all the

9

knowing certitude of one who has had a bellyful of religion.

So it never occurred to me that after twenty-five years of confident agnosticism I could, in the space of several days, become obsessed with a religious dream experience. And the reader may wonder what kind of dream it was that could have produced such a reaction.

It all began in New York City, where I had arrived from London on a publishing trip that was to take me 3,000 miles through the United States. On that first night, in a hotel in midtown Manhattan, I went to bed exhausted with jet-lag and fell into a deep sleep. The context of the dream I had that night was remote from any of my professional preoccupations, or my role as a husband and father. And yet, it seemed to illuminate in a mysterious way my entire life:

I am walking in the garden of what appears to be a college campus, with a range of low, red-brick buildings in the distance. The sun is shining in a bright blue sky. The air is clean, cold and sweet. Beyond the buildings the tops of tall trees wave slightly in the breeze, the foliage gold, silver and scarlet. The place is unfamiliar, and yet there is a sense of sacred presence mixed with nostalgia and melancholy.

There is a pathway bordered by recently planted shrubs. Young men dressed in black robes are approaching in twos and threes. They are contemporaries of my seminary days, and yet their faces glow with youth and innocence. This is all the more painful as I am aware that I have aged by comparison; I feel ashamed of my appearance, conscious of my sins, convinced that I will be condemned and rejected.

To my relief, however, the first two figures acknowledge me cheerfully. I begin to experience an overwhelming sense of grief, as if for lost happiness; a sense of having returned to where I belong.

When I woke the next morning I had the impression that the dream had recurred a number of times during the night. The pillow was wet.

After a morning of business appointments I set out in a hired car to drive to Philadelphia. That night I had the dream once more, every detail identical with the dream of the previous night: the sense of sacred presence; the young men in black – the apparent contemporaries of my youth – greeting me; the sense of loss.

The dream continued to recur, night after night, as I drove on down through Baltimore, Washington DC and on to Atlanta, a blur of newspaper offices, filling stations, fast-food restaurants. The dream sequence finally came to an end in New Orleans. I checked into a Howard Johnson Motel; after dark I went out to look for a restaurant. I walked several blocks, then lost my bearings; the streets were deserted and ill-lit, but I had no sense of danger until I found myself in the open space of a car park adjoining the rear of the Hyatt Hotel complex. The building was perhaps 200 yards away; I had begun to head briskly across the lot towards the hotel, remembering as I did so that I had $2,000 in traveller's cheques in my pocket, when I heard a voice somewhere to my left:

'Hey man, can we talk with you?'

Four young men emerged from behind a car about fifty yards away. One appeared to be carrying a wrench. In an instant I took off, sprinting on my toes. As they came after me I could hear their curses, the sound of their soles on the gravel lot. Ahead was a system of wire security cages and a staff entrance. I was convinced I was going to die. I was thinking: 'God, please spare me and I'll believe in you!' The men were no more than a few yards behind me, and one had already punched me on the shoulder, when I seemed to be swept forward and away from them with incredible speed. I stormed through a doorway and collapsed in front of an armed security guard. As I passed out I saw the young men in black in my dream coming towards me with all the vividness of waking reality, as if they were now mixed with my attackers.

I eventually returned to my hotel in a taxi and went straight to bed. That night I slept soundly and, for the first time for many nights, dreamlessly.

Next morning I wondered whether the series of dreams had not given me some sort of psychic energy and readiness. This was a vague, illogical feeling, not so much connected with the dream's content as a sense that during the previous two weeks I had somehow been in an unusual psychic state of expectation, a feeling of being affected by a presence or power.

I did not give my bargain with God another thought.

I flew to St Louis, where I hired another car, and checked into a Holiday Inn on Route 55. On Sunday morning a week after the mugging attempt I got up early, planning to spend the day touring some of the townships along the Mississippi. The road was empty, sparkling with ground frost and sunlight. After twenty minutes a white circular church like a stranded spacecraft came into view, and I felt an urge to go inside. I parked the car and entered the building by a ramp.

A service had been recently performed and shafts of sunlight penetrated the tentacles of incense smoke that lingered above the high altar. The exotic scent was entrancing but I felt panicky and hot. I went out of the nearest exit, but being a circular church it was not the door by which I had entered. I burst from the building in a state of nervous excitement. Outside the air was cold, fresh, autumnal. I looked about me and my heart was immediately suspended with terror.

Ahead were pathways and lawns bordered by low, red-brick buildings beyond which stirred the tops of tall trees in their fall glory – silver, gold and crimson.

I had stepped into my dream, of this I had not the slightest doubt.

Ahead was the door through which the young men in black should emerge. Appalled by a sense of inevitability I stood paralysed on the pathway for several minutes. Then the door opened and a small old man with pure white hair came out. I almost laughed at the bathos of the sight. He was dressed from head to toe in the black habit of a Benedictine monk. He limped very slowly along the path and as he drew level he stopped.

'Where am I?' I asked.

'St Louis Abbey,' he said in a clear English accent. Then he added with a bleak smile: 'I have to set off early because I'm so lame. I'd stop for a chat, but I mustn't be late for prayers.'

He made a gesture of farewell and shuffled away. As he entered the church a bell rang somewhere in the building ahead and I continued to stand on the pathway.

After a minute or two the door opened once more; first one monk, then two, then three, began to spill out of the building to hurry along the pathway on their way to the church. They came in order of age, the youngest first. With their shorn heads and ascetic features they had a common stamp of appearance. As they passed by none spoke, but they all gave a brief nod – as if of recognition.

A dozen or so monks passed along the pathway, and after the last one had gone I followed them to the door of the church. I did not enter; I stood outside listening to the sound of plainchant echoing in that strange, space-age building.

*

This is not the place to describe the serenity, the healing quality of Benedictine hospitality. I spent a day and a night with the monks of St Louis Abbey, eating with them as a guest in their refectory and enjoying their company in the common room. This small monastery was founded in the mid-1960s by the English Benedictines of Ampleforth Abbey in Yorkshire and, as if to further confirm the prognostication of the dream, I was to find among them several contemporaries of my student days who had been permanently transplanted from England to America's Midwest.

It seemed clear to me as I sat among them that I had been confronted with a peculiar intellectual and emotional challenge. The million-to-one coincidence with my past in a suburb of St Louis would have been extraordinary enough; but the foreshadowing dreams gave the episode a 'miraculous' quality.

As I drove away from the monastery the next day I continued to sense something of an indefinable longing for a presence, associated with the nostalgia of the dream and with St Louis Abbey. It was a feeling that never left me during the rest of my journey – to Chicago, Cleveland, Pittsburgh and beyond. I was in a state of obsession, constantly mulling over the implications of the dream experience and its fulfilment.

2   *Professor Ayer's Drogolus*

B ack in New York I had an oddly appropriate encounter for somebody in need of an antidote to mystical experience. I went out to dinner in Greenwich Village with a party of friends and found myself squeezed into a corner with the world-famous atheist Professor A. J. Ayer, who was the stepfather of our host.

The professor, who was in his late seventies, looked spry for his years, although he had recently suffered a bout of pneumonia which had put him in hospital. His hooded eyes and hook nose, his slightly drooping, sardonic lips, gave an impression of sensuality, an air of fastidious disdain. He looked rakish in a well-cut English suit and a floral-patterned silk tie.

When he laid down the menu card, I asked him what brought him to America.

'My pension is worthless,' he said, 'so I am obliged to spend my declining years debating the existence of God with Bible-belt Christians. I take on 500 of them at a time.' I wondered how his audiences coped with his logical positivism – the view that all propositions are nonsense except those of mathematics and the natural sciences, and those that can be verified, directly or indirectly, by sense-experience.

Were the debates worthwhile, I asked him.

'If you mean was I paid well, the answer is yes,' he said.

'From an intellectual point of view, though, hardly so; the debate about God is long dead.'

'Have you never had a mystical experience?' I asked him, hoping to draw him further.

'The ghost-hunter Brian Inglis once invited me to witness him levitating,' he said with a sniff. 'Well, I went along to his house and watched him as he shook and heaved about on the carpet; but he failed to get airborne.'

'What surprises me about your story,' I said, 'is that you should have bothered to walk five yards to witness such a thing.'

'Not a bit of it,' he snapped. 'I'm a follower of David Hume. I'll believe anything if you show me the evidence. And you'll remember that Hume said that the difficulty with miracles is deciding between the likelihood that they have occurred, and the veracity of the report of them.'

'Are you still a logical positivist?' I asked. I was wondering if I could needle him a little. 'I'm no philosopher,' I went on, 'but people tell me that it's logical positivism that is dead.'

'It may well be that the principle of empirical verification is open to criticism,' he said airily. 'But perhaps you would like to suggest a better way to test propositions about God and the mystical?'

I pointed out (I was getting, perhaps, a little over-confident) that Wittgenstein seemed content to say that the mystical simply manifests itself and therefore requires no other proof, or verification, other than its sheer impressiveness.

Ayer took a swig from his glass.

'Yes, indeed. Wittgenstein believed in the mystical,' he chuckled, 'and he believed in sin; but this was because he was a homosexual and suffered guilt. Belief in mysticism made him feel better. I do not believe in shame, guilt, unworthiness, punishment. I do not accept the concept of *deserving*; and yet we behave in life as if these things are a reality.'

He paused for a moment as if waiting to see whether I would come back at him.

I was in no position to bandy further words on the question of Wittgenstein, but I thought I would draw him a little more on verification.

'In 1916,' I said, 'more than 100,000 people claim that they saw the sun spinning and falling to the earth at Fatima in Portugal after a claimed apparition of the Virgin Mary. I've read newspaper accounts of this phenomenon. Would this satisfy your Humean criterion of evidence for the truth of such a statement of fact?'

'No it would not,' said Ayer, 'for the simple reason that the phenomenon was reported nowhere else in the world, so we must conclude that the sun stayed in its proper place and that 100,000 people were subject to some sort of mass hallucination.'

Ayer sat back in his seat and cocked his head at me. 'After all,' he went on, 'how do we know whether *anything* is real or purely an illusion? I learn that I've had an hallucination because the further course of my experience assures me that the object that I thought I saw does not exist. Simple as that.'

By this time he had gained the attention of the rest of the party. He seemed to be perking up with the prospect of contention; although he was clearly aware that I was no match for him.

'The only people who have ever given me a decent argument on God's existence are the Jesuits,' he went on. 'I once took on all the Jesuits at Campion Hall in Oxford. I think I converted a few of them to atheism.'

This got a laugh.

Then he said, 'I upset them by working out how far the Virgin Mary must have travelled into space from earth after her Assumption . . . But you know, I don't think any of those Jesuits believed in a personal God.'

17

I asked him whether he ever had a sense of religious experience in music.

'No such experience can ever be regarded as a source of knowledge about reality other than the purely subjective experiences of the so-called mystic in question,' said Ayer. 'So it tells us nothing about the real world. In any case we'll soon be building computers that can compose music as well as Mozart or Bach. There is no mysterious transcendental quality beyond the computable activity of the brain. The brain is just a very clever computer.'

One or two of the party groaned. A young woman said, 'Oh, Freddy!'

After our food arrived he continued to range over the stock objections to arguments for the existence of God. And the more we talked the more I realized that he would be impervious to any propositions that failed the stringent test of his principle of sense-experience verifiability.

Eventually we moved on to other subjects; but later in the evening he stopped in mid-flight.

'I have a problem,' he said suddenly. 'I don't accept the notion of public morality, so I would be logically encouraged to accept Huxley's *Brave New World*: the idea of us all taking happy drugs. Life, after all, comes down to our needs and their fulfilment, and provided one does not offend against another – why not do anything you want? My problem is this: I can see this argument intellectually, but I know in an instinctive way that Huxley's vision is wrong.'

As we were walking away from the restaurant, he suddenly clutched me by the arm and shouted, 'Hey! What's that drogolus behind you?'

I looked behind me and saw nothing but the railings.

'You see!' cried the professor with glee. 'It's there; but

you can't see it, or smell it, or taste it. Just the same as God!'

As I set off for my hotel I reflected that Ayer's opinions might have once constituted for me a serious opposition to the reality of a mystical element in the world. That night, however, in the light of my dream, they struck me as superficial and altogether unconvincing.

3   *Accounting for It*

A s I returned across the Atlantic on a night flight I found myself thinking about my dream. I usually spent such flights writing up business reports and hatching private schemes of profit and advancement while listening to music on my Walkman; there was something about the isolation of long night flights home that stimulated reveries of material optimism. My dream, I realized, was intruding on the satisfaction I usually derived from making all those plans for myself and for my family that were to do with money-making, vacations, possessions, enjoyment . . . I had tried to relegate it to where I thought it belonged – to the realms of executive stress; but it seemed to offer confirmation that I was being challenged to review my whole way of life.

Back in England, I seemed to be heading towards a personal crisis. I began to spend much of my days and nights reading books and articles in specialist journals on the science of dreams, dream interpretation, the anthropology of dreams.

In Freudian and general psychiatric terms dreams are principally associated with problematic resistances, transferences and counter-transferences. Freud, who had little patience with mysticism, attributed religious belief and the religious content of dreams to wish-fulfilment generated by unconscious conflicts. A fashionable scientific view of dreams, on the other hand, considers them of no more importance than the 'refuse-

20

collection' process of overloaded computer software, a 'cleaning-up' system that blows out the flues, as it were.

And yet the significance of dreams in the religious traditions of Jews, Christians, Muslims and Hindus is generally considered a crucial element of spiritual growth and revelation, just as it is in the lives of American Indians and many other cultures.

Religious dreams are widely associated as a cultural phenomenon with an individual's rediscovery of an inner self, a conversion process or even a spontaneous, ecstatic experience that leads to dramatic deliverance. In an article by Lloyd Siegel in the journal *Jewish Contemporary Psychotherapy* I found descriptions of the 'miraculous dreams' of Holocaust survivors who claimed that their dreams, which often came when they were at the brink of despair, gave them strength and courage to overcome extraordinary obstacles.

There is plentiful evidence, it seems, that we are capable of making contact through our dreams with a wider sense of self and belonging. In a 1975 contribution to the *Mental Health Society* I found a report by Mirjam Viterbi of the unconscious Jewish content in the dreams of Catholic patients of Jewish descent, despite the fact that the patients were completely unaware of their Jewish ancestry: of a young man, for example, who dreamed continually of a kiddush cup and only later discovered that his mother was Jewish and had converted to Catholicism prior to her marriage. Later he established a relationship with the Jewish psyche that his mother had discarded, and a trip to Israel became a decisive experience in his spiritual awakening.

Amongst all this reading I was especially impressed with Carl Jung's autobiography, *Memories, Dreams, Reflections*. Jung's father was a sceptical theologian whose doubts had driven him to 'irritability and discontent'. Jung commented:

21

He had to quarrel with somebody, so he did it with his family and himself. Why didn't he do it with God, the dark author of all created things, who alone was responsible for the sufferings of the world? God would assuredly have sent him by way of an answer one of those magically, infinitely profound dreams which he had sent to me even without being asked, and which had sealed my fate.

Had I been sent, I wondered, such a magical and infinitely profound dream?

According to Jung, the supplanting of mystical and spiritual realities by materialist values has created a deep hunger which is frequently manifested in our dreams, when our conscious lives attempt to connect with reconciling symbols of inner wholeness. Writing in 1983 in the *American Journal of Psychotherapy* a Jungian psychiatrist, Richard Gunter, makes the following huge claim: 'Dreams, I believe, lead us to symbols that enhance personal growth and health. It can be comforting to know that religious symbols in their varied expression of the divine live in our dreams ... God is alive and well, living in the unconscious, and is sending us nocturnal messages for inspiration, growth, and health.'

My first instinct was to reject this sort of stuff as simplistic nonsense and get back to my normal life, which for so many years had been both healthy and fulfilled without religion. Yet the power of my dream and its intrusion in waking reality continued to obsess me. I went to see a Jungian analyst friend and told him the dream story.

'It's hazardous to attempt to interpret a dream outside of therapy,' he said, 'but I'll say one thing, you can always tell an anxiety dream because it's recurrent and you sweat.' After some hesitation, he added, 'Mind you, the blackness of the robes is interesting. That might be indicative of the shadow. In Jungian terms that signifies an unacceptable part of yourself which you need to come to terms with. That's a crucial process Jungians call individuation. And the trees are interesting, too ... the tree of life. It sounds to me as if you are entering something of a crisis. Perhaps your younger self is trying to get in touch with your mature self; or perhaps it's the other way round. And it's difficult to tell which self is finding it more difficult to forgive and make friends.'

I next told him about the dream's fulfilment.

He shook his head and smiled. 'People have a way of projecting their waking experiences back on to their dreams; and sometimes the other way round. On the other hand, it could be pure coincidence, or what Jungians call a synchronicity. If you accept the supernatural route then you're accepting a decidedly mystical viewpoint. You're going to have to decide on the implications of that.'

As a result of this conversation I started to extend my interest to parallel areas of the mystical and miraculous. I pored over accounts of prophecy, miracles of healing, apparitions, visions, bilocation, stigmata, prophecy, out-of-body experiences, levitation. I took out stacks of books on mysticism and the supernatural from the London Library. I enrolled in the theology faculty library of London University at Heythrop College in Cavendish Square; plundered the Catholic library at the back of Westminster Cathedral; made contact with a number of organizations, including the Alistair Hardy centre for the science of religion in Oxford and the newly formed Arthur Koestler psychical research foundation in Edinburgh.

Combing the shelves of bookshops in the Charing Cross Road I was fascinated by the popularity of extensive sections that lumped religion, philosophy, the occult all together in a mystical mish-mash. Jungian psychology and John of the Cross rubbed spines with New Ageism, transcendental meditation, Zen, Gai ecology, witchcraft, Satanism, UFOs and ley-lines. The great Christian mystics, the understanding of any one of which would take a lifetime, were given a voguish equivalence with the vast ephemera of parapsychology, self-help and horoscopes. The idea of reading John of the Cross or Teresa of Avila in order to procure some self-help and uplift struck me as very funny. But looking through these shelves helped concentrate my mind.

What, after all, did I think I was up to? Was I asking myself whether I was prepared, in mid-life, to subscribe once again to a belief in an alternative world beyond the veil of appearances? Or was I asking this: does God give us evidence for his existence? Does he interfere in his own creation in the sense that Jung suggests? I was conscious that such questions were hedged about with a host of further, tricky philosophical and theological questions. What sort of God would it be, after all, that could be conceived of as an object competing among other objects for my attention in the world? I was aware of the endless ramifications of the debates between materialists and vitalists, reductionists and animists, empiricists and metaphysicians; but the notion of direct, personal evidence of the supernatural had a new, outflanking simplicity.

Of all the books I gutted during those first weeks the most absorbing was a collection of papers entitled *The Physical Phenomena of Mysticism* by the late Father Herbert Thurston, an English Jesuit who had spent fifty years studying evidence for the operation of the Christian supernatural. The scope of his book, which was published in 1952, seemed to establish sensible limits to the broad area of phenomena in which I had an interest. He convinced me that the traditions of Christian mysticism, as opposed to the realms of the non-religious paranormal or the occult, contained the best documented, the most fascinating and the most accessible range of 'marvels' or 'prodigies' available for scrutiny in the Western world.

I had little doubt that I could find parallel prodigies in the experience of the other great world religions, and I had positive confirmation of this one afternoon in Cambridge. I was having tea with the Indian writer Anita Desai, who was staying at Girton College. I asked her whether Hindus experienced visions and miracles as a rule.

'It would be rare,' she said, 'to find a single Hindu who had not experienced at least two visions and a miracle in their lives. As for holy dreams, they could be counted by the score.'

If I was going to embark on a quest for the supernatural made visible I would restrict myself to Christendom, not out of a prejudiced favour for the religion of my childhood but in the interests of cultural accessibility. This, at least, is what I told myself at the outset.

Thurston's legacy was a crop of superbly researched and analysed case-histories, which seemed to lay down the ground rules for procedure and provide an excellent list of precedents. His approach was sceptical and empirical, which suited me, for although I was obsessed with the possibilities, I was in no mood to give the notion of supernatural origins the benefit of the doubt.

All the same, in the midst of my growing absorption with the supernatural, my friends began to assume worried expressions in my presence, and one or two even intimated that I was perhaps going off my head. It seemed to them unhealthy that a journalist would interest himself in anything so intangible and irrelevant as the mystical element in life, which, as far as most of them were concerned, came under the heading of 'freak news'. An old friend gave me a cynical smile as he handed over a cutting of a story about a woman who thought she saw the face of Jesus in one of her pancakes. Another colleague, a practising Catholic, said to me acidly, 'I find your interest in that stuff *distasteful*.'

I was upset and frustrated by this, not so much because it hurt my pride (which it did), but because they were ignoring, just as I had done for years, the fact that a mystical element lay behind fanatical religious conflicts the world over, and I was beginning to see every reason, both personal and objective, for trying to understand that element.

The tendency on the part of journalists to draw a strong and unquestioning demarcation line between everyday experience and the mystical – 'freak news' – came home to me strongly as a result of a conversation I had at about this time with my paper's editor, Donald Trelford.

Trelford had recently published an article in the *Spectator* claiming that many years earlier he had seen the mysterious apparition of a schoolfriend one winter's afternoon in Coventry. He and his friend (they were both in their early twenties then) had agreed to meet under the town-centre clock-tower at six in the evening, after playing in separate rugby football matches. Trelford was waiting at the appointed hour, and eventually his friend came walking towards him on the crowded pavement. But instead of stopping he carried on walking and disappeared in the darkness. Baffled by this behaviour Trelford returned home, where he discovered that his friend had been killed in a road accident earlier that afternoon. The article had not been written up as a curious, paranormal episode for Hallowe'en or Christmas, but as a deeply felt reminiscence of a sadly missed friend; it was an eloquent, finely observed piece of unfinished business.

Not long after the publication of this story I had dinner with Trelford and asked him how he accounted for this experience. Had he seen a ghost? 'No! I don't believe in ghosts.'

Had he been mistaken and seen a look-alike? 'No! It was definitely my friend.'

Eventually I said, 'But Donald, if it happened and you're not making it up, you surely have to account for it.'

'Well it definitely happened,' he said with finality, 'and I *don't* have to account for it, and I *won't.*'

I could sympathize with Trelford's conviction about the vivid reality of his experience, just as I was equally certain of the reality of my own dream's fulfilment. But the major difference between us was that I felt bound to come up with an explanation, even if that explanation turned out to have uncomfortable implications. And the fact that such an explanation might make not just a particular difference to my life (as would be the case if Yuri Geller were to bend one of my spoons), but *all* the difference to my life, was a risk I was prepared to accept.

At about this time I had another boost of much-needed confidence in what I was doing when I travelled up to Nottingham to meet a marine biologist, Dr David Hay, who was then director of the Alistair Hardy Research Centre in Oxford, which seeks links between science and religion.

Hay had been closely involved in work on the relation between statistics and religious experience and showed me some recent national opinion-poll figures carried out for the Oxford centre by the Gallup Poll of London. According to the poll about a third of all Britons believe that they have had some sort of religious experience, in the sense that they have been 'influenced by a presence or a power'. More surprising still was the poll's finding that nearly three-quarters of those who took part in the survey thought that spiritual experience was very important in a positively beneficial sense in their lives. The dramatic difference between the two sets of figures seemed to me fascinating, for it indicated that it was arguably the norm for people to be open to the idea of the transcendental even though they might not be church-goers or have had an actual religious experience themselves.

Did this mean that it was 'human' to be open to the notion of the transcendental? And was it possible that statistics could be used to tell us about the validity of transcendental experience?

Hay was quick to emphasize that neither the statistics nor people's 'experiences' could prove the existence of God. (I needed no reassurance on this point.) On the other hand he insisted that such data should not be ignored if we wanted to make sense of our world. 'Statistics show that religion is hardly about to die out,' Hay said. 'But they also indicate, perhaps, that religious awareness is becoming isolated from the mainstream of modern life. Human realities that are resolutely ignored tend, as Freud pointed out, to return in bizarre and fanatical forms.'

'That's the negative view,' I said, 'so what can you, a scientist, say positively about the benefits of religious awareness?'

'I'm a biologist,' said Hay, 'so I'll take a biological perspective. We need to attend more openly to our religious awareness, so that at the very least its constructiveness and creativity can be used for the benefit of the species. People who become religiously aware seem to experience directly their solidarity with their fellow human beings and their responsibility towards them. Tasks that had previously appeared impossible begin to look less formidable. They are less inclined to be seduced into the amassing of goods, because they perceive there are other sources of security. Life gains meaning. In a world threatened by environmental disaster and the depletion of natural resources, these would appear to be advantages of our biological heritage not lightly ignored.'

But was this true? Was this contention about the benign

28

consequences of religion as simple as all that? My meeting with Dr Hay only heightened my curiosity, and served to raise new questions.

Shortly after Christmas I decided that I could not in good conscience both pursue my obsession and continue working on the newspaper. I talked it through with my wife, who was supportive although somewhat anxious as to what I was getting myself into, and I eventually applied to the chief executive of the paper for a year's leave of absence without pay. Calculating that I would be of little use to the newspaper enterprise until I had worked out of my system whatever mid-life crisis I seemed to be tangled in, he gave his reluctant blessing to the idea. At one point in our discussion he wondered whether it would not be better for me to apply to my doctor for sick leave, a measure I am glad I rejected.

So it was that for the first time in more than twelve years I found myself a free agent and ready for a journey that seemed on the face of it enticing in its simplicity. I would go in search of the supernatural made visible in the world, seeking out current evidence, wherever I could find it, that God intervenes in the affairs of humankind in literal and observable ways; asking what difference it makes to the lives of those who are prepared to accept the authenticity of such evidence.

And pondering the problem of a starting point, I found myself reflecting for the first time in many years on the story of my early faith and the path towards scepticism and agnosticism, that had become such a well-trodden highway for so many Catholics of my generation.

4   A Catholic Boyhood

As a boy I carried a profoundly disturbing memory of an experience I could never quite locate in time, except that it may well be my very earliest recollection. As I grew up I sometimes thought of this experience as an encounter with Satan; at other times I believed that I had seen the true face of God, and had discovered what no one else knew – that he was entirely, eternally evil.

I am lying on a bed in a room high in a building. It is a summer's evening and I am gazing through a deep window out over rooftops and chimneys. Suddenly the door opens and people enter at a rush with masks and scissors. They lean over me and I can hear a sound of sighing and crying as if the trees are calling to the rooftops, and the rooftops to the distant hills, the sounds ever-expanding in the twilight.

There is a presence in the waves of sound, like an ageless, all-powerful, dark being, and it gathers strength and purpose in a series of sickening, irresistible pulses. I am about to be engulfed by the monotonous rhythm which intends taking me to itself forever.

This I know is the only reality, the ultimate and inescapable truth, all evil, and without end. As it ebbs away, like a mighty ocean of darkness, it lets me understand that its departure is only temporary. Finally, inevitably, it will return to take me to itself forever.

This memory, I believe, had much to do with my turning at an early age towards religion and religious things. I felt safe in the presence of holy objects, and reassured that I had glimpsed the Devil rather than an evil God. I carried holy water and wore a medal of the Virgin. I felt a sense of security at early-morning Mass, and I became a daily communicant from the age of eight.

Through these regular visits to church I met an old woman who was to have a considerable influence over my life. Miss Racine used to hang around the church door looking for companionship after Mass. She had whiskers and misshapen feet; people tended to shun her. One day she invited me to her house, a gloomy, unkempt suburban villa where she lived in one cluttered room amidst holy pictures, statues and devotional books. She had an inexhaustible stock of gossip about religious communities, priests and nuns. I got into the habit of visiting Miss Racine from about the time that I was eleven, drinking her rancid tea and eating her stale biscuits, despite my mother's anxious warnings that she was a religious maniac.

Miss Racine painted an enticing picture of life in a junior seminary, where young boys could start their studies for the priesthood in a monastic routine far away in the countryside. She encouraged me to believe that I had a vocation and gave me a relic of St Thérèse of Lisieux, the modern French saint who was venerated as the patron of priests. She also persuaded me to wear an item of devotional apparel known as a scapular, two pieces of cloth not much larger than postage stamps attached to each other by silken threads. The scapular, a symbol of the Virgin Mary's protection, was reputedly given to

St Simon Stock in England in 1247, and is to be worn around the neck beneath one's clothing. It wards off evil. Those who die wearing this object, she told me, are guaranteed entry into heaven on the first Saturday following their death.

I was prepared to give its miraculous properties a chance. Wearing the scapular I knelt before the statue of the Virgin in the Catholic church in Woodford, in Essex, and begged her to make me a priest. The following year the curate took me to see the local bishop, and it was arranged that I would be boarded at St Wilfred's, a junior seminary in the Midlands.

My mother, who had been oddly tolerant of my religiosity despite her doubts about Miss Racine, took me to St Pancras Station and installed me on the train. She stood waving mournfully from the end of the platform, as if knowing that she had lost a son. I was unmoved by my mother's tears; there were after all, I reasoned, three more brothers and a sister at home. When I could see her no longer I settled myself back into the seat and began reading a mint-new edition of the *Imitation of Christ*, a medieval work of spirituality written specifically for the formation of religious of enclosed orders.

I opened the book and read: 'It is no small matter to dwell in a religious community, or congregation, to converse therein without complaint, and to persevere therein faithfully until death. Blessed is he that hath there lived well, and ended happily.'

I was thirteen years old.

The rural setting of the junior seminary in the high moorlands of north Staffordshire seemed the fulfilment of my deepest yearnings and fantasies. I felt safe at last, sleeping beneath the same roof as the Blessed Sacrament.

One hundred and eighty boys and twelve priests lived in a sprawl of cloisters, stairways, attics and garret dormitories.

The building was perched on the side of a gorge-like valley with steep woods and waterfalls. Below the college, in the depths of the woods, was a shrine built by Father Faber, the Victorian spiritual writer. Whenever I could get permission to visit Faber's Retreat I would spend time there saying the rosary and listening to the rushing waters and the wind in the larch trees, identifying myself with the romantic figments of my imagination – St Francis, St Bernard, St Anthony.

Our teachers were a team of diocesan priests who put the lid down firmly on anything that smacked of excess, extravagance – the *mystical*. They were men of abundant faith, and they were convinced that belief was all that was required to make contact with the supernatural realms. They would have firmly disparaged the idea of more direct encounters with the supernatural in the form of miracles, visions, voices.

I was comfortable with this ethos, but in common I imagine with most of my contemporaries I developed a rich fantasy life to lend reality to the propositions of faith. Ideas of Christ in the Sacrament, the presence of angels, demons, heaven, hell, the Virgin Mary, grace, sin, were fed by imitations of Pre-Raphaelite art in the stained glass that filled the church, and the prints that lined the walls of the corridors and cloisters. Our role models were the saints, whom we read about daily in our spiritual reading. The romantic seclusion of the landscape encouraged a picture of reality that bore little relation to the harsh industrial wastelands of Stoke-on-Trent that began just twenty miles west of us, beyond the edge of the moors.

Throughout these years, from thirteen to eighteen, we learned to define ourselves in terms of monastic regulations and identification with Christ, Mary and our guardian angels. There was no feminine influence, save for the members of the elusive enclosed order of nuns who cooked our meals. Relationships with 'special' friends were discouraged, and we had no notion of being part of the local rural community. Our doctrinal studies were sustained by a sort of half-baked medieval intellectualism. The main articles of Christian and Catholic dogma – the idea of the soul; the distinction between nature and person expressed in the Holy Trinity; the transubstantiation, the turning of wine into the body and blood of Christ – these complex and mysterious notions were clarified and explained by a crude version of the thinking of the medieval philosopher and theologian Thomas Aquinas. Philosophy as we were taught it at St Wilfred's treated ideas as if they had the same sort of reality as a child's coloured building blocks. It was held that there was a *real* distinction between a thing's substance and its observable appearances – shape, size, texture; that a thing's essence could be distinguished from its existence; that ideas like justice, beauty, truth, had a sort of separate existence in a universalized world of pure forms, independent of individual minds and actual objects and actions. It was thus easy to accept, without the aid of sense experience, that a supernatural realm, far more important and durable, lay beyond the veil of appearances.

And yet I believed that I was happy and that I was enjoying a foretaste of heaven. I can see myself, aged fifteen, on the Feast of the Immaculate Conception coming in from a hard afternoon's manual labour and going into church to pray alone before tea. The sky is cloudless, with a rich December light streaming in through the west window; there is a keen wind that can be heard in the lime trees outside. As I kneel before the Blessed Sacrament in the empty church, imagining the real presence of Christ before me, I feel a deep sense of holiness and peace. After tea there will be choir practice, and we will be singing Palestrina, or Vittoria, or Carissimi.

After my eighteenth birthday I was sent to the senior seminary of the archdiocese, at Oscott College, Birmingham, a sooty, red-brick pile with commanding views of a landscape of chimneys, concrete cooling towers, factories and housing estates. The routine of the day was much as it had been at junior seminary, although we were now trussed up in black soutanes and Roman collars. The emblematic romanticism, the liturgical formalism, the monastic routine continued; but it had gone sour on me.

In the rural idyll of St Wilfred's I had managed to linger in a state of late childhood. Now on the grim city's edge, the storms of adolescence, with accompanying ravages of scrupulosity and guilt, were unleashed. I suffered migraines and stomach-aches; I lay awake at night and fell asleep in chapel and through lectures in the mornings; I took up smoking and drinking; against the severe rules of the house I escaped whenever I could to the cinemas down in Birmingham. I was desperate for affectionate companionship, wracked with sexual torment.

My fellow students struck me as self-absorbed, sanctimonious, gullible. (I doubt whether they found me preposessing either.) Most of the teaching staff I considered to be narrow, lost without their course books. I was sceptical about Thomistic philosophy, which I began to see as a precarious building with grand, soaring pillars and buttresses; so much interlacing, so much analogous patterning, without true foundations. Pull away one pillar and the whole edifice would collapse.

I began to read and to be influenced by modern British philosophy, which demonstrated the fallacies of metaphysics and nourished my growing scepticism. I became interested in science, astronomy and anthropology. One day I read an article in a journal about a tribe in Australia that put its god into a stone in order to control the deity. I saw an exact parallel with Catholic priesthood.

Reading Hegel on the function of the Catholic clergy as

keepers of the Eucharist I was deeply impressed by this reflection: 'The Holy as a mere thing has the character of being taken possession of by another to my exclusion; it may come into an alien hand, since the process of appropriating it is not one that takes place in the Spirit but is conditioned by its quality as an external object.' This comment was responsible for the loss of my belief in the mystery of the real presence of Christ in the Eucharist.

I took delight in attempting to undermine the beliefs of my fellow seminarians with what I regarded as clever arguments; I quarrelled with the lecturers in class and flagrantly ignored the rules of the house. At the end of my second year I received a reprimand from the Rector. Either I must mend my ways or a poor report would be sent to the bishop who sponsored me in the college. I forestalled further acrimony by slipping away without warning and without farewells several days before my twenty-first birthday.

I felt no sense of loss on leaving Oscott, nor was I unhappy about relinquishing a vocation that had begun to fill me with foreboding. But what had happened to all that accumulated religious experience at St Wilfred's? Somehow I had managed to bury it deeply as if it had never been. In the meantime I threw myself into a new life. I went to Oxford to read English literature. For the first time in my life I felt intellectually and emotionally stretched. I fell in love with a girl who was not a Catholic and religion began to recede from my conscious everyday life.

I turned to literature and found spiritual sustenance in the Romantic poets. Wordsworth's 'spots of time' in 'Tintern Abbey' and 'The Prelude' described a sense of transcendent mystery that was far more impressive, and true, I felt, than any of the sterile propositions about God composed by the 'Angelic Doctor', Thomas Aquinas.

And I have felt
A presence that disturbs me with the joy
Of elevated thoughts; a sense sublime
Of something far more deeply interfused,
Whose dwelling is the light of setting suns,
And the round ocean and the living air,
And the blue sky, and in the mind of man:
A motion and a spirit, that impels
All thinking things, all objects of all thought,
And rolls through all things . . .

This I could feel and understand. This was an acceptable prayer.

After Oxford I went on to Cambridge to do postgraduate work in early-nineteenth-century English literature and philosophy. I had stopped going to church, and I knew that I would soon come to a firm decision about Christianity itself.

During a long vocation I went to stay in Maidstone with a doctor called Gabriel Fielding, who happened to be a novelist and a Jungian analyst. He offered to talk me through my childhood. With the aid of hypnosis he discovered that my childhood experience of the 'Evil Eternity' was nothing more than the confused memory of a badly administered ether anaesthetic which I had undergone at the age of three for an operation for tonsilitis.

Back in Cambridge I was walking one afternoon across Parker's Piece, an expanse of open ground close to the centre of the city. I could see the huge Gothic spire of the Catholic church in the distance and the very sight of it provoked in me a feeling of unbearable tension. I understood for the first time, in a vivid flash of insight, that I had been striving for several years to live my life with two entirely irreconcilable cosmologies in my head. One picture involved a supernatural realm, just beyond the veil of appearances, in which resided the Holy Trinity, the angels and the saints, the souls of the dead – in purgatory, in hell, and in heaven – all of which depended on belief rather than knowledge and reason, and which one could only imagine inadequately as in a fairy-tale. The other, and it was, admittedly, a vision of youthful optimism, centred on the wonders of the universe; the stupendous fertility of life on the planet; the dignity, the genius, the resourcefulness of humankind. All of which could be ascertained by means of direct knowledge, and understood by the light of unaided reason.

How was it possible to hold two such utterly opposed pictures of reality together? And yet, despite its purely speculative, shadowy nature, the supernatural realm made outrageous demands, claiming for itself, paradoxically, a greater sense of significance, grandeur, importance, even though it required a greater suspension of disbelief, and was less reconcilable with life as one had to live it in this world.

I could no longer hold these two worlds together. I would have to choose. But even as I turned the dilemma over in my mind I knew that I had made my choice. It was a simple decision that brought immediate relief. There were no pangs of conscience; no heart-searching; and I was determined that I would not look back. The transition to agnosticism was painless, guiltless and immediately rewarding in a psychological sense. I could get on with my life unhampered by scruples of conscience or intellect.

After university I took up journalism. I worked as an investigative reporter and as a foreign correspondent, and travelled the world. I married and raised a family. As the years passed I became increasingly convinced that human beings were morally, psychologically and materially better off without a belief in God. Morality was the avoidance of actions that might bring painful consequences on our fellows; we owed no duty beyond our obligations to family, community and society.

As I entered middle age nothing short of a miracle could have changed these firm convictions.

5   *The Jesuits*

In the weeks before starting my sabbatical leave I had been collecting cuttings from newspapers and newspaper libraries under the broad category of 'miraculous'. Two-thirds of this material was about sightings of the Virgin Mary, and strange phenomena linked with Marian statues. In the previous four or five years such prodigies had been reported in Burundi, Cameroon, Costa Rica, France, Haiti, Ireland, Italy, Japan, Lithuania, Nigeria, Peru, the Philippines, Poland, Rwanda, the Ukraine, the United States and Zaïre.

The most frequently reported instance was the daily visitation of the Virgin to a group of children in Medjugorje, Yugoslavia, where some 17 million pilgrims had travelled since 1981. There were also numerous reports of secondary phenomena: many thousands of people had said that they had seen the sun spinning and changing colour, and there were stories of various luminous prodigies in the district.

These apparitions of the Virgin, still in progress, seemed to offer the most public and varied examples of alleged supernatural manifestations. What was more, the Catholic Church, normally cautious about such matters in modern times, was encouraging the cult. It was inevitable that I should start by attempting to make a first-hand study of this most available token of the supernatural made visible in the world today.

In a bookshop near Westminster Cathedral I picked up a

magazine entitled *Medjugorje Messenger* and decided that an appropriate starting point would be a meeting with its editor, who turned out to be a London Jesuit, the Reverend Father Richard Foley.

So I found myself walking across Berkeley Square and approaching the front door of the Jesuit mother house, known as 'Farm Street', an Edwardian orange-red sandstone building opposite the Connaught Hotel. There was a cloister with bikes and a sign announcing 'Confessions'. A man in a grey suit, he might have been an accountant on his lunch break, passed by and walked purposefully towards the sign, disappearing into the dark interior of a corridor. The sight did nothing to inspire me with confidence.

As I rang the bell the door was immediately opened by a man in a black zip-up bomber-jacket who introduced himself as Father Foley. He had been expecting me. He had a face like a boxer: flattened nose, high cheekbones fiery with broken capillaries, and overhanging eyebrows. He greeted me breathlessly, calling me 'my dear'.

Talking all the way he marched on squelching shoes down polished stairs to a self-service cafeteria in the bowels of the building. There were a dozen or so priests eating lunch at hexagonal tables; some looked ceremonially academic in traditional Jesuit gowns with fussy false sleeves; others were dressed in dark-blue shirts reminiscent of New York cops in summer garb. They looked lean and studious. There was a hum of machinery in the room, air-conditioning perhaps, lending the atmosphere of a powerhouse.

Father Foley took his place at a table where there was one other priest, who introduced himself as Father Frederick Copleston, whom I knew by repute as the author of a prodigious history of philosophy that had been a staple diet in the seminary. Father Copleston, unlike his companions, was dressed in civilian clothes, brown corduroys and a plaid shirt; his eyes were screwed up myopically and he wore a faintly sardonic grin.

Father Foley launched immediately into the business in hand, while his companion listened in silence. 'If you are setting out on an investigation into current evidence for the Christian supernatural, my dear, you cannot do better than visit Medjugorje.' He wagged a finger: 'Attend the apparitions! Examine the phenomena! Interview the visionaries!'

He rehearsed the story of the apparitions. Walking in a field near the village of Medjugorje in southern Yugoslavia, on 24 June 1981, a fourteen-year-old peasant girl, Ivanka Ivanković, saw a light which she identified with the Virgin Mary. Ivanka had been in good health and had never suffered any psychological illness; her mother, however, had died eight weeks previously. Within the space of a few hours five other children, three girls and two boys, ages ranging from ten to seventeen, had joined her and claimed to have witnessed the same apparition. They said that they saw a woman with long dark hair, wearing a grey gown. All the time she was covering and uncovering something she held in her left hand.

In various combinations the children continued to 'see' and 'speak' with the Virgin each day. The visionaries would line up to pray, facing a wall in a room in the parish house. Suddenly they would drop to their knees in perfect coordination while observing and speaking to a presence that remained invisible and silent to others. The apparition normally lasted no more than three to four minutes; afterwards a Franciscan priest would debrief them to write down the Virgin's messages.

Within weeks of the commencement of the phenomenon a trickle of pilgrims turned to a flood of hundreds of thousands.

The regional Communist government reacted with hostility; the children were interrogated and bullied, the Franciscan parish priest was imprisoned and tortured. The Roman Catholic Bishop of Mostar, at the outset sympathetic, was soon to call in question the authenticity of the events; but the phenomena were to achieve worldwide fame and approval among devout Catholics. The impact on the local community, according to Father Foley, was dramatic. The villagers now attended Mass each day, fasted twice a week, and were to be seen walking in the fields and lanes with rosaries in their hands. Men had given up drinking and swearing, enemies had been reconciled.

'Nowhere in the world,' said Father Foley, 'will you witness so many signs and wonders, spinning suns, moving lights, religious pictures filling the sky, rosaries turning to gold. The phenomena are as plentiful as the rocks that are strewn about the hillsides!'

There had been many claims for miracles of healing, and many answers to prayer; the most impressive evidence for the supernatural authenticity of the happenings, according to Father Foley, was the many thousands of conversions to a devout life.

'My dear,' said Father Foley, 'it's like a veritable Disneyland of the supernatural. And the world needs it so much. We need a bit of starlight and stardust. But you go there and you've never seen anything like it: it's a cross between a pop festival and the Sermon on the Mount. The fervour, the devotion, the real prayer; the mystical and miraculous events sparking off all over the place.' The priest was red in the face, his forehead glistening with enthusiasm. I looked at his companion, Father Copleston, who continued to eat stolidly, as if Father Foley were talking about the weather.

'And what message,' I asked, 'is the Virgin Mary giving to the children?'

'Pray, say the rosary, fast,' said Father Foley, 'otherwise there will be a great chastisement. There will be ten signs, terrible scourges to be visited on mankind. One of the visionaries, Mirjana, wept when she was told of the chastisement. She cried out: "Oh no, does it have to be like that?" The third secret will be a great sign, one of the wonders of the earth, which will appear on the hill of the visions. The visionaries will inform a certain priest when all these things are going to occur, and he will notify the media. Three of the children have now stopped having their visions because they have been told all ten secrets. The remaining active visionaries have their full quota still to come.'

As Father Foley was imparting all this, I was conscious of having winced. It had not gone unnoticed. He laid a hand on my arm. 'This shocks some people, John; but, you know, a religion without Apocalypse is like a dragon without teeth.'

With this he trundled off in the direction of the self-service hatch.

'What do *you* think?' I asked Father Copleston.

He considered the question for a moment. 'I've never had any visions,' he said flatly.

'What did Thomas Aquinas have to say about mystical phenomena?' I asked. 'Didn't he say that all he had written was straw compared with his mystical revelations?'

'Yes, that's true,' said Father Copleston. 'It seems that he had a mystical experience while saying Mass a few months before he died in 1274. As a philosopher, though, he had nothing to say about mysticism.'

He seemed to smile inwardly to himself. 'There is no distinction,' he went on, 'between Christian philosophy and good philosophy. Some people believe that mystical experience is problematic, that it calls for an explanation involving the intervention of God. There are plenty of other people around, however, who are prepared to accept that there are alternative explanations. You ask about Aquinas: as a philosopher his position was that transcendent being, or God, is indicated not by mystical experience but by the universal mystery of dependent or contingent being. How can an infinite series of dependent being, which does not contain within itself the reason for its own existence, get started in the first place? That is something we can all ponder, irrespective of our religion or lack of it. And you certainly won't have to go to Medjugorje to think about it.'

'But not all philosophers would agree that it is meaningful to talk about transcendent being in the first place,' I said. 'Doesn't that indicate that there is a sort of mystical aptitude in some philosophers?'

Copleston shook his head. 'There are students of Aquinas who argue that there is a sort of metaphysical *intuition* of being, equal to a privileged mystical experience. I don't think that Aquinas ever accepted this. He was a thoroughly professional philosopher and as such he saw philosophy as the striving of the human mind after truth. This striving can only be fully satisfied in the vision of God, but this does not mean that he approved of substituting mystical experience for proper philosophical inquiry.'

At this point Father Foley appeared, carrying our desserts. He appeared a little flustered, as if guessing that Copleston might well have been ridiculing Medjugorje during his absence.

'At Medjugorje,' Father Foley began again, 'people look at the sun quite painlessly, as if it were in eclipse . . .'

With this Father Copleston rose, made his apologies and walked away. He was still smiling enigmatically to himself.

Father Foley leaned towards me confidentially. 'Of course, John, Medjugorje has its sceptics. The local bishop in Mostar, as you will discover, has turned his back on the events. He's resisting the enormous opportunities Our Lady has given him. He's even accused the saintly parish priest of having fathered a child by a Franciscan nun. Just imagine. Then he accused another priest of having had erotic designs on one of the visionaries . . . You know, the bishop is looking awfully old for his age.'

I felt vaguely uncomfortable; the austere talk of Father Copleston was preferable to this sort of cranky gossip.

Before I left Farm Street that afternoon Father Foley gave me a pile of books, a list of contacts in Medjugorje and letters of introduction.

'If you go, take plenty of small bottles of whisky and lots of tea-bags,' he advised. 'You'll find that will soften people up. Take bags of sweets for the children.'

As he let me out of the front door he said: 'If you get to Medjugorje I hope you have a quiet time; but if you see anything you're going to be very busy.'

As I walked back across Berkeley Square I was suddenly overwhelmed with misgivings. Father Copleston had in a few sentences warned me of the danger of deducing a God of the gaps from a few allegedly paranormal occurrences. On the other hand, Father Foley's enthusiasm for his spiritual Disneyland had filled me with dismay. Here I was planning an expensive trip to a country I did not like and to a place where the people were almost certainly suffering from mass hysteria.

But I had made a start, and there was no turning back.

PART TWO

A Spiritual Disneyland

6 Baffled Scientists

On a cold and rainy afternoon I left London on a Yugoslav Airlines flight mostly composed of elderly holiday-makers on their way to the Adriatic Riviera. Sitting next to me was a Yugoslav pop-singer with dark gypsy looks and an evil-smelling cigarette. Over a meal of unidentifiable meat and roly-poly cake I told him of my destination.

'Those people up there behind the mountains are the smartest,' he said. 'They make good business with that St Mary – the Gospa, we call her. I just wish I could find something like that in *my* back garden!' He rubbed his thumb and forefinger together earnestly.

I spent the rest of the flight examining a publication Father Foley had given me. It was entitled *Scientific and Medical Studies on the Apparitions at Medjugorje*, the work, principally, of one Professor Henri Joyeux of Montpellier University, described as 'hospital surgeon and director of a nutrition and experimental cancer laboratory'.

The book began:

Never before in the history of the Church has the phenomenon of ecstasy been subjected to modern scientific tests. The Medjugorje visionaries have undergone electro-encephalographs, electro-oculographs, eye-reflex tests and a study of evoked auditory responses

A Spiritual Disneyland

... These are the 'firsts' offered by our book: the tests and their implications.

Joyeux usefully described the various empirical tests that had been applied to the visionaries to date. There had been inconclusive psychiatric interviews, attempts at hypnosis and several unscheduled tests of an amateurish nature. There had been a horrifying 'prick' test, administered by a priest who leapt forward with an apparently unsterilized needle and stabbed one of the girl visionaries, mid-ecstasy, straight through her clothes. The visionary did not appear to notice anything although a bloodstain appeared on her dress. On another occasion a zealous cleric had suddenly thrust two fingers at the eyes of one of the visionaries as if to gouge them out; seeing the girl blink, the perpetrator had lost all faith in the authenticity of the apparition.

Setting aside these crude scrutinies Professor Joyeux and a half-dozen French medical specialists, including a brain surgeon, an ocular surgeon and an ear, nose and throat specialist, had made a new, 'wholly scientific' start. They had travelled to Medjugorje on five separate occasions with a quantity of electrical contraptions. After consulting their apparition and receiving the go-ahead, the visionaries allowed themselves to be trussed up with wires, headphones and suction pads while they experienced their visions up against the empty wall of a room in the parish church.

The results, according to the medical team, were as follows:

1 No clinical signs of individual or collective hallucination.
2 No signs of individual or collective hysteria.
3 No neuroses or psychoses.

The team also concluded that the visionaries were not experiencing pathological ecstasy, which they defined as the sort of trance suffered by hysterics, the chronically delirious or those suffering from hallucinations. Pathological ecstasy, declared Joyeux, 'is normally accompanied by a web of erotic and religious fantasy in which excesses of exaltation alternate with lewd excitability'. He could also definitively exclude the existence of dreams, sleep or epilepsy during the apparitions. He was convinced, as a result of lie-detector tests, that the visionaries were not consciously deceitful.

The electro-encephalographic recordings positively indicated the presence of alpha rhythms, which, according to the publication, were consistent with 'an attitude of expectation, during relaxation and meditation exercises'. Mystics and contemplatives, apparently, are capable of an extensive range and 'abundance' of alpha rhythms in meditative states.

In their conclusions the medical men professed themselves baffled by just two phenomena. First, they could not understand how it was that in ecstasy the children managed to use their lips and larynxes as in normal speech while not uttering a sound. Secondly, they were astonished at the way in which all six children, or any lesser numerical combination of the six, managed to coordinate their eye movements in exact synchronicity while observing the arrival and departure of the apparition.

But what had the scientific tests proved? Granting that Professor Joyeux was all that he said he was, and assuming he was unbiased and motivated by genuinely scientific objectives, his testimony was nevertheless purely negative; and yet there was something about the circumstances of the experiments that had moved me.

The medical men had taken a number of photographs of themselves and their electrical devices as they went to work on the visionaries. Coming in to land at Dubrovnik, I was gazing at a particularly poignant picture. The visionaries were kneeling looking up in wonder at a blank wall while the medical men leaned forward in the act of twiddling the knobs of their sinsister black machines, as if they could capture the Virgin in the dials and print-outs. Somehow it exemplified a frantic longing for a degree of certainty about the existence of authentic mystery, and the futility of achieving that certainty by empirical means.

At Dubrovnik I stayed in a state hotel where a desultory band played *The Godfather* theme tune to a scattering of dejected guests in the lobby. In a vast, deserted basement dining room, overseen by a waiter in scarlet dinner-jacket with gold epaulettes, I sipped a glass of wine that tasted like cough linctus.

That night I fell asleep over a book about Medjugorje extolling the Virgin's special messages to the children. I dreamt that I was in a church that celebrated the cult of the Virgin as a pagan goddess. Priests with moustaches and wearing scarlet skull caps and gold copes pranced around an altar on which her statue had been erected. They were inviting me to join their rites, and I was fighting to escape. I woke up panic-stricken in the small hours.

7   *Jakov the Visionary*

The next morning I left the city in a hire car and took the coastal road towards Split. Steep mountains descended abruptly to the sea; there were sudden bays with shingle beaches; misty islands basked like humped-back whales on the horizon. In the peaceful morning sun it was easy to forget that these mountains had been the scene of atrocious acts of inhumanity in the Second World War, some of the worst of them committed by Catholics against their Orthodox neighbours. In 1941, just a few miles from Medjugorje, I had read, Catholic Fascists had thrown some five hundred Orthodox men, women and children over a precipice to their deaths.

At length the road descended to a fertile valley where a deep, dark-green river flowed swiftly towards the sea. The sun was high as I drove inland to Čapljena, a quiet garrison town where a phalanx of soldiers marched up and down in front of a deserted hotel. The road north, towards Medjugorje, now twisted through undulating country until the fertile uplands gave way to a high plateau encircled by mountains.

To the west was a tawny hill surmounted by a concrete cross; this, I knew from my reading, was the famous Mt Križevac, dominating Medjugorje. Nestling at its foot was a series of lower hills, thinly wooded. Why, I wondered, should the people of this remote place receive visions of the Virgin Mary? Was there a connection between the visitations and the harsh, desolate landscape, as in other great Marian shrines of Europe – Lourdes, Fatima, Gaudaloupe, Rocamadour . . .?

At the junction for Medjugorje I was stopped by a policeman controlling long lines of traffic coming in from the north. He looked inside the car and asked to see my passport before waving me on. I followed a convoy of air-conditioned German buses towards the village; on either side of the road were box-like chalet houses set in a oasis of fertile fields. There were vineyards, tobacco plants and well-organized market gardening; the soil was a deep, rich red.

The road turned at a primitive bridge running across a dried-up river bed filled with garbage. A white stuccoed church loomed ahead, a concrete block with twin towers that might have been designed by a child. Either side of the approach road was a turmoil of traffic and pedestrians; stalls and booths with festoons of belts, handbags and religious knick-knacks; luminous bottle-statues of the Virgin with garish blue stoppers, poker-work plaques of the Crucifixion, key-rings of the Sacred Heart. Groups of gypsy women with peroxided hair were sunning themselves in deck-chairs; as each vehicle passed they cried out and gesticulated towards their wares.

I left the car in a makeshift car park and went in search of the young visionary Jakov's house, where Father Foley said I might get a bed for the night. I struggled along a narrow lane choked with buses, horse carts and knots of overheated, sweaty pedestrian pilgrims. Some of the groups were led by priests who were saying the rosary and singing hymns; but the devotees were rubbernecking in every direction and chatting among themselves. In the background I could see two police-men lounging against a blue Fiat car.

Jakov's house was at the end of a farm track well off the village lane. It was a white stuccoed villa with a roof-top balcony approached by an exterior staircase. A woman, perhaps in her early forties, sat on the doorstep in conversation with an elderly priest in a black beret. As I approached, she stopped talking and looked at me coldly.

'Jakov's aunt? Stoika?' I asked.

She nodded.

As I began to speak, slowly, in English, I produced from my shoulder-bag a quantity of presents. I handed over two bags of sweets, two cartons of cigarettes, a box of cigars, a box of tea-bags and two bottles of whisky.

She took them unsmilingly and called to somebody in the kitchen. An unshaven man with a cigarette in his mouth came to the door and the woman passed him the gifts. He examined the bottles of whisky carefully, then, without looking at me, he started to talk with the priest.

'They are saying it is not possible for you to stay here,' said the priest.

At that moment I saw somebody moving at the top of the outside flight of stairs that led to the roof. It was the visionary Jakov. He was prowling nervously, looking down and immediately glancing away. He was dressed in a blue-denim suit with wide shoulders and a cossack-style front; his collar was turned up stylishly, his hair highlighted and spiked up in punk mode. He looked young for fourteen, sickly, and the whites of his eyes glistened, hare-like.

He persisted with these nervous antics for a minute or so as he came and went and pirouetted on the balcony, tossing his head and flinging his shoulders in strange flicking movements. I was longing to speak to him, and gave him a little wave and a smile of encouragement. But this only served to throw him into an even greater display of frantic behaviour until I realized, to my shame, that he was trying to work up courage to come down the steps and pass the doorway without being accosted by me.

Despite my years of doorstepping as a journalist, it made me feel wretched to think that people like me had made a freakish curiosity of this simple boy, to the point where he was half-crazed with self-consciousness. I therefore studiously ignored him and looked at Stoika, who seemed to be discussing some sort of deal with her husband and the priest. I sensed a mercenary atmosphere, a certain hardness of heart between them; they were evidently discussing money.

The priest had seen me looking at Jakov the visionary; at length he said in English in a low voice: 'You know that both his parents died of drink!' Out of the corner of my eye I saw Jakov flitting down the staircase and flashing past within an inch of me. He looked vulnerable, stricken.

8   The Sun Spins

I left the problem of a bed for the night to providence and made my way back to the parish house, where the pilgrims were already flocking for the evening's apparition. At the top of the steps leading to the door a young American priest was leading the rosary in English; immediately beneath him, squeezed in tightly on each of the steps, were priests, friars and monks of all ages who had formed a ragged queue to gain admittance to the apparitions' room. Many of the priests carried plastic supermarket bags containing religious objects that the faithful had passed to them for the Virgin's blessing. Even as the priests jostled on their uncomfortable perches, the pilgrims continued to approach them with more bags.

The reciting of the rosary seemed to have a mesmerizing effect on the crowd, but there was an atmosphere of suppressed excitement and restlessness. Here and there a group of women would suddenly gabble in high-pitched voices. Many of the people were squinting up at the sun, which was just dipping below the pine trees next to the church, casting dramatic fingers of light and shade over the pilgrims.

At about six o'clock the door of the parish house opened and a priest appeared on the balcony; he was pale and he had grown his sideburns long, until they almost covered his cheeks. There was a pause in the prayers and a strange murmur, like a low growl, went through the crowd. The priest was choosing the privileged ones who were to be allowed into the apparitions' room. He signalled admittance by laying a hand on each applicant's shoulder; some were firmly rejected by a prod in the chest; others he brought forward by pointing and then beckoning.

I pushed my way to the front, holding out my letter of introduction from Father Foley. The priest snatched it and read it almost at a glance. 'Yes!' he said. 'But not today. You come here tomorrow, understand?' And he retreated.

A few moments after the door had shut behind him the rosary recommenced with even more fervour.

Fifteen minutes passed, then a shudder went through the crowd and people began to cry out: 'The children! The children!' Several strapping young men were approaching, making a way through the throng towards the steps. They passed within a foot of me; then the 'children' came into view: Jakov and two girls whom I recognized from photographs as Vicka and Marija. They were walking at speed, arm in arm, three abreast. Jakov was in the centre; the girls were blushing, their eyes aglint, their heads raised high, swaggering as they went; they looked like brides on the eve of their weddings.

Pilgrims were calling out to them and holding up rosaries, crucifixes, devotional medals and even babies, as if seeking blessings. Several women leapt forward to touch them, and one managed to grab a lock of Vicka's hair, but they were roughly pushed away by the young men.

As the party reached the steps of the parish house the young men made a way through, pressing the priests up against the wall to enable the visionaries to leap up the steps.

At this point the rosary praying began again, in Italian, while in different parts of the crowd the chanting of Alleluias and Ave Marias broke out spasmodically. Some people were on their knees, their arms raised above their heads. Those nearest the parish house leant against the walls, stroking and fondling the stucco as if the very fabric of the house would bestow virtue.

After a few more minutes another cry went up: 'Oh! My God! The sun! Look!' Large sections of the crowd were pointing through the trees; they seemed to be able to gaze directly into the sun's rays. Others were screwing up their eyes and shading their faces with their hands.

Most of the crowd had abandoned their prayers and were trying to observe the sun-visionaries or gabbling together with their neighbours. I felt nervous. 'What is it?' I said out loud. 'What on earth are they seeing?'

An American woman standing next to me held me by the arm. 'That's their present from Our Lady,' she said. 'I saw it yesterday afternoon. After coming out of church I looked into the sun for about four minutes; it was painless.' She was looking searchingly into my eyes, pleading with me, as if under a strange compulsion. 'You see the corona,' she went on, 'then the disc spinning and shooting out colours. I saw reds and yellows.' She shaded her eyes and gazed up into the sky. 'But I can't see anything now,' she said.

I looked up towards the sun and was instantly blinded. The woman was moving away from me, sharing her experiences with anybody who would listen.

The young American priest who had led the rosary earlier was taking charge of the crowd once more. 'Brothers and sisters, I beg of you,' he cried, 'be sensible and don't stare directly into the sun. The visionaries in there need your prayers; so let us now pray the rosary all together.'

With this he began to intone the prayers and carried the pilgrims with him in a great roar of fervour.

After half an hour's prayer the crowd suddenly fell silent.

People were pointing at the window that faced out over the yard.

'The light is on!' I heard somebody whisper. 'The vision is beginning. Our Lady is here!'

Then, quietly, like a tremor of wind, people were kneeling down where they were in the gravel. An eerie silence descended over the entire village, the only sound a distant murmur of traffic up on the main road.

They knelt, statuesque in the silence. Some gazed up towards the parish-house window, mumming prayers with their lips. Others were bent down almost to the ground. Those closest to the house itself pressed their foreheads to the walls.

I remembered a phrase I had once read referring to the pilgrimage as the 'therapy of distance', symbolizing the needs, the yearnings, satisfied by departure, by discomfort and the rigours of travel. I was conscious of the enormous distances these pilgrims had travelled to be here; I was also aware that they had made sacrifices, many of them journeying despite sickness and handicaps. But pilgrimage is also arrival, and I felt that in these moments I was witnessing the goal of every pilgrim's journey to Medjugorje: the hoped-for presence they had come to encounter.

The silence, the stillness, lasted for some five minutes. Then, without warning, the door opened and the visionaries came out on to the veranda almost at a run. There was a burst of applause from the pilgrims, who in an instant rose to their feet, clapping and cheering. Marija came first, her hands joined in an attitude of prayer, then Vicka and Jakov, attended by two nuns and the young men. The party turned right at the corner of the parish house and walked quickly towards the church, the rest of the crowd following.

There was a great throng of pilgrims already collecting outside the church in readiness for the evening Mass that was now to follow. As I pushed slowly forward I could see lines of people waiting in a file next to the church for confessions. The priests sat on folding chairs, bent double; some put their hands on the penitents' shoulders or foreheads. I saw a priest dressed in a white robe with Hi-Tec sneakers gleaming under the hem; a rascally-looking Franciscan in conversation with a beautiful young woman was wearing fashionable blue canvas deck shoes under his habit: quite unreasonably I found myself shocked by the inappropriate footwear, which seemed to me to symbolize unorthodoxy.

By the time I reached the door the building was packed. I wormed my way through and craned my neck. There were thirty or more priests at the altar. The congregation was singing the Kyrie – 'Lord have mercy' – with a devotion that took me straight back to my childhood, to the parish mission weeks when the powerful preaching of visiting friars brought about an epidemic of religious fervour, church attendance and resort to confession.

I made my way out again to the fresh air. Most of the outdoor pilgrims were kneeling in the dust and following the service on loudspeakers which were attached to the trees; but I saw a young couple smoking cigarettes and several gypsies were wandering among the praying pilgrims attempting to sell crucifixes.

I came away and wandered around the side of the church until I stood on the edge of a field looking towards Mt Križevac and the setting sun. Halfway up the mountain I could see a gleam of light, as if the rays of the sun were reflecting on a piece of glass or metal. Out of the corner of my eye I saw a small fat man approaching. He seemed to be covering his mouth with both hands in a gesture of emotion.

He stood right next to me for a while in silence. Then he spoke, in a clear Scottish accent: 'You've seen the light on the hill, have you not!'

A Spiritual Disneyland

I turned to take in the man. He was balding, sandy-haired and bespectacled, wearing a worn tweed jacket. He was rocking slightly on his toes and kept taking one hand away from his mouth to point up towards Križevac.

'Yes, I see the light,' I said. 'Surely it's a reflection of something on the hill.'

'No way!' he said with quiet emphasis. 'That there's a special light. Just for us. I saw Jesus on the wall of the church this same day last year: I've got a photo to prove it. I've seen Mary, she appears in all kinds of guises. I've seen Jesus and I've a photo to prove it. I've seen a massive ring around the sun taking in the whole church.'

I moved away from the fat man and headed for the car park. I looked back just once to see him still standing, eating a bar of chocolate straight from the wrapper while squinting up at the sun.

Later, after the Mass had ended, I walked from house to house in the semi-darkness looking in vain for a bed for a night. In most of the houses there were bands of pilgrims sitting down to a simple evening meal around a communal table. Their faces glowed in the lamplight; there was an impression of nervous excitement, anticipation, unaccustomed fellowship. I felt envious of them, disappointed that there was no place to welcome me in.

9 Fra Zovko's Voice

Unwilling to put providence to the test any further I had driven to a town called Ljubuški, just ten miles from Medjugorje, and spent the night in an empty, echoing hotel called the Biggeste. At breakfast I was served hard-boiled eggs while the hotel manager at the next table tucked into a plate of pork chops and pickled gherkins, washed down with white wine. He wished me good-morning with a blast of wicked breath.

Later that morning I drove out to Tihaljina, twenty miles from Medjugorje, to meet Fra Jozo Zovko, who had been pastor at Medjugorje when the apparitions first occurred, and who had spent almost two years in prison for his part in the promotion of the phenomena.

I found a youthful-looking man in his early forties, with an innocent, rounded face and a gentle voice. We sat in the back pew of his empty, whitewashed church and he immediately launched into his story.

'During the week the apparitions began,' he said, 'I was absent from Medjugorje. I came back through Mostar and a woman yelled to me from a passing ambulance. It was one of the parishioners, she was swathed in bandages from an accident; something had collapsed on her. She wasn't interested in her injuries. She shouted: "Hey, Father, get back to Medjugorje. Our Lady is appearing to a bunch of our children!"'

So I raced back to find the village in uproar. People were coming in from all over the region.'

Fra Zovko sat with his hands resting in his lap with a diffident, inward-looking expression.

'How did the children strike you?' I asked him.

'They were confused,' he said. 'Their reactions were childish, and they were quarrelling among themselves. I didn't know what to do for the best.'

Fra Zovko continued with his story in a quiet voice. The police suspected that the children were on drugs; they also speculated about political motives. At the beginning of the Second World War there had been an attempt to establish a Catholic Fascist state in Bosnia-Hercegovina; any kind of Catholic manifestation made the Communists suspicious. One morning a police car drove up to the church where Fra Zovko was standing with his assistant Fra Zrinko after Mass. A man got out and handed them an envelope on which was written: 'Monk Number One and Monk Number Two'. It was a summons from the local Communist party to attend a special session at Čitluk. The priests turned up to find the party officials furious; they were told they must stop the children and the parishioners going to the hill.

'I would have been more than happy,' said Fra Zovko, 'to see all those people in my church rather than on the hillside.'

At this point the priest stopped and began to swallow compulsively, as if trying to suppress his emotions.

'The people were abandoning the church,' he went on. 'They were leaving me, their pastor, and the Mass and the sacraments, to search for some sort of phantasm on the hill. I felt a failure; and I felt terrified, because I didn't know what to make of the apparitions.'

One afternoon he was in the church praying. He did not know it at the time, but the police were chasing the children to prevent them from going to the hill. The children had successfully eluded the police and were running through the vineyards towards the church.

'I had my Bible in front of me,' he said. 'I opened it at random to see if God would send me a word of guidance and I lighted on the passage in Exodus where Moses stands helpless before the Red Sea. I was crying out to God from the depths of my own darkness; I was placing before God all my doubts and despair; all the broken pieces of my life . . .' Fra Zovko was breathing deeply with emotion. One hand was splayed across his chest.

'In that silent and deserted church,' he continued, 'I heard a voice, a human voice as real as my own, not a voice in my head. It was a voice that seemed to echo across the whole of my life.' Fra Zovko stopped; he seemed on the point of tears.

Eventually he said, 'The voice said, "*Go outside and protect the children.*" I rose immediately and went quickly to the door of the church. At that very moment the door opened and the children came rushing up, crying that the police were after them. I took them straight to the priests' house and hid them. That evening the children had their first visions indoors. They had come in under the protection of the house of God . . .'

The priest sat in silence for several minutes. There were tears in his eyes; he hugged himself.

'You witnessed the children experiencing their visions on many occasions, Father. Did you ever see the vision yourself?'

'Yes,' he said, 'I did see Our Lady . . . But, I have to say that this vision was not really for me . . .' He raised his hand in a gentle gesture, as if to forestall any further questions on the subject.

I said eventually: 'How did you come to be arrested, Father?'

'Communist officials sat in the midst of the congregation

and took notes on my sermons,' he said. 'I had preached about the Israelites in exile in the desert; about one of my parishioners who had been taken in sin for forty years and had recently returned to the Church. One day I spoke about the need for courage, even to the point of shedding our blood ... It was the year of the fortieth anniversary of the founding of the Yugoslav Communist Party; I was arrested and charged with fomenting political violence. They bundled me into a car and I was taken to a jail in Čitluk. The place was unknown to me; we went through a tunnel, and there we were. I was thrown in with criminals and drug-addicts.'

When the case came to trial, he said, they refused to hear the testimonies of 300 parishioners, who would have spoken on his behalf; nor would they allow him to explain the spiritual significance of his sermons. He was sentenced to three years' imprisonment, later commuted to eighteen months.

The priest's voice trailed off into silence. He was unwilling to speak further.

'I have to go,' he said. 'There are people waiting for me.'

As I drove away from Tihaljina I felt curiously saddened and moved by Fra Zovko's story. He had a strong charisma that seemed to transcend the drama of the alleged miraculous events in his former parish. It was one thing to believe in visions and voices and to go in search of them as a pilgrim during one's vacation; it was something else to end up in prison. His story about the voice telling him to protect the children seemed to me both impressive and authentic.

Impressive, because the voice had imparted an accurate message; authentic, for it seemed to me inconceivable that he could be lying.

10 Nada, Nada, Nada

I returned to Medjugorje the next morning to mingle with the pilgrims. In the church there were about fifty people deep in prayer before the Blessed Sacrament. Many of them were old peasant women in black. As they prayed their beads they seemed to be summoning enormous reserves of concentration. The church had an almost tangible atmosphere of stillness and peace.

But outside I could hear the constant murmur of querulous voices. Curiosity overcame me and I wandered back out and walked into a group of young men who were squabbling heatedly. In their midst was a Swiss youth who was passing round a colour photograph. It depicted what looked like a pretty Italian model posing as the Virgin Mary.

'What's the problem?' I asked.

'The problem?' said the young man. 'Some priest has been saying that he captured this in his camera while taking a picture of the Križevac. I don't believe it. Why do these people have to do this? It spoils the truth.'

'I believe it!' insisted a young American. 'You've got to have faith.'

Before I could say anything a man in a red singlet drew me to one side. 'My name is Dermot, I'm from Belfast. Where are you from? What's your name? Is this your first time?'

Before I could reply he launched into a testimony: 'Before I came here, I had just enough religion to put under one finger-nail. I think I've found something here. It's changed my life; I'm praying; I love to go up on the mountain – the animals and birds up there never seem to sleep, there's a ceaseless chorus all through the night. Last week we went up with Marija to the cross, there were about 2,000 of us. She said that we would all receive a kiss from Our Lady. And sure enough, when we knelt there in the darkness and prayed, each and every one of us felt the firm imprint of a kiss on the cheek.'

Before I could question him more closely Dermot had vanished, only to be replaced by another informant, then an-other: a stream of buzzing pilgrims seeking willing ears for their testimonies.

One of them drew out his rosary. 'See this? When I came here the links between the beads were silver. Now they are gold. You'll find hundreds of people who've had this happen. A man told me yesterday that he had had his rosary beads assayed and the jeweller said the gold was of a unique kind found only in the Middle Ages.'

During the next hour I wandered slowly through the picnic area greeting pilgrims who were only too happy to 'share' their witness. Testimonies of curious luminous experiences abounded, and there were more claims of rosaries turning to gold. But the most popular anecdotes featured coincidences, all of which were said to be 'amazing'.

A man wearing a label that said 'Peace Tours' accosted me. He carried an open beach bag in which there were dark glasses, a camera, suntan lotion and a crucifix. 'I called the cab service the morning of our departure from Dulles airport. Who turns up? A Yugoslav! Can you credit that? You can't tell me that something like that wasn't *meant*.'

The witnesses buzzed about the place, swapping their testi-monies. Yet there were many more who remained silent: people who seemed closed in on themselves, who could be seen sitting alone looking out towards the mountains.

One such was a middle-aged woman from New York City whom I found reading a book on a bench near the parish house. I apologized for disturbing her and invited her to tell me why she had come to Medjugorje.

Her name was Lois and she was single. She had spent her life working among addicts in Hell's Kitchen. She looked exhausted. 'I could have gone anywhere for a vacation,' she said. 'The Caribbean, Florida, California. I came here because I felt empty. I wanted to get *close* to something.'

When I asked her whether she had found what she was looking for she said, 'Sure!' And left it at that.

There were others whose feelings were more ambivalent, as was the case with a priest I spoke to by the coffee bar. I had seen him making his way slowly but purposefully towards the church as I arrived that morning. He was tall and stooped. He had wispy grey hair, and a kind, contemplative face. He clutched a plastic supermarket bag that appeared to be stuffed with a white Mass robe. I sat close to him and introduced myself. I told him of my experience on the steps of the church and he shook his head.

'There are a lot of people here who need their heads examined. Myself included! Eh? You shouldn't be surprised at that. Almost everyone here, God love them, has brought a problem.'

Then he launched at once into the story of his life in a soft Irish brogue. 'I'm a Carmelite. I entered the order in 1960 after being a printer on the *Irish Independent* all my working life, from the time I left school. I'm a late vocation. I raise funds for the order. I have to raise £100,000 a year, or we're in trouble. Talk about stress . . .

'This is my second visit here. The first time I came just to accompany a friend and it did nothing for me. This time I've come on my own account, hoping for something to happen.'

'And what have you seen?' I asked. 'Anything that's convinced you of the authenticity of the apparitions?'

He gave a short laugh. 'God, what am I saying! I'm a firm believer, John, in the principle of St Paul's second conversion, where he puts reason and logic and proof to one side and goes for the illogical. It's a question of belief, not of proof. I believed deeply in another set of apparitions, at Garabandal in northern Spain; I believed in them because the visionaries were obedient to the local pastor, and because of the support of Padre Pio, who is the most powerful saint of our era. But the church came down against it. Now Medjugorje has been endorsed by Sister Briege McKenna, who is the only living equivalent we have to a Padre Pio. What a wonderful woman. She prophesied the events here several months before they occurred.

'I don't think you can set out to find God as if he's at the bottom of a drawer someplace,' he went on. 'He reveals himself *to* you. I can only dispose myself for revelation. That's all I can do, you see. The growth of the spirit is an extraordinary thing; it's the work of a lifetime. St John of the Cross said that most of us get stuck less than halfway on our journey to God because we think we've made it. What a man he was! He was a spiritual *mountain-climber*, that's what St John of the Cross was ... What on earth did he mean by that thing he said? – *nada, nada, nada!* Finding God in the vast emptiness.'

He scratched his ear and smiled to himself. 'I spoke to Marija outside her house the other day. She said to me, "How long are you staying, Father, are you staying until Pentecost?" And I said to her, "Why, Marija, is there to be a sign on that day?" And she just winked at me and said, "You'll see! You'll see!"'

Nada, Nada, Nada

'You're looking for a personal sign?'

The priest shook his head. He looked weary. 'I don't know. I pin everything on the promise that Jesus gave to Peter and his disciples – the promise of Peter's authority. It's the only thing we've got to hang on to, the one straw. And at the very end of it all, there may be a precious small remnant hanging on. I'll tell you, if the Pope says that Medjugorje is false I'll burn my books on the subject and never set foot here again.'

With this Father Keogh collected his things together. As he made ready to leave, he said, 'Remember, John, it's not the big politicians that make the decisions in the world, it's the little people and their little prayers.'

As he trundled away with his supermarket bag I felt depressed. Nearly thirty years a monk and Father Keogh seemed beset with contradictions: a contemplative religious, harassed by financial problems; hanging on to faith, yet looking for a sign; declaring his trust in Church authority, yet hoping for private revelation; searching for God, yet insisting that God would find him. And all the while puzzling over that stark riddle of John of the Cross: '*Nada, nada, nada!*' Nothing, nothing, nothing!

11   *In the Apparitions' Room*

By 5.30 I was in a position once again by the balustrade of the parish house, hoping to gain admittance to the evening's apparition. The huge crowd of pilgrims pressing in on all sides behind me were again being led in prayers and hymn-singing from the steps.

At 5.45 the door of the house opened and the pale Franciscan with the sideburns emerged to select those who were to be admitted. The priests went up first, pushing and jostling; such was the crush of people behind I despaired of being spotted. The priest was looking about in the crowd while hundreds of devotees, some holding up sick children, cried out, begging to be noticed and admitted.

At last he saw me and shouted, 'You! Mister! You come up now, quickly.' I put my best shoulder forward and squirmed through; as I went a woman thrust a supermarket bag full of holy objects in my hand.

'Get it as close to the apparitions' wall as you can, honey!' she implored.

Once inside, the door was slammed to by a young woman. I was out of breath and perspiring. I turned to her and said, 'How do you cope with this?'

'You say *no*,' she said grimly, 'and you mean it. Otherwise you're dead.'

The pale priest introduced himself as Father Slavko, and

ushered me to the study bedroom, the room where the apparition was to take place. Some thirty priests, their faces drenched in sweat, were crammed together in uncomfortable kneeling postures in a space no more than twelve feet by twelve feet; they were praying the rosary in Latin. There was something peculiarly primitive and shamanistic about the scene, as if the clerics were there to ward off evil. There was only one woman in the room, an elegantly dressed, bejewelled, highly made-up lady with false eyelashes, who had clearly been introduced into the room in a more dignified fashion than the rest of us.

The attention of the priests was focused on the wall opposite the window, where there was a low bookcase on which stood a vase with a single red rose, and a crucifix. There, in the blank space above, the Virgin would appear. I found myself wondering whether one day, like Fatima and Lourdes, this simple room might not be the site of a vast and ornate basilica.

The priests now began to sing the Veni Creator Spiritus, stumbling uncertainly over the words; only one of them appeared to be fully confident – a corpulent Passionist who, despite the heat, was dressed in the full rig of his order, cassock and cloak with various badges, belts and buckles. Scanning the assembly I fancied I could see Irish, German, Spanish, Chinese and Mexican faces. I wondered if they were indeed all priests, or whether some of them might be imposters. One cleric looked particularly suspicious. He was dressed in a soutane with a sash around his middle; his hair was a mass of greasy ringlets and there was something bogus about his demeanour. His eyes were turned up so that only the whites were visible; but every so often he would come down to earth for a few seconds and take a swift, canny look about him before resuming his ecstatic expression.

In the midst of the hymn there was a sudden commotion at

the outer door. Two women and a little boy had somehow gained entrance. One of the women was the mother of the boy, who, she insisted, was suffering from an incurable illness, although the child seemed more likely to die of imminent choking from the scores of rosaries that were hung around his neck. The doorkeeper managed to eject one of the women, but the mother had wrapped herself up in a ball, sitting on the floor of the corridor, with her hands over her head and her knees drawn up to her ears. She was refusing to speak or to budge.

But the site of the apparitions was spared further disturbance by the arrival of Jakov, Marija and Vicka. There was an excited hush as the priests stopped their praying to stare at the young people. Jakov was dressed this evening in a pink linen suit and his hair was freshly spiked up again; scowling and avoiding eye-contact he immediately went down on his knees, attempting to crouch out of sight. Marija, despite the heat, was dressed, for modesty I imagined, in a pale blue sweater, a woollen plaid skirt and dark woollen stockings. Her oval face glowed in the heat; her nose was longish and strong, and she had a rather pointed jaw. She looked directly at those about her with tranquil grey eyes. There seemed to be nothing artful about her. She looked a trifle nunnish. Guileless. Vicka, who had a wide mouth and slightly crazy eyes set in a Slavonic face, had her hair swept back and held by an elastic band; she was dressed in a simple green dress. Both girls went down on their knees and began to recite the rosary out loud in Croatian while the priests responded in various languages.

Father Slavko, the Franciscan, had joined us now and was squatting next to Marija. I was still standing, no more than a foot away from her, studying her face closely. Once or twice she looked directly back at me and I felt a sense of peculiar excitation in the momentary eye-contact.

In the Apparitions' Room

The voice of Marija was dominant; she spoke slowly, enunciating each word clearly. And the longer she prayed the more she drew the attention of everybody in the room. Was it the highly charged intensity of expectation, or the stirring of some barely understood, primitive undercurrent? Whatever the case, with every passing minute this plain girl seemed to me to become more radiant, more mysterious and more graceful. I found it impossible to take my eyes off her. For much of the time she was kneeling upright, although occasionally she would rest back on her heels in a swan-like movement for a few moments before resuming an upright position once again. Meanwhile it was clear that the majority of the priests found the unaided kneeling excruciating; they fidgeted and attempted all sorts of squatting contortions, while the perspiration rolled down their faces. Jakov was hidden from sight, his head bowed. Outside, the crowd could be heard reciting the rosary and singing, and as time passed the responses became a steady, concerted roar; it was as if they were willing something to happen in the room by their fervent pleading.

After forty minutes, when we reached the end of the complete fifteen mysteries of the rosary, Slavko stood up. He pointed to the window and asked the nearest priest to shut it; then he switched on the light, a simple naked bulb hanging from the centre of the room. The crowd suddenly fell silent. He said simply: 'Let us pray now that the children will receive an apparition.'

Jakov and Marija and Vicka stepped forward, causing the priests to squeeze together even tighter so as to make room. The three stood before the wall, their hands in an attitude of prayer. They began to pray out loud in unison. I was now standing to Marija's left, slightly in front of her so that I could see her full face and profile; she was no more than a foot away. Suddenly, in perfect coordination, they went down on their knees and continued to pray some more; then together their heads rose; they were now speaking silently, their lips and throats moving quite rapidly, gazing intently as if at a real object. They had entered their ecstasy.

It was at this point that I witnessed something truly astonishing, and for which, in principle, I could find no ready explanation. For about three minutes, I saw Jakov, Marija and Vicka speaking silently and in turn to the invisible figment that hovered in front of them. The extraordinary fact was that when one of them stopped 'speaking', the other, in that same split second, would begin. Yet they were not uttering a sound, nor were they capable of observing each other's lips; I could see no bodily movement whatsoever by which they could cue each other in order to achieve such a feat.

Marija, on whom I now began to concentrate, did not appear ecstatic in any melodramatic or histrionic way, but her face radiated a striking loveliness, innocence and wonder. Her gaze was steady, unblinking, tender; the whites of her eyes seemed to shine with an unearthly light. 'Transfiguration' was a word that came at once to mind. And when I focused my attention on Jakov I saw that same transfiguring quality in his face, made all the more poignant because of his adolescence.

While I stood watching them I became aware of the stunning silence and stillness, both inside and outside the room; momentarily a child cried a long way from the building, and the sound and the distance lent depth and gravity to the silence. As I watched the visionaries in the deep peace of those few minutes I had an experience that was as fascinating as it was unexpected and unbidden.

The cliché about seeing the whole of one's life in an instantaneous panoramic vision on the brink of sudden death was certainly not something that I had ever experienced personally, and I had always thought it an exaggeration; but I now believe that I have an inkling of what such an experience might be like. For as I stood in the apparitions' room I saw in my mind's eye, with great clarity, each and every one of the images of Mary before which I had prayed throughout my childhood and youth: from the statue of Mary in my mother's bedroom in my infancy to the carved stone Mary Queen of Heaven that adorned the Lady Chapel at Oscott College in my young manhood. And in a mysterious expansion of a single moment I was somehow *aware* of each and every prayer I had prayed, and hymn that I had sung, to Mary from my earliest Hail Marys to the poignant Salve Reginas at the end of Compline in later years.

As the experience faded I found myself thinking that these memories gave new meaning to the phrase 'full of grace', and for a moment I had the impression of something unblocking inside myself. Somehow, unawares, I found my heart inclining.

Then the moment was past.

All this took, I believe, a matter of seconds. Then, without warning or any indication of a cue, the three young people whispered something together; they leaned back slightly at the same instant, their faces awestruck; they gave a little sigh. They were now praying out loud and I noticed that Marija's voice was thick and throaty and full of emotion. Then all three stood up and the ecstasy was over.

As the pale Franciscan led the visionaries from the room the priests began to chant over and over again: 'Ave, ave, ave Maria . . .' The debriefing, which was a strictly private affair in a separate room, took no more than three minutes. When he reappeared the priest said: 'Let us go now to the church.'

Next we were walking from the apparitions' room and facing the crowds outside, looking up at us expectantly, enviously, shading their eyes in the rays of the setting sun. A man who was wearing four crucifixes around his neck shook me by the hand. Then the woman came to retrieve her supermarket bag; I was grasping it in my hand with a bloodless iron grip. I had not noticed it from the moment she handed it to me.

During Mass I went off to sit alone on the edge of a tobacco field to try to get the experience of the apparition into some sort of perspective. How could one define what was happening to these young people day after day in Medjugorje? To say that it was an illusion would imply that they were in some way mistaken about a visual stimulus corresponding with an extra-mental reality. It was quite possible, it seemed to me, that they had indeed been in a state of illusion during the original apparition, when they might have extrapolated a presence around a light in the mountain mist. But in the confines of the parish room it was clear that the young people were now engaged in 'perceptions' without a material external stimulus, and from this point of view they were, by any clinical definition at least, in a state of hallucination, as opposed to illusion. At the same time these hallucinations, to refine their status a little further, were aural and visual and projected an external rather than an internal presence.

They were not asleep and dreaming, nor did they appear to be on drugs (after such a long period that possibility would by now have been exposed). Nor could I accept that all three were simultaneously suffering from epilepsy or schizophrenia.

So what were the remaining possibilities? It seemed to me that they were limited to the following:

1   That they were engaged in a deliberate and sustained hoax. To put it bluntly, they were lying.
2   That they were affected by hypnosis: either by one or several of their number, or by self-hypnosis, or even hypnosis controlled by somebody outside the group.

3 That they were hallucinating spontaneously in a powerful act of the imagination.
4 That they were 'given' the hallucinations by a supernatural agency.
5 That the Virgin was there in reality, and that we, the onlookers, had been deprived of normal sight.

My natural inclination was to discount the latter two possibilities and plump for some sort of combination of 2 and 3. Hypnosis, as I had gathered from reading around the subject, is a far more elusive phenomenon than is widely understood. For example, the common notion that people forget their hallucinations or behaviour outside hypnosis has long been proved false, as has the idea that one needs to be on a couch and focusing on a hypnotist's eyes. The forces and laws of hypnotism are powerful, extraordinarily flexible and deeply mysterious, although hardly in a mystical sense. The mechanisms of hypnotism undoubtedly involve complex neurological considerations and the explanation as to what is happening, and how, must surely lie at the frontiers of cognitive science; the problem is that we simply do not understand enough about those mechanisms as yet.

All the same, having seen these young people in action, it seemed to me that there was no reason why a Christian believer might not accept the idea of there being no contradiction in the spiritual presence of the Virgin Mary being combined with a process of hypnotic or imaginative hallucination. This would come within the Christian idea of grace building on nature, and would outflank the extreme debunkers and reductionists, while doing no violence to the views of those who sought rational explanations. Yet even for a believer the question still remained as to whether an authentic spiritual or moral resonance was occurring at Medjugorje. And was this resonance something that only the 'children' were experiencing? Or was it something that the pilgrims were encountering too?

This reflection brought me to my own reactions during the apparition. In the strange otherworldliness of the place, in the peculiar psychic atmosphere that seemed to attend the behaviour of Marija, my imagination and emotions had been stimulated in a quite dramatic fashion. I felt touched. I could not deny that the experience was arresting and even slightly uncomfortable. But had I been in receipt of a genuine moment of what Christians call grace, or was it something more akin to powerful sentimentality?

My personal experiences in the room offered no token or proof of a supernatural agency beyond the vague (but daunting) conviction that I had felt myself drawn towards some sort of 'higher power'; but neither did they disprove a supernatural agency.

I felt aroused, confused, even harassed and restless. But these feelings did not amount to any kind of new-found religious conviction. As for evidence of the paranormal, there remained only the strange phenomenon of the synchronized behaviour of the children.

12   On the Mountain

I made my way to the foot of Križevac hill and began to climb. I had gone no more than twenty yards up the steep rocky path when a little crone leapt out from behind a boulder. She held out her hand for money and mumbled something through her toothless gums; as she did this her face folded up like a concertina. I gave her a note and hurried on.

The path twisted upwards, marked at intervals by the Stations of the Cross. I passed a young man who was walking slowly and painfully up the hill on bare feet; his soles were bloody with lacerations. I tried to smile encouragement through my ill-concealed disgust, and he said: 'It's tough, but it's good for me!'

Another man passed me on his way down; he was carrying a rock on his shoulder. He was shouting with laughter. He cried out at me: 'I'm taking a bit of this little ole mountain with me.'

There were wildflowers – foxglove, purple heather, brilliant poppies – in the rusty soil that clung around the tawny rocks. The scrub resounded with crickets.

A man surrounded by several teenage girls was standing by one of the shrines; he was dressed from head to toe in a sort of pale-blue religious habit. He caught my eye. 'I'll take my vows,' he called out to me, 'on the feast of the Assumption; Our Lady planned it all, a whole host of coincidences; she planned my vocation, everything . . .'

A Spiritual Disneyland

Panting and bathed in sweat I eventually emerged on the summit, which was still flooded with light from the setting sun. There was a platform of rock into which a huge concrete cross some hundred feet high had been set. A man wearing a combat jacket and dark glasses stood to the side of the cross with a tape-recorder to his ear; he was listening to plainchant. A dozen or so pilgrims squatted among the rocks praying in silence.

The stone on the platform had a curiously luminous quality, evidently scorched by votive candles. Stuck in the crevices of the rocks were hundreds of wooden crosses to which were attached thousands of rags, gloves, scarves and handkerchiefs, blowing in the wind like fetishes in a Buddhist graveyard. Pilgrims evidently liked to leave something of themselves behind in the holy place. But what did all these pieces of rag signify; was it the detritus of their sins, their miseries, their lives?

I sat down and looked out at the vista. Medjugorje lay in the foreground, like a picture of a village in a fairy-tale book, its farmhouses spread out in a great loop amidst the fertile fields, with a winding road leading to the very doors of the church. It was a landscape of fable.

Here was the home village of the visionary children, living among devout peasants led by the saintly Franciscans. And up there in the north, beyond those snow-clad mountains, dwelt the wicked bishop in his palace, plotting to stop the visions and to persecute the children and the friars.

What was extraordinary about this fairy-tale was the fact that it was a living, continuing drama, with the protagonists and the antagonist permanently on stage in a long-running show.

The time had come to hear the bishop's side of the story. I started the descent down the mountain.

13   The Bishop of Mostar

At Hotel Biggeste I telephoned the Bishop of Mostar's secretary to arrange an appointment. Bishop Pavao Zanić was not only eager to speak to an English writer about the Medjugorje apparitions, but there should be no delay, he insisted; and the bishop himself would provide an interpreter.

The next morning I drove to Mostar, a grey modern town nestling in a valley beyond the mountains north of Medjugorje. The Baroque episcopal palace on the outskirts of town faced a hulking concrete cathedral across a busy highway. I peered through the glass doors of the cathedral, which looked as enticing as a public toilet; there were nuns inside, polishing the parquet floors.

At the door of the palace I was greeted by a dapper young priest with a halo of curls, who ushered me into a parlour; lace curtains were hung across the french windows and there was a bright modern oil painting of the Assumption of Mary into Heaven. The interpreter had arrived, a young suntanned Yugoslav in a T-shirt; he shook my hand and told me that he had been to California and to Oxford Street.

Bishop Zanić appeared almost instantly, limping a little, as if slightly arthritic. He was somewhat overweight, his silvering hair well trimmed and oiled, his face puffy and purplish around the jowls. He wore a long black linen frock-coat and the black stock below his Roman collar was blemished with food stains. He scrutinized me balefully through horn-rimmed spectacles.

We sat at a long polished table on which he drummed his fingers.

'Look here,' he began, breathing noisily. 'I'd like to say straight off: there's nothing supernatural going on over at Medjugorje. *Nothing!* Understand that and you've grasped everything.' His delivery was explosive, his face bright with emotion.

'In this diocese,' he went on, 'there are about 180,000 Catholics. We have a difficult enough life under the Communists without a gang of kids saying they see the Virgin Mary every day! These Franciscans have been a nuisance to Rome for generations. They are disobedient. They've been in conflict with me for years, because they don't wish to accept my authority over the allocation of parishes. And they're using these so-called apparitions to attempt to get their own way. The Virgin, if you please, is intervening and giving verdicts on the question!'

I said, 'Monsignor, are the children in your view lying! Or are they hypnotized, or what!'

As this was translated I could see Bishop Zanić's leg trembling nervously.

'These so-called visionaries,' he snapped, 'probably experienced something to begin with. I acknowledged that and I said I didn't think they were liars; but the important question is, did they experience something supernatural or was it merely psychological? Most of the reports just take my first words and say that I originally said the children are not lying. You see? They try to make out that I've contradicted myself.'

The bishop was gasping now between sentences, holding on to the table as if it would run away from him.

'Listen,' he went on, 'I have a book in French called *True and False Apparitions.* Out of 230 sets of apparitions of the Virgin Mary in this century the Church has acknowledged only two as authentic; so you have to look on these things with a lot of scepticism.'

'But what makes you so certain that the Medjugorje apparitions are false?' I intervened.

The bishop pointed at a row of some twenty box-files on the sideboard behind him. 'If you could see,' he fumed, 'all the things the visionaries have said from the very beginning . . . And they write that the Pope has said this and said that about Medjugorje, and you discover that he's said nothing of the sort . . .'

'What sort of things did the visionaries tell you?' I asked.

The bishop clenched his fists and shut his eyes tightly. 'When I spoke to the visionaries I got everything they said down on tape,' he said, 'and I caught them out in *lies*. One minute they're saying one thing; the next minute they're contradicting themselves. It would take *weeks* to demonstrate all their lies and contradictions.'

'Anything else?'

'Anything else!' mimicked the bishop. 'It's endless! I saw the notebook of one of them, conversations she'd had with the Virgin. And it was just full of − silliness . . . that the blessed Virgin Mary is talking unfavourably of me, the bishop, and on the side of the Franciscans; that the Virgin Mary is saying that all religions are equal. Then they're saying the Virgin has announced a different date for her birthday. Next, I suppose, they'll want a different date for the Immaculate Conception.'

The bishop fell silent; he was staring, eyes wide stretched, at the french windows. He looked as if he were about to have a fit of apoplexy.

He leapt up from his chair. He paused for a moment, his head cocked. In the shocked silence I could hear the furious buzzing of a bluebottle. Suddenly he lurched across the room towards the windows and began to flail at the curtains until, with a grunt of satisfaction, he had destroyed his quarry. Limping back to the table, he resumed his seat. He took a deep breath and looked at me directly.

'Listen!' he said. 'A Jesuit came to see me and said he'd got hold of this diary of one of the visionaries. It was full of the most complete nonsense that Our Lady was supposed to have said. So I asked to see the diary, and he starts to give me the runaround. First there *was* a diary, then there *wasn't* a diary. Next he's *going* to bring the diary; then he's *not* going to bring the diary. You see, there are so many people playing games!'

'Tell me about the commission of inquiry,' I said.

The bishop seemed to calm down a little. He put his hands together and assumed a more moderate, even defensive, expression.

'The commission? Well, it was very thorough. I had fifteen experts on it. There were thirteen theologians and two psychiatrists, and over a period of three years they studied everything the children said. And at each meeting a member would receive statements and they would be given a job to study a certain statement and bring the answers back at the next meeting. Then we'd examine the answers, discuss them and take a vote on them. At the end of the three years eleven members of the commission voted that there was nothing supernatural going on there; one member abstained; just two voted that the visions were authentic, and those two members were Franciscans! In my opinion all the arguments put forward by those Franciscans were poor.'

'Were there any miracles put before the commission?' I asked.

The bishop threw back his head and laughed. 'They speak

of 300 miracle cures!' he roared. 'They sent documentation on fifty of them to the medical tribunal in Lourdes. Each and every one was turned down.'

'So if the happenings at Medjugorje are bogus, my lord, what is your theory about the children?'

He shifted around uncomfortably in his chair, took off his spectacles and started to wipe them with a handkerchief.

'I was never present at any of the psychiatric examinations,' he started cautiously, 'because I didn't want to show any interest or give any importance to that. But all the results were brought to me, and it's proved that some of the children are not mentally healthy . . .' His voice trailed off vaguely.

'You mean one or more of them are mad?'

The bishop raised his head. 'Please. The doctors' ethic does not allow that to be publicly stated. All I will say is that one of the visionaries has been taken to a mental hospital many times under a false name.'

'Are you referring to Vicka, the one that has a brain cyst? Surely that's common knowledge?'

'No, no, no, no! I'm *not* referring to Vicka. And in any case her cyst is not dangerous.'

The bishop was conscious, it seemed to me, of being on shaky ground. Suddenly he started to flutter his fingers in front of his face, as if to ward off a swarm of flies.

'But all this is beside the point,' he insisted. 'You've heard of the visions at Garabandal in Spain in the sixties? Well, I think those had much more claim to authenticity than these at Medjugorje. But look at the difference between the two cases. The moment the bishop in Spain declared against the visions everybody accepted his verdict and was obedient to him.'

Suddenly the bishop jumped up from his chair and banged his fist on the table. '*Why* do they behave towards me in this way?' he cried. 'Why do they hate me so much? They have written books and books and books, and I have only written twenty-five pages. But they are frightened of my criticism. Those people over there, who are misleading the good, ignorant faithful who come here, deserve to be thrown into the deepest pit of hell!'

The bishop was so beside himself with impatience to get the words through the interpreter I thought he would start pummelling the unfortunate young man, who was struggling to keep up.

'Now!' The bishop's chest was heaving; there were tears in his eyes. 'If Our Lady gives a sign to me of her genuine presence I will be the first to walk all the way to Medjugorje on bare feet! You hear? *Bare feet!* But what will those people over there say to the poor faithful when it is finally proved that the visions are false? What will they say? Eh? And make no mistake about it, many people will abandon the faith when it becomes apparent that the Medjugorje events are false.'

The bishop was beginning to look exhausted.

'One thing seems certain,' I said. 'There are a lot of conversions over there. Don't you think that counts for something?'

'Ha! Conversions! That's the same propaganda given out by the Adventists, the Jehovah's Witnesses, even the Muslims.'

With this the bishop had risen from the table; he was talking to the interpreter. Then he gave me a brief nod and started limping from the room.

The interpreter looked at me a little awkwardly.

'The bishop says he has to go to his lunch now and wishes you good day and *bon voyage*. He says he doubts whether you will be any better than anybody else at getting over his point of view, as nobody wants to hear what he says and report it faithfully. He also says . . . that you are to pay my interpreting fee.' The young man shrugged. 'Which is $10, please.'

14   Marija the Visionary

In the church porch at Medjugorje a group of pilgrims were peering at a bulletin on a red baize noticeboard. They were reading the message that Our Lady had given the visionaries at the previous evening's apparitions; it was typed out in French, German, Italian and English:

Dear children! I desire you to be the reflection of Jesus, who enlightens this unfaithful world which is walking in darkness. I wish that all of you be a light to all and to witness in the light. Dear children, you are called to darkness, you are called to light. Therefore, live the light with your life. Thank you for your response to my call.

These were the supposed actual words of the Virgin Mary.

But what did they mean, 'you are called to darkness, you are called to light'? Was it a riddle to be pondered reverentially? Was it nonsense? The result perhaps of poor translation?

My reverie on the subject was interrupted by Father Svet, a slightly built Franciscan with a huge bald dome of a head, who had run in from the picnic area, his cowl up against the light rain. He had come by arrangement to take me to meet the visionary Marija.

*

A Spiritual Disneyland

There was a flight of steps to the living quarters of Marija's parents' farmhouse. Svet led the way into the kitchen; the walls were painted bright yellow and there were pictures of the Virgin, the Sacred Heart and the Pope. Marija was standing by the stove; she was wearing blue jeans, a blouse and sneakers; her hair was tied with a scarf, peasant-fashion. She greeted me with a hard handshake and ushered us through to a sitting room.

There was just enough space for two armchairs, a sofa and a coffee table. One whole wall was papered with a lake scene against a backdrop of pine woods. Cut-outs of a bumblebee, St Francis of Assisi and the shape of a heart had been pasted on to the side of the lake. There were statues of two child shepherds on the sideboard. Two stickers in English had been fastened to the curtains: 'Praise the Lord,' said one. 'Try God!' said the other.

No sooner had Marija shut the door behind her than she went straight up to Father Svet and launched into a diatribe in Croatian, eyes blazing, face flushed.

While this tantrum was in progress I sat down, placed my mini tape-recorder on the coffee table and switched on. She noticed this action and immediately swooped forward; picking up the little machine she deftly, without a moment's hesitation, pressed the 'off' button and continued with her harangue. Then suddenly she stopped and started to laugh, throwing herself into an armchair opposite me.

Svet smiled. 'It's nothing,' he said to me. 'She's overwhelmed with housework, you know, and the demands of the pilgrims. There was a row this afternoon about a pilgrim group.'

Marija the visionary now gazed at me with bright eyes. She was wearing a T-shirt with a map of Louisiana printed on the front. Down the side of one of her socks was printed' 'MY FRUIT'. When she laughed her gums were prominent. Her looks were unremarkable but her face had something of that appealing luminous quality I had noticed during the apparition.

As I asked my first question she leaned over to her side and moved a vase of flowers on a low table to reveal an effigy of the infant Jesus with white spun-wool hair. She fiddled with the effigy as she began to piece together her story, Father Svet translating sentence by sentence.

'They refer to us as "children", but I'm now twenty-three years of age,' she began. 'As a child I was maybe more delicate in health than my brothers and sisters and more sensitive in my feelings. They doted on me more when I was small, especially my father.

'Among grandfather's belongings I found a book about the life of Dominic Savio, an Italian child saint. Dominic was one of ten children and he died very young from TB, after a life of great holiness. He once remained in ecstatic prayer for six hours. He died having a vision of heaven. He is now the saint whom I love more than any other, even more than St Francis of Assisi.

'The day of the first apparition I was in Vicka's house with a lot of other people from the village listening to her story. Everybody was arguing and laughing, saying that it was probably a flying saucer or shepherd's lantern in the mist. But I begged Vicka to call me if the Virgin appeared again. I told her that I didn't mind if I couldn't see the Virgin, but I wanted to be there.

'The next day, during the second apparition, she came running down off the hill to fetch me; I was with Jakov and he came along as well. When I got up there I could only see a light about a hundred metres away from where the others were standing. It was like a mist clearing; I gradually saw the shape of a figure in a long grey dress and a white veil. I could see her face quite clearly although she was a long way off, at the top of the hill. The Virgin was summoning us and we threw ourselves to the ground. We prayed for a time, then Ivanka asked the Virgin about her mother, who had died two months before. Our Lady told Ivanka that her mother was well and happy. After a quarter of an hour Our Lady told us to go in peace. As we came down the hill Ivanka was in floods of tears.

'The visions have changed my life. As I grew up I had a very different future planned for myself than all this. I trained to be a hairdresser, I thought of getting married, having a family, things that normal little girls think about. Now everything has changed. When my visions have finished I plan to go into a convent. It never occurred to me that I might do something like that. For me a convent was just a prison.

'After my visions began I experienced a steady growth in my faith. I began to feel God more like a friend. Before that I feared God, and my religion was an obligation. Now it's what I want to do, the whole purpose and goal of my life. It's been a kind of school. My faith grows not only from the apparitions, but from my prayers and my meditations, and the sacraments.'

Marija had been talking with great fluency all this time, her face animated, her expressions mobile. She had a very positive, confident personality, and once again I began to be struck by her peculiar beauty, which seemed to bloom the more she became the centre of attention.

I had felt repulsed by her tendency to see her own life in terms of hagiography, but this was somewhat mitigated by her playfulness with the priest. Frequently she laughed at him; several times she kicked him through his habit as he questioned her about a term or phrase she had used. Once or twice she looked at me curiously and winked, as if to say, 'I hope you're getting what you want.'

It occurred to me that she was the strangest mixture of homespun vivacity, peasant shrewdness and priggishness. I wondered, too, whether she might just be capable of fraud, but I rejected the thought even as it came to me.

'People don't understand,' she went on. 'They think of me as a walking saint, but I have my own feelings. There are times when I find it difficult to restrain myself. But then I say it's all for the greater glory of God: for the conversion of sinners, and at that moment I can cope with it.

'There was an incident just today when somebody accused me of refusing to come out to see pilgrims. This woman had simply made it up. So I said to her, "Lies are short-lived." I wanted to show her that I knew she was a liar and that I wasn't some sort of deaf-and-dumb holy statue. I know what's going on!

'I lead an extremely busy life because of the apparitions and the pilgrims. Sometimes I take a cushion, go to the hill, sit down on a rock where nobody can see me and remain in prayer and silence. That's when I have the best rest, when I pray by myself.

'If you devote more time to your friend, then you will come to know his secrets. It's the same with God. The more time we devote to God the more we shall know him and the easier we shall find it to talk about him because we have experienced him.

'I am conscious that my life may not always be so well protected. Our Lady once said: "You are in an oasis but Satan is lurking outside." I'm not afraid because I have a great trust in God. And yet God has given us freedom. Each of us can decide for or against God.'

With this, Marija's story or homily had reached a natural conclusion, and she stood up, signalling that our meeting was at an end.

She shook me by the hand and looked solemnly into my eyes. 'Do you have any special intentions or personal requests,' she asked, 'to put before Our Lady?'

The question threw me. I knew that for a confirmed believer this might have seemed a wonderful privilege. In my state of complicated scepticism and obsession it made my blood turn cold. Instead of answering it, I said, a trifle meanly, 'Marija, am I right in saying that you think yourself holier than others because of these visions?'

Father Svet was unhappy with the question, but he translated it all the same.

She was unruffled. 'Certainly I am not better,' she said. 'What's more, I could have passed on the messages without obeying them myself. But Our Lady says time and time again: live and testify with your lives.'

As I picked up my tape-recorder I said, 'Marija, when Our Lady speaks does she say the same thing to all of you? Simultaneously?'

'Not necessarily,' she said. 'She says different things to us at the same time.'

'And another thing. Can you describe how Our Lady speaks? I mean, is there anything special about the way she says things that is different from the way ordinary people like you and I speak?'

'She speaks in Croatian,' said Marija promptly, 'and you get the impression that every word is exactly the right word and that it is in exactly the right place.'

At the kitchen door she shook me vigorously by the hand.

I said, 'I'm very grateful for the time you've given me. I'm sorry if I've added to your troubles.'

'It's no extra burden,' she said, 'and even if it were, I would welcome it, because it means I would get to my Father in heaven more quickly.' She said this without the slightest hint of self-mockery.

As Father Svet and I came out of the house a band of pilgrims had gathered below the balcony hoping for a glimpse of her. Svet stood in the lane looking at me.

'That was remarkable,' he said. 'Did you hear that? If you devote more time to your friend then you will come to know his secrets. And it's the same with God. That's beautiful.'

We walked a little down the lane together. Father Svet still seemed captivated by the interview.

'She's different from the others, you know. Vicka is ill a lot of the time, and she is a great example of suffering. The other two girls, I believe, have resisted their vocations as seers – they would never have given interviews like that. But Marija has said an unreserved "yes" to the call; she is cooperating fully with the opportunities God is giving her.'

Further down the road he stopped and looked about him at the thronging pilgrims. He placed his hand on his chest. 'You know,' he said, 'even if Our Lady is not appearing here in reality, I have to say that the fruits of Medjugorje are good. I do not think God will punish us for what we are doing: we do everything in good faith. How can anyone say that this is bad?'

After Svet had gone I went to sit in the church. I was watching the peasant pilgrims kneeling at their long, silent vigils before the statue of the Virgin, trying to weigh up in my mind what I thought of Marija.

I found her priggishness distasteful and yet I was impressed by her comments about the vision's mode of speech, which was as close to a definition of poetry as one could wish from a girl of her education and background. I was convinced that she was not a liar. I felt that she had a strong, charismatic personality, and I wondered if she had taken on the role of a ringleader capable of manipulating the others and engaging in unconscious hypnotic practice.

It occurred to me, too, that in a former age a young woman such as Marija might well have been hauled before the Holy Inquisition to explain and defend her revelations. Historians are only now beginning to discover the extent to which investigations into the religious paranormal were projected substitutes for the clergy's unconscious inclinations towards doubt and apostasy, their deep fear and hatred of the power of women. Having seen Marija in the midst of the priests, it seemed to me that her role was anomalous and fraught with risk. Her status as seer, as prophetess, had raised her above the male-dominant priesthood; but it would be foolish to imagine that the priests were not ultimately and firmly in control. Her situation, it seemed to me, was precarious, and I found it difficult to believe that there might not be a heavy price to be paid in the fullness of time.

15 Satan's Free Hand

As I passed the steps of the parish house I ran into Father Keogh. He was listening to a tall monk who sported a goatee beard that quivered as if with the vehemence of his utterance.

Father Keogh, who was evidently trying to escape the man's clutches, grabbed me by the wrist. 'You should talk to this fellow here,' he said with a wink. 'He's an exorcist. When he exorcises people they vomit up the demons.'

The monk eyed me speculatively. He was stroking his hairy wrists and forearms as if contemplating a fight. Before I could say a word Father Keogh had taken off with a chuckle.

'Does the Virgin speak of Satan?' I asked politely.

He looked stern. 'Listen!' he said. 'In 1890 Pope Leo XIII had a vision that Christ was to give Satan a free hand in the world for exactly one hundred years. This explains many things in the world. The end of his time is near, and he is getting more and more angry and desperate.'

The priest spoke rapid English with an American accent.

'The time of Our Lady, she who in the book of the Apocalypse crushes the serpent under her heel, is now coming,' he went on. 'But the World Wars, the rise of Communism, are explained by Satan's grip over the world in the past one hundred years. You are about to see a vast change in the world as we approach the year 2000: the demise of world

97

Communism, the re-establishment of the Kingdom of Christ. The day will come when you will see a statue of the Virgin surmounting the Kremlin. Maximilian Kolbe, the Franciscan saint of the death camps, saw this in a vision. And it all links with the Virgin of Medjugorje: AIDS, the disaster at Chernobyl, the shuttle disaster, the Armenian earthquake . . . These are clearly the chastisements Our Lady refers to in the children's visions. But we see many wonderful signs of conversion and transformation, too, all linked with the warnings. There are wondrous prospects as we turn to the Virgin. On the Eve of the Feast of Our Lady of the Immaculate Conception last, President Reagan, President-elect Bush and Gorbachev stood together at the foot of the Statue of Liberty. President Reagan said: "Read our smiles!" The very next day Gorbachev flew back to Russia as a result of the earthquake in Armenia. What does it all mean? Who knows! We must ponder these things in our hearts. Our Lady is very busy. Last week she failed to appear to the children on Thursday. We puzzled and prayed over this . . . then I read in the *International Herald Tribune* that she had appeared to a nun in the Philippines on that very same evening. We can only ponder these things in our hearts . . .'

As I drove back to the hotel I remembered a cutting remark of one of my colleagues: 'A good journalist doesn't entertain mumbo-jumbo, even to debunk it!' I was beginning to feel sympathy for the view.

I went into the restaurant in search of something to eat. As I sat at a table reading my notes I heard a strange noise to my left from behind a curtain: 'Da-da-da-da!'

I looked up to see the hotel manager shooting at me with two fingers. He giggled with childish glee. 'Here comes the Mafia! Da-da-da-da!' he cried, and retreated again behind a curtain. At length a waiter appeared and took my order for dinner.

After a while a lean, sallow man of about fifty sat down at the next table. He carried a suitcase from which he took several books. He told me that he was an American, a Catholic publisher and tour operator.

When I told him that I was a writer, he held up a colour booklet. 'See this?' he said. 'We're reprinting this thing at the rate of 10,000 every month. Every month of the year. I bet you never saw sales like that.'

Between mouthfuls of dubious-looking stew and nervous drags on a Marlboro cigarette he reeled off facts and figures about back-to-back flights, publishing reprints and video productions. Everything was 'looking good!'

'What do you make of the visions?' I asked.

'The most fantastic thing is that they keep going,' he said. 'But I think I know why. Do you realize that this is the first set of apparitions in the modern age of the media? I think that Our Lady is keeping the visions going so we can get market penetration.'

As I began to laugh he said, 'No, I'm not kidding you, buddy. That's what I really think! And I'll tell you one thing, we're dead worried the Pope's going to pronounce against it. If he does, it will show everybody's been taken for a ride and it'll kill the thing stone dead. There are a helluva lot of buildings going up, including a hotel with 500 bedrooms. It's all private money, all private risk.'

'You're saying, then, that a lot of people are going to be ruined if the Church says that the visions are false?'

'Actually, if you want my honest opinion, and I wouldn't like you to quote me by name on this, it's a no-win situation no matter what happens. People come here, *I* think, because they like the unspoilt village atmosphere, but that's all disappearing in uncontrolled development. The place is going to lose out eventually whatever happens. That's just my personal opinion. But in the meantime, we're reprinting that thing at the rate of 10,000 a month!'

'Do you believe in the apparitions yourself?'

'I don't know,' he said. 'I was brought up to believe that it's all about faith, about believing in what you can't see. But this younger generation is different – it needs to see and hear. Perhaps it's something to do with the effect of television.'

When he had finished his stew he came over to my table to say goodbye. As he shook hands he said, 'Mind you, I've seen people witnessing these strange visions of the sun. I've seen more than a hundred people witnessing it spin and change colour. I don't know. I just wish we could get it on video.'

16   *Vicka's Descent into Hell*

O n the eve of my departure from Medjugorje I went to the parish house to meet Father Svet, who this time had arranged a meeting with the visionary Vicka. He seemed curious about my reactions; eager to discover whether I had formed any strong objections to the cult.

'I suppose,' I said mischievously, and without quite understanding what I meant by it, 'one of them could be a medium for the others.'

Svet looked at me solemnly and shook his head. 'Look, there's an Italian priest-sociologist called Gramaglia who suggested this without ever having been here. How can somebody make pronouncements without studying the phenomenology? Anyway, I think I can prove that the medium idea is nonsense, because the apparitions have occurred with every combination of the group, one, three, four, five and all six together, and a problem never arose because somebody was missing. Unless you are going to say that they are all mediums.

'And if one of them was a medium,' he went on a little heatedly now, 'how do you explain that they're doing it at a distance? If you can't answer that question, what you say makes no sense.'

With this Vicka arrived and threw herself into an armchair, as if feigning exhaustion. She was a sturdy young woman with a wide face and wild almond-shaped eyes. Her speech was rapid and excited.

A Spiritual Disneyland

Using Father Svet as interpreter she told me first about the appearance of the Virgin: her height, her apparel, the texture of her flesh, the sound of her voice, the manner in which she moved from place to place. I learnt that the Virgin never showed her feet; that the cut of her clothes was always the same, although on special feast days she wore cloth-of-gold. She could be touched, and indeed even kissed. One day a child with dirty fingers had left marks on the Virgin's veil.

I asked her about the manner in which the visions commenced.

'She used to come in the form of a light,' said Vicka, 'then we would go to her. We prayed, sang, asked her questions; later she would start to appear as soon as we prayed. It was like a light-picture approaching us, then in a second she was in front of us, clear, beautiful, smiling; we would kneel down. Sometimes she would come the moment we crossed ourselves, sometimes we would pray ten to fifteen Our Fathers before she came . . . She eventually got into a routine. She usually left more quickly than she came.'

'Did anybody else appear in these visions?' I asked.

'In Marija's house in 1981 four of us had an apparition: when Our Lady arrived she was holding in her hand a picture of Pope John Paul II that had been hanging on the wall in the room. Our Lady kissed the Pope's picture. The picture is still at Marija's; Our Lady said we should keep it in a safe place.'

Vicka went on to describe how she had had visions of Christ – both as the child in the Holy Family, and in the form of a bust depicting the crowning with thorns. She explained how the Virgin had said that the local bishop 'made a mistake'. She added: 'But it's well known that anybody can make mistakes.'

'Have you had any other sorts of visions?' I asked her.

'Our Lady showed us heaven; it's beautiful beyond words;

we saw Ivanka's mother there, and another woman we knew. One day Our Lady disappeared and in front of us appeared hell. Jakov, Marija and myself saw a local woman with blonde hair that we knew, a woman that had died; she had horns, and there were devils jumping sort of sideways towards her.'

I stared at Vicka for a few moments in silence. At length I said, 'How did it come about that you visited heaven?'

'I was over at Jakov's house at about 3 o'clock in the afternoon,' she said. 'His mother was out somewhere. Our Lady appeared and said, "Glory to Jesus," and told us that she was going to take us to heaven. We were frightened; Jakov started screaming. He said he didn't want to go because he was an only child and I could go on my own. Our Lady didn't say anything. We were on our knees and she took our hands – me by my right and Jakov by his left, and she stood between us with her face turned towards us, and we started to rise up immediately, right up through the ceiling. The house disappeared and we were going upwards. I was afraid but I tried not to think. We reached heaven quite soon.'

'And what is heaven like?' I asked her.

'It's full of beautiful flowers and angels. Just like people say.'

'What else did you see?'

'Purgatory. It's a dark abyss, a dark space between heaven and hell. It's full of ashes and it looks horrible.'

'Did Our Lady tell you why she had shown it to you?' I asked.

'She wanted us to know that it's the place where souls have to cleanse themselves,' said Vicka. 'And they are in need of a lot of prayers.'

'And how did you return to earth?'

'The same way we went up,' said Vicka confidently. 'She took us back inside the house and said goodbye and left. We started to adjust slowly; it took us a little time. Jakov's mother saw us first, she asked us where we had been hiding. She said she had been looking for us. She started to cry because Jakov was in such a state.'

I had heard enough of Vicka's testimony. I turned to Father Svet and told him that I had finished.

With this he said something to Vicka and they both rose and left the room. I sat for a while musing. Up till now most of what I had heard about the visionary content of Medjugorje had kept just on the right side of the traditional expression of pious private revelation on the one hand and prophetic Marian conventions on the other. Vicka's account, however, went well beyond that pale; all the same, I was intrigued by the psychology of her experience. Assuming for a moment that she was not lying, I could only speculate that she had vividly imagined and acted out the entire episode and related it in turn to Jakov, who had responded to her suggestions as if to a real experience.

After a few moments Father Svet reappeared; he was peering at me owlishly as if expectant for a reaction.

'Very interesting,' I ventured. 'But I must say that I'm worried a bit about Vicka's hell.'

'All you have to understand,' he said, 'is that when God reveals a supernatural truth, he does it according to our capacities. Vicka is a simple peasant girl; there is a maxim in scholastic philosophy: "*Quicquid recipitur, per modum recipientis recipitur.*" Whatever is received is received in the manner of the receiver. Do you understand my meaning?'

I nodded.

'And what are you going to do now?' he asked.

I thought for a moment. I wanted to be truthful with the priest, not merely polite. 'I think,' I said, 'that I am going home to read the Gospels again.'

The priest smiled and put a gentle hand on my shoulder.

'Wouldn't it be better, Mr John, to go home and read the messages of Our Lady?'

17   Mystery and Manipulation

That evening by the light of a full moon I made my way to the summit of the hill of the apparitions one last time. The ragged rocks seemed luminous in the pale light and I could make out pilgrims huddled in silence among the primitive wooden crosses and votive candles. As Dermot had promised, the birds were singing in unrestrained chorus in the trees and bushes below, lending an atmosphere of peculiar excitement to the night vigil.

I looked out on the amphitheatre of the mountains: the whitewashed church gleaming in the lunar light, the fertile valley fragrant with night scents. I felt confused about my experience in Medjugorje. My witnessing of the apparition had somehow opened up my heart, and yet I was deeply troubled by many aspects of the shrine.

Huddled up with my back against a rock, I tried to sort out my thoughts about the 'children'. It occurred to me that whatever their genuine spiritual experience, they were open to considerable manipulation and exploitation on the part of the cult's impresarios and promoters. Their visions now seemed to be structured into a daily routine that had become part of the liturgical ritual. The daily timetable of the visions before Mass every evening had the effect both of creating a daily expectation and of associating the phenomena with the Mass itself — as if the visions were part of the most powerful cere-

106

mony in Catholic worship. This seemed to me to provide not only the circumstances of subtle coercion, but to lend liturgical authority to the proceedings in the eyes of the pilgrims.

And the pilgrims at Medjugorje were being told week in, week out, through Our Lady's messages, that things would go well in the world if there was a return to the rosary, but things would go very badly if there was not. To the gullible sensation-seekers who flocked to the place in huge numbers this was a clear signal that history was merely the capricious plaything of the supernatural. Among these people there was not so much an atmosphere of genuine prayer as a feeling that the Virgin required appeasement.

This fundamentalist tendency in Medjugorje, with its authoritarian and exclusivist programme based on primitive fear and propitiation, was clearly at odds with the post-conciliar model of the Catholic Church, which had committed the faithful to a middle ground of pluralism. Nothing so strengthens a strident, fundamentalist agenda as apocalyptic revelation, accompanied by alleged paranormal phenomena.

The principal means of manipulation at Medjugorje, it seemed to me, involved the amplification of folk religious experience (the ancient Mediterranean tradition of local Marian apparitions), via the skilful use of publishing and the pilgrim-tourist business, into a species of designer pop-religion. The by-products ranged from a type of 'Dungeons and Dragons', do-it-yourself 'Star Wars' mysticism – spinning suns and sky pictures and talismanic weapons against the powers of darkness (alchemies to turn rosaries to gold) – to supra-scientific 'beam-me-up-Scotty' theories of the supernatural, of which the magic photographs and the scientists' encephalograph machines were typical examples.

Father Foley had described the Medjugorje cult, with approval, as a 'veritable spiritual Disneyland'. The phrase was an accurate, if unconscious, description of the promise of make-believe phenomena that was being peddled worldwide by promoters who were bringing 2 million people there each year.

The tour promoter I ran into in the hotel had boasted that he had a mailing list of more than 100,000 'pilgrims' who had spent an average of $500 each on videos, books and devotional items connected with the cult. The travel arrangements, moreover, probably involved gross sales in many millions of dollars a year. 'We've only scratched the surface,' he had told me with satisfaction.

But money alone was clearly not the prime objective. The ultimate goal was an attempt to deal a blow against the perceived enemy of the Christian right: the bogeys of socialism, rationalism and secular humanism. The principal casualty, however, was likely to be the tolerant, moderate middle ground.

And yet I was nevertheless convinced that despite the exploitation on the periphery, Medjugorje was an unusual focus of spirituality in modern times, one that outweighed the sum of its drawbacks.

The old peasant people who knelt hour after hour in the silent church were a reminder that the shrine was a place of amnesty from the world's doubts and miseries and evils; a deliverance from helplessness. Against the background of injustice, famine, violence, war, ecological disaster, race hatred, drug abuse, Medjugorje offered a message of hope. Under its auspices pilgrims could renew their confidence. Here on pilgrimage there were no class or racial distinctions; all were equal in the eyes of the Mother of God; money, clothes, possessions, counted for nothing; few came here by car; the lodgings were simple, many people sleeping on the floors; many fasting as often as three days of the week. People who normally saw themselves as powerless, disenfranchised, help-less, weak, believed that they could do something about the world, about their predicament, and would return streng-thened and refreshed to their homes, their communities and their work.

Medjugorje, then, seemed to me a curious mixture of im-pressive spiritual drama and obnoxious manipulation. Its neg-ative aspects had by no means encouraged me to dismiss the phenomenon as fraudulent, nor had its positive qualities demonstrated an overwhelming sense of supernatural authen-ticity. My principal conviction was that the cult raised far more questions that it answered.

PART THREE

Real Presences

18   Briege McKenna

Father Keogh, Father Foley and others had told me of the crucial role of a nun called Sister Briege McKenna in the Medjugorje story, and referred to her as one of the most charismatic figures in the Catholic Church: she had, they claimed, astonishing healing powers, as well as gifts of prophecy, bilocation and the ability to 'see' into people's hearts. According to Father Foley, Briege McKenna had foretold the Yugoslav Marian apparitions during a prayer meeting in Rome before a large number of witnesses a month before they began.

On my return from Medjugorje I decided that I wanted to meet her, to see whether I would be impressed with her powers. When I called on him once more at Farm Street, Father Foley promptly volunteered to effect the introduction. 'Such an extraordinary woman,' he said. 'She's the successor to the great Padre Pio! You must see her; but you must be prepared, she is a most daunting person.'

Father Foley then proceeded to fill me in on her background as a prelude to my meeting her in Dublin.

Sister Briege left school in Northern Ireland at fifteen to become a member of the Poor Clares, one of the most austere religious orders in the Catholic Church. Now aged forty, she had an unparalleled reputation as a healer; she was, moreover, an outstanding spiritual director of bishops and priests, with legendary gifts of discernment.

113

Sister Briege was currently ministering to many thousands of prelates, priests and monks on five continents: including bishops and cardinals, and even national leaders. President José Sarney of Brazil had gone on television holding a rosary in his hand to announce that a meeting with Sister Briege had transformed his spiritual life. No one in the contemporary Church, according to Father Foley, could rival this Irish nun for her 'supernatural' reputation.

Her ministry had begun from a convent in Tampa, Florida, fifteen years earlier. Her education was slight and she had never had any formal training in theology. Her inspiration was said to come from between three and five hours' daily prayer and the exercise of visionary powers that, again according to Father Foley, could unnerve the most hardened and cynical.

Her special ministry to priests and religious was set against the background of a major shift in the Church. Following the upheavals of the Vatican Council in the late sixties, more than 100,000 priests had abandoned their ministries, leaving an overworked and largely demoralized clergy. A great many priests suffered from sexual difficulties and alcoholism; and there were other, darker problems on the periphery, especially in America, associated with witchcraft, paedophilia, New Ageism and even Satanism.

Sister Briege had broken through the normal time-consuming process of counselling. She would see each priest alone. Taking him by the hand, she would put an arm around one shoulder and bow her head towards him. After a few brief prayers she would begin to perceive what she called a 'word of knowledge' that came unbidden into her head: it was a vivid allegory or emblem. Invariably it illustrated a deep-seated spiritual problem or anxiety; sometimes she would confront a priest with a grave habitual sin. She would begin to speak to him in the words of Christ or the Virgin Mary, using the first person. Frequently it was a message of comfort and sympathy; sometimes a severe reprimand. The experience was often so stunning that many priests broke down in tears. She had been know to pick someone out of a crowd of thousands and say, 'Hey! You! If you don't shape up, you'll burn in hell!'

For ten years now she had been travelling – always by invitation – ministering to scores of priests daily at special retreats. In the previous year her itinerary had included Brazil, Nigeria, France, Holland, Australia, Taiwan and the United States. She was block-booked solidly for the next two years. These were not lightning calls to capital cities, although she had regularly filled whole stadiums in Brazil and Nigeria; she travelled the length and breadth of each country, visiting remote parishes and mission stations. And she would continue to communicate with her charges by telephone and by sending out a daily flood of hand-written 'little notes'.

The more I heard of Father Foley's glowing report, the more I was reminded of the large energies of the great saints of history, and especially women like Catherine of Sienna, Teresa of Avila and Catherine of Genoa. I was excited at the prospect of meeting a woman who might one day be looked upon as one of the outstanding spiritual figures of the twentieth century.

But it struck me that by the same token her so-called powers might be no more significant than a clairvoyant's or a fortune-teller's. By any criteria, it seemed to me, she appeared open to accusations of exploiting men who lived unusually stressful and lonely lives and who came to her with high expectations.

A week after my second meeting with Father Foley I flew to Dublin to meet Sister Briege McKenna. The taxi took me from the airport through driving rain towards the city. At length we turned off an avenue lined with suburban villas and entered the gates of a spacious park surrounded by a high wall. There was a sweep of drive through oak trees, and ahead lay a long, slate-grey, barrack-like building with high, curtainless windows; at the far end of the building stood a gloomy neo-Gothic church with flying butresses. This was All Hallows College, Drumcondra, the largest missionary seminary in the world. The students were now away and it was Sister Briege's headquarters for her retreats when she was in Ireland.

A cheerful lady called Barbara met me at the administrator's desk in the lobby and took me to my room on the first floor. The house was deserted and our shoes echoed on the granite stairway.

'All the fathers are in church,' she said crisply. 'Lunch is at 1.15.'

The room was cell-like. There was a single narrow bed, a small desk and chair, a cupboard and a wash-basin, a piece of grey drugget on the bare floorboards. There was a crucifix hanging above the bed.

I stood at the window listening to the rain falling in a steady curtain, smudging the distant mountains in the west. A flock of seagulls wheeled about a flood-pool on the seminary's playing fields. The houses of Drumcondra were hidden by a line of flourishing horse-chestnut trees. I sat on the bed and felt a sense of strange languor associated with memories of the religious institutions I had inhabited in my youth: the smell of beeswax polish, the heavy stillness of a large house where time stands still, waiting for the next church service or communal meal. Something about my destined encounter with Sister Briege was nagging me. The atmosphere of the seminary was creating a strange mood in me, evoking shadowy, fearful recollections of guilt in the presence of Irish nuns and priests, figures of strict authority and discipline throughout my childhood.

At length an electric bell rang in the house and there was a knock on the door. Barbara had come to take me to lunch.

Priests by the score were spilling from the church into the cloister. They seemed mostly in their early fifties, many of them with brick-red Irish complexions. They walked in twos and threes, hands behind their backs, in earnest conversation.

Uneasy at the sight of this clerical conclave, I was on the point of considering withdrawing to the safety of the playing fields when I was suddenly accosted and overwhelmed by the presence of the woman herself. She came upon me in a bustling rush. Her face was squarish, rather pasty, with a hint of freckles around the nose. A widow's peak of dark auburn hair and wide, rawboned features confirmed her Irish origins. Her grey eyes scrutinized me with a daunting frankness. She looked exhausted, there were deep lines about her eyes and mouth, and yet her face had a gentle, youthful appeal of humour and kindness. She grabbed me by the forearms and gave me an affectionate little pat. Her hands were pale, freckly, delicate.

She was physically close, and talking insistently, urgently, although I could not seem to concentrate on anything she was saying. I felt a delightful bat-squeak of feminine allure, and yet she exuded an unassailable chasteness as bracing as convent soap and cold water.

As befitting a thoroughly modern nun she was dressed in comfortable blouse and hand-knit cardigan. Her two concessions to religious status were a silver crucifix and a short brown veil.

She was leading me to the refectory and explaining the gathering of priests in a rapid, melodic brogue with a hint of Ulster. The participants, she was saying, had travelled from as far as Papua New Guinea, Brazil, Nigeria and Australia. There were clerics from a variety of religious orders – Jesuits, Franciscans, Dominicans, Carmelites – and several bishops. Many of them, she said, were Irish missionaries.

Suddenly I found myself seated beneath the glowering portraits of nineteenth-century prelates and a man was serving me boiled bacon, potatoes and watery cabbage.

Sister Briege was looking at me very directly. There was something both deeply mature and yet extraordinarily childlike about her, an impression of wisdom, experience and innocence. I was conscious of a sense of holiness, and yet she was very ordinary. Her features were unremarkable, almost plain, but her eyes and mouth had an impressive, mobile beauty.

I managed to ask, 'What is it like, having miraculous powers?' I was conscious, even as I said it, that it was a stupid, journalistic question, but she treated it with seriousness.

'Nobody could have been more reluctant than I was to believe I had special powers,' she began. She had slowed down now, and she was choosing her words carefully. 'I used to pray, "Oh, God, please keep your miracles to yourself." But they're not my powers; I give them back to God every night of my life.' She laughed. 'And if I get a headache I usually take an aspirin.'

It all began, she went on, with a dramatic healing of her own body. When Briege was twelve, her mother had died of a cerebral haemorrhage. In 1962, at fifteen, she had left behind her tenant-farmer father and four brothers to enter a strictly enclosed convent in Newry, County Armagh. Her father was heartbroken, but he told her, 'If that's what you want, go ahead, and if it's not what you want, you'll know it.' Two years later she developed crippling rheumatoid arthritis in her feet and hands. She remembers the sisters had to put plaster boots on her feet to prevent deformity. 'I used to faint with the pain.' She was transferred to a community in Tampa, Florida, but the humid climate only made things worse. 'By 1968 I was a cripple, on high doses of cortisone. My feet were completely twisted and I had sores.'

During this period she was suffering problems with her religious vocation and sat for many hours in the chapel close to despair. 'One morning I felt a hand on my head. I opened my eyes and no one was there, but I felt a power going through my body. I looked down. My fingers were limber, the sores were gone and my feet were no longer deformed. I jumped up screaming, "Jesus! You're right here!"'

The summer after her healing she returned to Ireland for a holiday and cured a woman dying of cancer in the hospital in Newry. Sister Briege laughed happily again: 'The town was in an uproar looking for the healing nun. Every time they saw a nun in a brown habit in the street they would dash after her.'

But the 'miracles' were a mere prelude to what she saw as her real mission – the renewal of the Catholic priesthood. She received the call while alone in prayer in 1975. She had been kneeling in the convent chapel thinking about the defection of priests throughout the world and she cried out loud: 'Oh God, what is wrong with the priesthood?'

She began to receive a sequence of visions that appeared vividly 'as on a television screen' above the tabernacle on the altar and lasted four hours. 'I found myself weeping as I watched the unfolding of this powerful revelation of the priest-hood.' A voice told her to go out into the world and lead priests back to God.

As she talked I could not help being impressed by her natural gaiety and frankness. She had the unusual ability to talk about religious matters without seeming nunnish or prig-gish. But this naturalness and vitality seemed to mask a core of obsessive determination and seriousness. Everything she said was to the point; there was no small talk. And in the rare moments when her smile failed, she seemed hag-ridden with effort. Sitting in the midst of the noisy refectory her attention was devoted entirely to me.

As the refectory began to clear, she stood up, her meal barely touched. She said she would find time to talk with me after supper in the evening. 'You must stay for two or three days,' she said with a final pat on my forearm. 'Don't run away from us just yet.'

I wandered out into the cloister. The walls were lined with ordination-day photographs of students. They told their own story. Up to the 1960s there had been thirty or forty priests ordained every year; in more recent photographs there were no more than four or five.

When I came out into the grounds the rain had stopped and I could see the clergymen strolling slowly together in pairs along the cinder paths. I decided to take a walk in the direction of the deserted outer reaches of the football pitches.

'How curious,' I thought. 'I'm on retreat!' Then I realized that in the past two weeks or so I had also been on a pilgimage, and during all this time I had given very little thought to the world of journalism and business. And yet I had not prayed. As I walked around the cinder track at the far end of the grounds I began to worry about whether I should attempt to pray or not. In Medjugorje I had been too busy studying those about me to think of myself. It had not occurred to me that I should want to pray, nor had I even pondered the question of the existence of God.

I had not prayed for nearly twenty-five years. Nor did I feel any great need to do it now. But somehow, in the wake of my meeting with Briege McKenna, the idea had taken a strange grip on me. 'Why not do it just to see what happens?' I thought. But almost as quickly I said to myself, 'No!' Prayer meant submission, a loss of independence and self-confidence. I turned towards the college buildings.

Back in my room I fell asleep on the bed and began to dream about putting sheets of paper into a typewriter; every time I took a fresh, snowy white sheet and rolled it through, it came out stained with black ink.

Perhaps an hour into my sleep I began to have a recurring dream. I sensed that Sister Briege was 'working on my soul': I had no clear idea what this meant, but it was a phrase that kept recurring in the dream. Was she talking to me? Praying for me? Then I became conscious of a cynical voice that kept saying, 'There can be no life or experience that is in any way imaginable, or knowable, beyond this body. This is an *absolute* truth.'

When I awoke I looked out of the window and saw that it was raining again and that the priests had disappeared.

I wandered down to the ground floor and walked along a corridor looking into the public rooms. At length I opened the door of an oratory. It was a spacious room full of light, furnished with stripped-pine chairs and white carpets. Six or seven priests were praying in various postures; some of them were lying face down on the floor, their heads pointing in the direction of an inner room where I could see a red sanctuary lamp and a tabernacle.

I entered the oratory and found myself a seat. Out of sight of the priests I sat for a while contemplating the silence and the stillness. The traffic, the streets, the city, seemed infinitely distant. I felt a sense of admiration for this small band of priestly survivors. They reminded me of the peasants in black in the church at Medjugorje. They were irrelevant, impotent, in terms of the daylight realities of the world, and yet their faith in the presence of God in that little box on the wall gave them a kind of majesty. I tried to imagine what it must be like

121

to believe that Christ was actually present, a living, thinking being, hidden within the tabernacle; but I found it difficult even to simulate the frame of mind of somebody who accepted such a notion.

Sitting in the silence of the chapel I was suddenly gripped with terror and disgust. I was not ready for this, I thought. I was not ready for Sister Briege McKenna. I rose and left the chapel and went straight to my room to pack. I wanted to be out of All Hallows College as fast as my legs could carry me.

Five minutes later, as I stood by the desk in the lobby waiting for the administrator to call a taxi, Sister Briege appeared smiling.

'Off so soon?' she said. 'Never mind, we'll meet again.'

With this she took both my hands in hers and kissed me on the cheek.

19   The Clever Horse Hans

Back in England I spent several days reviewing my notes and considering the next move. Although I was keen to travel by instinct, I needed an overall plan of the terrain. I was beginning to see a rough shape to the categories of supernatural evidence available in the Christian tradition, and I hoped to seek out contemporary examples of them all – although not necessarily in strict order. This was my first list:

1   Apparitions, visions, voices of supernatural figures, including the Virgin Mary, saints, Christ, Satan, angels, demons.

2   Prophetic utterances as a result of intuition or dreams, and gifts of discernment such as seeing into a person's past life.

3   Miracles of healing.

4   Synchronicities, or extraordinary coincidences with a spiritual or moral significance.

5   Physical prodigies such as stigmata, odour of sanctity, levitation, bilocation and speaking in unlearnt languages.

6   Material prodigies such as the Holy Shroud of Turin, the liquefaction of blood of St Januarius in Naples, weeping and bleeding statues.

7   Psychic experiences with moral and spiritual significance, such as a sense of having returned from the dead, and feelings of being possessed by evil spirits or demons.

I was mainly concerned with investigating phenomena that were above suspicion as far as fraud was concerned. And while I wished to observe and probe, I was not at this stage principally interested in formulating strict, rational or scientific answers. Yet the question of 'authenticity' was important: if I were not to consign all mystical experience to subjectivism, I would have to run the risk of getting personally involved, as I had learnt from my experience in Ireland. One needed to approach the religious paranormal with all one's antennae engaged in order to grasp the world, the milieu, the culture, of these phenomena on their own terms. I had no answer to the problem of getting personally involved, except to acknowledge that I must follow my obsession, my feelings, wherever they led.

But where next?

I was talking one evening in London with a neurologist friend about the synchronized behaviour of the 'children' and the spinning suns of Medjugorje. He dismissed the latter as a simple case of saturation of the retinal pigments, commenting that people can 'actually get better at doing it'; but he was more intrigued by the synchronized mannerisms and silent speech gestures of the visionaries.

'This sort of synchronized behaviour is almost certainly accounted for by cues,' he said. 'And the fact that you couldn't see the cues doesn't mean that they were not happening. They might be cueing each other by a faint auditory sign, such as a slight intake of breath. Have you never heard of the case of Clever Hans?

'Clever Hans,' he went on, 'was a German horse that supposedly could do arithmetic. This involved stamping with its hoof a simple signal for yes or no, in response to suggested answers to arithmetical problems on a board in front of it.

Hans was rumbled by Osker Pfungst in 1911, when he demonstrated that the horse failed to perform when its trainer was not in view. The animal had apparently been sensing signals imperceptible even to the trainer, who had been unconsciously relaxing when the correct answer was given.

'The curious synchronized behaviour of the children at Medjugorje may well have been managed, perhaps unwittingly, by cues that were invisible to the onlooker,' said my friend.

The phenomenon of cueing seemed to provide a partial answer to the problem; and yet I was not altogether satisfied with this as a complete solution, for it seemed to me that there was something that we were missing in the *significance* of the synchronization in itself. I felt that I was far from understanding the symbolic nature of Marian apparitions, and I wanted to look at the phenomena from that perspective.

Shortly after this conversation I came across another case of highly synchronized behaviour in a recent series of Marian apparitions. Once more through the good services of Father Foley, I had received a curious video with some accompanying literature depicting the behaviour of four little girls who had reputedly received visions of Michael the Archangel, and later of the Virgin Mary, in a remote village called Garabandal in northern Spain in the early sixties. The Bishop of Mostar and Father Keogh had both mentioned Garabandal, and their reports of the phenomena there had stimulated my curiosity.

The video was composed of a variety of still photographs and home movies showing the girls in a variety of extraordinary postures and elaborate synchronized gestures and dances. They had received the apparitions mostly at night while on ecstatic or trance-like marches.

To see the Virgin they leant backwards until their heads almost touched their waists, and they rushed about the village in these astonishing postures, and up the hill behind the village, moving so fast – even over rocky terrain and ditches – that they appeared to be flying. If the video was to be believed the antics of these children portrayed an awe-inspiring demonstration of seemingly impossible physical feats; but what made their strange choreography all the more extraordinary was their swift, perfectly synchronized formation. They seemed, all alike, to be possessed by a power that played them like a musical instrument.

Were they possessed – by good or evil spirits? Were they merely cleverly cueing each other? Whatever the case, I was more intrigued by the meaning of the formation activity itself than by how it was done.

But Garabandal offered other paranormal feats. According to the written evidence, grown men had been outrun by the girls on their ecstatic marches, even when the girls were moving backwards. They had also astonished onlookers with acts of levitation, by alterations in body weight and by the way in which they fell backwards on the ground with such force that their skulls were heard to crack.

Another curious feature was the story of a priest, Father Louis Andreu, who became closely involved with the children and eventually began to experience the visions himself. Immediately after witnessing an apparition of the Virgin Mary in conjunction with the girls he had dropped dead without any apparent physical explanation. He was thirty-six years old and had been in perfect health. It was claimed that following his death he continued to speak in 'foreign languages' through the mouths of the girls.

At the centre of the Garabandal phenomena was the leading seer, Conchita Gonzalez, a girl of striking beauty. The camera lens had focused unrelentingly on her face. She, in turn, knew how to play to the camera, and took to her role as budding mystic with considerable skill and verve.

Characteristically, the Italian mystic Padre Pio was reported to be somehow at the centre of the phenomena, having enjoyed a parallel vision and having guaranteed the apparitions' authenticity. He had talked with Conchita and had specified that she should receive the gift of the lace veil that would cover his face as he lay in state after his death.

The Garabandal phenomena promised a fascinating mixed-bag of prodigies, including levitation, a Eucharistic miracle, apocalyptic prophecy and a promised 'Great Sign'. There was mention of an unusual miracle of healing involving an Italian-American millionaire called Joey Lomangino, who from New York had dedicated his life to the promotion of the cult. I was inclined to attempt to understand what had happened in Garabandal a quarter of a century ago, and to discover what had happened to the surviving participants in the meantime.

The four visionaries were still alive and presumably accessible, and I was particularly eager to interview Conchita. But first I wanted to visit Garabandal itself, to explore the village and to interview surviving eye-witnesses.

20 In Garabandal

On my way to Garabandal I stayed overnight in Burgos, where I had flown the previous day, and went into the cathedral the next morning. Twenty years after the Second Vatican Council the principal Mass of the day was still being said in Latin.

Sitting beneath the great Gothic lantern in the nave I remembered that this was Franco's capital during the Civil War. It was in this cathedral that the archdeacon had preached the virtues of Fascism and uttered a chilling curse on the heads of the Republicans: 'You who listen to me, you who call yourselves Christians, show no mercy on the destroyers of churches and priests; may their seed be trampled under foot, for it is the evil seed, the devil's seed.'

The celebrants of the late 1980s wore rose-silk fiddleback vestments edged with lace. They had grim, mask-like faces with pursed lips through which they gabbled their prayers as they hurried about the altar amidst clouds of incense. Meanwhile a bevy of pot-bellied canons minced in and out of the choir stalls, flourishing their velvet cloaks and wagging the scarlet pompoms of their birettas. The spectacle lent insight to Spain's long history of anti-clericalism and the subterranean resentment of women against the male-dominant clergy.

I was glad to be gone and on my way in a hired car. San Sebastián de Garabandal was a half day's drive to the north, beyond the Sierra de Peña Sagra, on the edge of the vast wilderness that contains the rugged mountains of Los Picos Europeos.

I arrived in the late afternoon in driving rain and wind. The road climbed a valley through hairpin bends, and beyond each steeply wooded spur was a hint of wild, high country to the west. A river boiled below, cascading through boulders and sudden ravines.

The village remained secret until the final bend in the road, which had only recently been laid. It nestled at the foot of a dark mountain, a huddle of stone houses with pantiled red roofs. On a lower hill, immediately above the village, stood a grove of pine trees. A Romanesque church-tower loomed above the houses on a platform of rock.

The air of Garabandal was wonderfully sweet, razor sharp. I walked through the deserted lanes until I came to a *pensión* called Meson Serafin; it was on the far edge of the village from the road and immediately below the hill of the pines.

As I entered the *pensión* the huge oak door was caught in a gust of wind and slammed with a mighty bang. I found myself in a simple stone-flagged hall with long refectory tables and benches and an open fireplace. There were various holy pictures on the walls – the Sacred Heart, the Virgin Mary and Michael the Archangel.

A dumpy woman with mild dark eyes and grey hair appeared and asked if I wanted a room and supper. Her name was Pacita Gonzalez, and she was the sister-in-law of the seer, Conchita Gonzalez. She told me that they would eat at seven o'clock, after rosary in the church.

My room was an attic under the eaves where the wind drummed on the shuttered mullioned windows. I slept until I was woken by the sound of a hand-bell ringing in the street.

Descending the oak staircase I found the Señora laying the table. She explained the bell. A woman walks slowly through the village each evening at sunset ringing a small bell, and it is customary for someone to approach, to kiss the bell and to recite the Lord's Prayer for a departed relative or friend.

As Pacita served a Spanish omelette from a pan, several more guests appeared from the attics above. There was a German – a monk-like young man with cropped hair, attended by a blond, uniformed chauffeur. The German nodded but refused to speak; he sat with his shoulder hunched and hands joined as if in prayer. The chauffeur informed me in poor English that they were driving to Lourdes and then to Medjugorje. A Frenchman with pure white hair and a large fiery red nose dispensed affable smiles to all present; but he appeared to have only one word in common with the assembled pilgrims, which was 'Fatima', whither, I gathered, he was hoping to make his way on foot. He refused the omelette, and when Pacita served him a bowl of watery soup he gave her a grubby holy picture in recompense. She stuffed it in her apron pocket without looking at it.

Opposite me sat a dapper man wearing a navy-blue blazer. To his tie-pin were attached a number of holy medals. When I commented on them, he said, 'Some people wear a pig's tooth or something like that, whereas I wear these sacred objects.' Then he drew my attention to a red cross on his lapel. 'See that?' he said. 'I am a member of the Order of the Holy Sepulchre, and I am a great supporter of pilgrimages there. I give money for the upkeep of the Holy Places.' He now shook my hand and introduced himself as the Filipino consul to Barcelona. His hair was an amazing pad of frizz, jet black and with the consistency of candy-floss.

Tucking into the substantial potato omelette, the consul told me his story: 'This is my second time here,' he began. 'I

came in 1972, but I stayed only for one minute. I had quarrelled
with my wife all the way up the valleys from Reinosa. She was
frightened of the road and the failing light. We went straight
up to the pines; we didn't know you could stay. Anyway, we
got up there and my wife was terrified. I begged her to stay –
you know, we'd driven across the whole of Spain to get here –
but she fled. We sat for forty minutes in the car without
speaking. Then I said to her, "Are you conscious of the smell?"
We had both experienced a wonderful scent at the pines and
we had somehow carried it with us into the car. I asked her to
check that it wasn't in her purse, but it wasn't.'

He reflected in silence for a while, then said, 'This time I
came on my own.'

The consul searched in his wallet and brought out a picture
of Padre Pio. 'See this? This is the great saint of our age. He's
at the bottom of it all. Here, take it, keep it. Padre Pio confirmed
that the apparitions here at Garabandal were authentic.'

I studied the picture of the peasant monk. 'Did you ever meet
him?' I asked.

'Meet him? I was given special introductions because of my
status. I served Padre Pio's Mass in San Giovanni Rotondo in
Italy and went to him in confession. We spoke in Italian, but
when we got into conversation I couldn't understand him; it
was as if he was speaking a dialect. I said to him, "Sorry,
Father, I don't understand." With this Padre Pio starts to
shout and yell at me: "Oh, you don't understand, you don't
understand! Get out of here. Come on, out of here . . ."'

'Well, that doesn't sound very holy, does it?' I said.

'You don't get it, do you?' said the consul, pointing his fork
at me. 'You see, I was very upset because I'm a proud man,
and certainly I wasn't used to being shouted at. I think it was
good for my pride; and I think in any case that he was angry
because I was wasting his time. His confession was mostly for

conversions and reconciliation. I had gone to him out of curiosity.'

With this the consul stood up and said an elaborate grace. As he shook my hand he said, 'I have a heart valve and a pace-maker and I've got a big journey tomorrow.'

Pacita and her husband Serafin came to sit next to me. Serafin, a lean, pale man, prematurely bald, was Conchita's eldest brother. We sat talking in Spanish for a while over a carafe of coarse local wine. I asked them about the apparitions.

Serafin began: 'When the visions started I'd been away working up at León. On the journey back I heard about nothing but the visions. As we came up the valley – there wasn't a proper road in those days – there were great crowds of people walking up here. The day after we arrived the children had an ecstasy. From that moment on I was absolutely convinced it was from God. I knew my little sister; I know what sort of people we are in this village. We're shy of outsiders, and modest. And here was my sister behaving as if the world did not exist for her. In fact, that's how she used to describe the experience – as if she were outside the world.

'There were all sorts of opinions being expressed by so-called experts,' Serafino continued. 'Eventually Conchita was taken up to Santander by members of the bishop's commission. They interrogated her. They told her that it was all a fairy-tale. They said it was a collective hallucination. But where on earth did all that behaviour and the messages come from? My sister is intelligent, but she was poorly educated and naïve. She would never have dreamt all that up. She disowned her visions for a time, but then she confirmed them. Life became impossible for her, so she went to America, where she lived incognito for a long time.

'I lost count of the ecstasies I've witnessed. I've even seen

132

them on my own with nobody else present. There were times in the depths of winter when I had to accompany Conchita around the village at two or three in the morning when there was deep snow everywhere. She would climb up to the pines and back again in appalling weather while I followed her.

'I've seen her in her ecstasy running backwards on her knees over razor-sharp rocks, and there wouldn't be a scratch or a mark on her afterwards. Nobody will ever convince me that the phenomena are natural. They *must* be from God.'

Pacita here interrupted, and began to speak excitedly: 'I saw one of the first ecstasies. I was sixteen at the time, I was rigid with excitement and I was completely obsessed with the idea that I was going to see the vision myself. A lot of people felt they would see the vision, but they never did. The children's faces were transfigured, like angels. They were beautifully healthy and normal, but there were times when they frightened us, including the men. They would scream and howl with terror at their vision: "Who are you? What are you?" – all of them screaming in unison together.

'I saw the Eucharistic miracle. The children said that the angel often gave them Holy Communion, and we would see them kneeling with their tongues out, although there was no other sign. Then Conchita announced a little miracle: the angel was going to make the host visible on her tongue. There were great crowds of people all pressing around her, shining torches on her because it was dark. I grabbed hold of the Guardia Civil's belt and he pulled me through to the front. And I saw it on her tongue, brilliant and dazzling as snow; it was thicker than the normal host and looked spongy. It just formed there on her outstretched tongue as if by magic.

'I've seen strong men unable to lift any of the visionaries off the ground. And one day Mari Cruz went into an ecstasy while she was holding another girl, Tere, by one finger. Tere was a big strong girl and she was dragged all over the village, unable to extricate herself.

'But the most extraordinary thing I witnessed occurred one night when Conchita was racing backwards down from the pines, alone in the pitch black in the middle of the night. It was an absolutely supernatural feat. Nobody could have done that normally.

'The most frightening thing was when they used to go to the cemetery and poke crucifixes through the barred gate for the dead souls to kiss. This kissing of crucifixes and medals and rings was remarkable. They would hold the objects up for the Virgin to kiss and then they would cross themselves, then they would pass it to a bystander also to kiss. All this was done with extremely reverential gestures. One day I was standing in the middle of the crowd and I found myself thinking that if one of them brought a crucifix for me to kiss my doubts would disappear for good. Within moments Conchita came straight over to me and applied the crucifix to my lips even though I was lost in this huge crowd and had only thought my wish in silence. I swear to you that this happened.

'Father Valentin, the parish priest, decided to isolate the girls from each other immediately after the visions to see whether their accounts of what the Virgin had said tallied. They always coincided exactly.'

'Senõra,' I said, 'where is Conchita now? Can you give me her address?'

Pacita looked at her husband and shook her head vigorously. She began to clear the table, and refused to be drawn any further. Her husband in the meantime brought me a cup of coffee and a book.

'You should read this,' he said. 'It's a copy of Conchita's diary. It's remarkable. Read it tonight . . . We don't give Con-

134

chita's whereabouts – she went to America to get away from the publicity. But there's a man called Joey Lomangino who lives in New York, he talks to people. You'd have to do it through him.'

21   Conchita's Diary

I sat up in bed reading Conchita's diary into the small hours. Outside the winds were so violent that the church bells were ringing of their own accord.

The diary, which was a combination of memoir and journal, was edited by a Father Joseph Pelletier from sixty-five handwritten pages in Spanish. Simple, economical, it clearly constituted the most authoritative subjective record of the Garabandal phenomena.

I was particularly interested in the starting point of the apparitions. According to Conchita the four girls were playing in the village square on 18 June 1961 when she and Mari Cruz went to steal some apples from a tree belonging to the school-mistress. With their pockets full of apples they ran off to eat them in a lane known as the *calleja* (which I gathered was immediately outside the Meson Serafin). It was half-past eight in the evening and she remembers that they heard a violent noise like thunder.

Conchita says that she regretted taking the apples and told the others: 'The Devil will be happy, and our poor guardian angels will be sad.' So they began to pick up stones to throw on their left sides, where the Devil was thought to be (their guardian angels, they believed, were on the right). When they tired of throwing stones they played marbles. At this point the vision began.

'Suddenly,' writes Conchita, 'there appeared to me a very beautiful figure that shone brilliantly but did not hurt my eyes at all. When the other three girls, Jacinta, Loli and Mari Cruz, saw me in this state of ecstasy, they thought I was having a fit, because I kept crying out, with my hands clasped. They were about to call my mother when they found themselves in the same state as I, and also started crying out together.'

Conchita went on to describe the almost daily apparitions of this celestial figure, which she identified with the Archangel Michael, from Sunday, 18 June to Sunday, 2 July, which was the first day of the Virgin's appearance. Only on Saturday, 1 July did the angel speak.

'We went to the *calleja* as usual to pray the rosary and the people accompanied us. That day the apparitions occurred very early, at 7.30, and it was still almost full daylight and the people were able to see very well.

'At the end of the holy rosary the angel appeared smiling very much and said to us, "Do you know why I have come? It is to announce to you that tomorrow, Sunday, the Virgin Mary will appear to you as Our Lady of Mount Carmel."'

Conchita records in this same entry, for the first time, a detailed description of the angel's dress. She had already described him as looking about nine years old, but of immense strength. Now she adds that he was 'dressed in a long, flowing and beltless blue garment. His wings were pale rose, rather long and very lovely. His little face was neither long nor round. His nose was very pretty, his eyes black and his complexion dark. His hands were very delicate and his fingernails short. We did not see his feet.'

In the entry for the next day she records: 'It was six in the evening and we left for the *calleja* to say the rosary. We had not yet arrived at the scene of the apparitions when the Blessed Virgin appeared with an angel on each side . . . They looked like twins. Beside the angel, who stood at the Blessed Virgin's right and at the same height as she, was a large eye which seemed to be the eye of God . . . The Blessed Virgin appeared with a white dress, a blue mantle and a crown of small golden stars. Her feet are not visible. Her hands are wide open with the scapular on the right wrist. The scapular is brown. Her hair is long, dark brown and wavy, and parted in the middle. She has an oval-shaped face and her nose is long and delicate. Her mouth is very pretty, with rather full lips. The colour of her face is dark but lighter than that of the angel: it is different. Her voice is very lovely, a very unusual voice that I can't describe. There is no woman that resembles the Blessed Virgin in her voice or in anything else.'

Reading Conchita's diary late into the night in that remote and wild spot, it struck me that while some aspects of the iconography of the visions referred to universal traditions going back to the origins of Christianity, there was also something even more primitive, perhaps pagan, and special to this secluded pastoral community.

22 Conchita Levitates

In the morning the wind had dropped and the sky was cloudless, crystal bright and with a cold, damp edge. While Pacita's coffee was brewing I walked out of Meson Serafin into the stone-walled lane that led up to the pines 200 feet above. A plaque on a post depicted Michael the Archangel, and the legend: '18 *Junio de 1961 (Domingo) acqui se aparecio por primera vez a las niñas el Arcangel San Miguel.*' This was the famous *calleja*. The rest of the way was marked with the Stations of the Cross in coloured ceramics cemented into ragstone cairns. The deep green fields on either side had been cropped down by sheep to a carpet smoothness.

The nine pine trees stood on a bluff looking out over the village and beyond to a circle of hills forming an amphitheatre reminiscent of the dramatic scene from above Medjugorje. The branches of the trees were tied with scarves and handkerchiefs, like the crosses on Križevac. It was here 'above the pines', according to Conchita, that a great natural sign would occur at some date in the future known only to her.

To the left of the pine grove I noticed an enclosure with a shrine made of aluminium. The gate was locked and I peered in to see a statue of the Archangel Michael striking a serpentine Satan with a lance. Pennants depicting the flags of various nations were stuck into the ground.

Standing at the gate of the shrine I was suddenly conscious

139

of an astonishing scent – a keen, pure, fresh smell, as of roses in blossom. There was a heavy dew but there were no flowers to be seen, nor herbs. Remembering what the Filipino consul had told me the evening before, I felt suddenly haunted and turned away to walk back down the hill towards the *pensión* and breakfast.

When I arrived in the house I found an elderly gentleman ensconced at the refectory table in the company of two ladies dressed in moth-eaten fur coats.

Pacita bustled in with coffee and hot milk.

'This is the Guardia Civil, he's come to pay us a visit,' she cried.

Brigadier Seco was a tall, upright man in steel spectacles. He was well groomed, with a trim moustache and white hair. He was wearing a starchy blue-striped shirt, a black silk tie and a well-cut dove grey jacket and waistcoat. But as he stood up to shake my hand I noticed that he was wearing blue waterproof trousers that made a sort of rustling noise.

He told me in sepulchral tones that his full name was Juan Alvarez Seco, and that he had once been the chief of the Civil Guard, Puentenansa sector.

He fixed me with a steely eye. 'What do you think of this government?' he asked gravely.

'What did *you* think of Franco?' I asked him guardedly in return.

He stuck out his chest and boomed, 'Generalissimo Franco was a man of destiny, without a doubt the greatest figure in the history of this century. What is more, he was a true Spaniard and a devout Catholic.'

The women in the fur coats, whose role, it seemed, was to act as silent witnesses to such utterances, nodded their assent.

'The brigadier will tell you about the ecstasies,' said Pacita as she poured the coffee. 'Ask him. He remembers all the details.'

The ex-policeman put six sugar lumps into his coffee and began to stir slowly.

'I first paid a visit to the village on 22 June 1961,' he began, 'so as to investigate personally the events taking place here, and to compose a report for my superior relative to the alleged happenings.'

Brigadier Seco spoke in constabulary parlance with pride and ease. It was as if he were addressing a courthouse.

'In consequence of my initial investigations,' he went on, 'I ordered two guards to be placed to watch over Garabandal. The news about the apparitions of the angel were going from village to village and throughout the surrounding countryside, and each day more and more people came, which necessitated increased vigilance. Some 3,000 people were witnessing the ecstasies at this time.

'Now. The people going up to see the apparitions were wondering if the children were hypnotized or being given drugs. This I investigated fully and satisfied myself that it was not the case. Other people were saying that Conchita was in control of her companions and that if they went at the same hour to the place of the apparitions it was because she was influencing them. They kept saying she was sick, and, upon the suggestion of Loli's father, they requested the presence of Dr José Luis, the incumbent physician for the region. This doctor said the girls were epileptic and sick and everything was happening because of that. But I could see this was nonsense. Why should four epileptics seek each other out as friends? Anyway, it was quite obvious that the girls were extremely healthy, mentally and physically. It is important to note that other expert doctors conclusively discounted the thesis of Dr José Luis at a later date.

'The parish priest then demanded that the children be separated, to verify if they would all come at the same time to the place of the apparitions when they felt the special urge that accompanied the onset of a vision. And in fact I can confirm that they did come from different places in the villages under these test conditions at precisely the same time.

'Then all sorts of doctors and priests turned up. During the ecstasies they inflicted pinches and scratches and stuck needles into them. I had to have this stopped. It was remarkable that none of the children ever reacted to these painful tests; but the marks were all clearly visible after the ecstasies had finished.

'I witnessed many apparitions and I saw hundreds of ecstatic walks and rapid marches, some of them backwards, through the streets of the village while in that state. And when the girls were running to meet one another, some in ecstasy and others in their natural state, no one could keep up with those who were in the ecstasy, not even the other visionaries in their normal state.

'I witnessed many times the way in which, while in full rapture, and after having had the objects kissed by the Virgin, the young girls would give such objects back to their proper owners without ever making a mistake.'

The brigadier pulled himself up stiffly and eyed me severely. 'I was a policeman, trained to observe accurately and truthfully. The phenomena took place over a long period of time and with great frequency and I was charged with reporting all these things to my superiors. At the beginning of these events I was a Catholic in name only and failed to practise or properly believe in my religion. As a result of the inexplicable nature of the phenomena I returned to full faith and practice.'

He turned to the womenfolk as if for confirmation, and they both nodded their agreement, vigorously and in silence.

'Was there any single event,' I asked, 'that impressed you more than any other as to its supernatural nature?'

142

The brigadier immediately began to nod and to shake his head all at once, in a sort of paroxysm of enthusiasm; at the same time he was winking at the women, whose faces were suffused with complacency.

'Now we're talking,' he said at last with emotion. 'On 28 July I was in the kitchen of Conchita's house. There were others there with me: namely, Dr Ortiz, a Father José Ramon Vasquez and a seminarian from Reinosa, and few other people. Conchita was in an ecstasy, begging us to help her up because she could not reach Our Lady's lips. We said to her, "Jump. Jump up!" But she said that she couldn't. So three of us, the doctor, the seminarist and myself, attempted to lift her, but we could not raise her one millimetre from the floor; she was like a ton of rock. Jacinta Gonzalez Gonzalez, one of the other visionaries, was with her, and came forward after we had become exhausted with our efforts. Little Jacinta, who was just a slight child, lifted Conchita upwards with the tips of her fingers. She lifted her right up to the ceiling.'

The brigadier made another dramatic pause and put his hand on his breast. 'What I am telling you, sir, is God's honest truth. After Conchita had made the gesture of kissing her vision all of us saw her float back slowly, right back, back, back, until she was absolutely horizontal. Jacinta brought her down holding only her legs. Then she let go of her legs and Conchita remained floating about a hand's height above the kitchen floor for several moments. We all stood absolutely amazed. I could have run my hand between the floor and her body, but I was rooted to the spot. I would also add that while Conchita defied the laws of gravity, her dress was never in immodest disarray!'

The women nodded gravely at this.

'Anyway,' boomed the brigadier, 'it was at this point that I was absolutely convinced within myself as a Christian and became a convinced believer in the supernatural events at Garabandal.'

That afternoon I went for a long walk in the lonely foothills of the mountains above Garabandal. Beyond the village the characteristics of the harsh farm economy of the region were clearly evident: the hay fields and arable plots were still worked by hand – mostly by women – and the annual cycle of winter and summer pastures could be clearly seen. It continued to prey on my mind that the ecstatic marches and trances of those prepubescent girls were as much to do with the ancient resonances of this mountain community as with their official religion. It struck me, too, that in less liberal times the associations of 'night-flying' and trances and communication with dead spirits, the Eucharistic mime, the magical ability to identify talismans, might well have been deemed the work of Satan. On just such evidence had girls of even younger ages been condemned by the Inquisition. In which case it made it all the more easy for me to entertain the notion that the phenomena had less to do with the Christian powers of good or evil and more to do with an aptitude for an ancient and primitive ritual.

My day and night in Garabandal had left me in a state of bemusement. I was deeply impressed by all that I had heard from the locals, and convinced that the children were not fakes. I had found the phenomena of Garabandal more dramatic than those of Medjugorje, and yet lacking in any obvious sense of spirituality. All the same, there was an undeniable atmosphere of sacred presence in the vicinity of the pines: but was it the sacredness of Christianity?

Later, when I attended the Mass of the day in the church, I noticed that only women were present and the devotion of the small congregation had none of the fervour of the Medjugorjean villagers. I passed the bar on my way back to the *pensión* and saw the men skulking around the space-invaders' machine or playing cards in a fug of tobacco smoke.

As I prepared to leave Garabandal later that day Serafin Gonzalez came to me with some assorted literature, including a magazine put out by Joey Lomangino which contained his address and a telephone number in America. I knew that I would have to do everything possible to meet Conchita Gonzalez, however reluctant she might be to be interviewed.

23   The Lads of Illfurt

On my return to England I came across a report of a recent case that had curious parallels with the Garabandal girls, and especially their synchronized behaviour, although the manifestations were patently evil and violent as opposed to sacred and benign.

In a document written by a Zurich psychiatrist, Hans Naegeli-Osjord, published in 1988, was the story of two German boys known as the 'lads of Illfurt'. The case, I gathered, was well attested by eye-witnesses and supported with plentiful evidence, including tape-recordings.

What seized my attention from the outset was the assertion that the experiences had begun, as at Garabandal, with the stealing of an apple from a woman – in this case a stranger who was passing through the village.

The phenomena started on 25 September 1985, when the boys, aged eight and ten, were observed to spin 'with incredible speed', like tops, while lying on their backs. Anybody who has seen children doing a 'break-dance' will hardly be over-impressed by this. But afterwards they proceeded to destroy all the furniture in the house in an exercise of strength that would have been extraordinary even in an adult. At the end of this demonstration, say witnesses, the boys showed no sign of fatigue.

From this point onwards the phenomena increased in strangeness and variety. The boys' legs often gained in plasticity so that they could intertwine them 'like supple rods'. In this state it was quite impossible for adult observers to untangle them; they were only extricated when the boys decided to exert, as if at will, their power to change the shape of their limbs again. Naegeli-Osjord was at pains to point out that the flexibility of the boys' bones bore no resemblance to *flexibilitas cerea*, a condition known in catatonic states of schizophrenia, where the notion of suppleness of bone is metaphorical rather than real.

More dramatic yet, the brothers were reported to have levitated, frequently floating 'in the air either on chairs or without chairs'. These episodes usually culminated in their being buffeted 'by what seemed like invisible fists' until they were thrown to the ground. Sometimes, when seated, the boys were thrown with incredible force to one side of the room, while their chairs hurtled in the opposite direction.

They were also subject to strange alterations in weight; they could sit, for example, on the slightest branches of trees without breaking them, as if their bodies had acquired an extraordinary lightness.

While these phenomena were in progress the boys spoke with the deep voices of men although their mouths were apparently shut. The 'voices' spoke in French, Spanish and English, including various dialects, as well as the boys' native German.

Since this behaviour defied the skill of psychiatrists and physicians, a Catholic exorcist was called. In his presence, it is claimed, the boys began to speak in Latin. The 'voices' then threatened to 'plague' the Father Superior of a local religious community, whereupon the priest in question, although several miles distant and unaware of the events in the brothers' household, was lifted into the air by invisible forces; all the pictures fell off his walls and his furniture tumbled about. The phenomena only stopped when the room was sprinkled with holy water.

On another occasion the boys were offered figs that had been blessed in secret by the exorcist. The brothers apparently cried out in unison, 'Away with the rat heads, the blackcoat has grimaced over them.' As the psychiatrist remarked, 'Such expressions are hardly common in the vocabulary of small boys.'

According to the report, house-hauntings spread throughout the vicinity of the boys' home to other Illfurt families: the Kleimers, the Brobecks, the Burbachs and the Dresches. Evidence was collated from all these sources.

The boys were immune to a variety of medical and psychiatric approaches; exorcism similarly failed, both in the boys' home and in the local monastery. Finally the bishop intervened and brought in two exorcists of outstanding reputation from outside the diocese: this at last yielded results and the boys returned to normal.

Hans Naegeli-Osjord, who is currently president of Switzerland's parapsychology society, was not inclined to accept an explanation based on psychosis, hysteria or hypnosis. He was convinced that he had encountered an exceedingly rare and outstanding instance of contemporary possession by evil spirits.

A characteristic of the case that I found particularly intriguing was the apparent flexibility of the bones, as I had come across a similar feature in an article by Herbert Thurston about Christina of St Trond, known as Christina the Wonderful, a thirteenth-century saint. 'The most remarkable feature,' says Thurston,

and the least likely to have suggested itself to the hagiographer spontaneously . . . is the flexibility of limbs, which seems to belong more to the character of an acrobat or a contortionist ... She melted, so to speak, like wax and rolled herself up into a ball ... She would suddenly and unexpectedly be rapt by the spirit and her body would rotate whirlingly like a child's hoop, revolving so rapidly that it was impossible to distinguish the outline of her separate limbs.

It is curious, then, that the same allegedly paranormal symptoms of sainthood in one age are to be found in the demon-possessed of another.

Naegeli-Osjord was principally swayed by the phenomenon of foreign tongues (also an ambivalent symptom, hovering 'twixt sainthood and possession); although, personally, I found this less impressive than the reports of levitation, which, if the witnesses were not suffering from delusions, would be evidence of one of the most elusive, albeit frequently claimed, paranormal events one could hope to observe.

My caution on the score of 'tongues' was largely owed to the writings of Samuel Taylor Coleridge. Coleridge, more than almost any thinker in the English language, had attempted throughout his life to reconcile the possibility of metaphysics and mysticism with rational and empirical methods of investigation; and the more I read him alongside Aldous Huxley, Arthur Koestler, Alistair Hardy, Colin Wilson and others, the more creative, and sound, I found his approach to the realms of the supernatural.

Browsing through his *Biographia Literaria*, I had come across a case which had occurred in what he describes as a Catholic town in Germany a year or two previous to his visit to Göttingen in 1799. A young illiterate serving-woman brought to the local hospital suffering from a 'nervous fever' was judged by local priests and monks to be possessed. The principal indication of diabolical influence involved her ability to speak Latin, Greek and Hebrew, which she did incessantly and 'in very pompous tones and with most distinct enunciation'. The clergy were all the more convinced that she was possessed since she was suspected of heresy.

The case had attracted the attention of many eminent physiologists and psychologists throughout Germany, some of whom came to the town and cross-examined the woman on the spot. Her ravings were taken down and found on careful scrutiny to consist of disconnected snatches of texts. Only a small portion of her Hebrew sentences could be traced to the Bible; the rest seemed to be in the rabbinical dialect. Fraud was soon discounted, and the doctors acknowledged that they were facing a genuine mystery.

A young physician, who was not prepared to accept a paranormal explanation, delved further. Eventually he discovered where her parents had lived and made the journey there. Both parents were dead, but he found a surviving uncle who related how the patient had been charitably taken in by an old Protestant pastor when she was nine years old and had stayed with him some years until his death.

The physician next discovered a niece of the pastor who had lived with him as his housekeeper and inherited his effects. On questioning the niece about the pastor's habits he discovered the solution to the enigma. It had been the old man's custom for years 'to walk up and down a passage of his house on to which the kitchen door opened, and to read to himself with a loud voice out of his favourite books'. The niece still had many of these books in her possession. Among them was found a collection of rabbinical writings, together with several of the Greek and Latin Fathers.

'The physician succeeded in identifying so many passages with those taken down at the young woman's bedside,' writes Coleridge, 'that no doubt could remain in any rational mind concerning the true origin of the impressions made on her nervous system.'

The case illustrated to Coleridge, at the end of the eighteenth century, a profound psychological truth evidently overlooked by trained psychiatrists towards the end of the twentieth century: 'that reliques of sensation may exist for an indefinite time in a latent state, in the very same order in which they were originally impressed'.

The 'lads of Illfurt' may well have picked up snatches of different languages from foreign radio broadcasts, and given the evident high concentration of Catholic clergy in the neighbourhood it is likely that they had heard Latin in one of the local churches.

But the importance of the parallel with Garabandal, it seemed to me, was the curious association of the apple stolen from the outsider. In Garabandal the 'outsider' had been the schoolteacher. The link between both stories and the Snow White motif from Grimm (and, of course, the Eve motif), with its implications of bewitchment, seemed to me irresistible. The apple incident had in both cases apparently triggered a series of parallel symptoms: synchronized physical actions, dance, abnormal strength, apparent levitation, clairvoyant insight about physical objects; at the same time, the phenomena were performed with the close involvement of clerical witnesses.

Considering both incidents anthropologically it would surely be unwise to discount the influence of traditional Catholic attitudes towards witchcraft and magic in rural Germany on the one hand, and the long tradition of Marian apparitions in Spain on the other. Moreover, it is surely intriguing that the *Rituale Romanum*, the clergy's handbook on exorcism, lists bewitchment as a cause of possession along with some familiar characteristics, including: the comprehension and speaking of foreign languages that are unknown to the subjects; knowledge

of secret matters; physical strength that exceeds comprehension; aversion to holy objects.

To what extent then was there unwitting collusion between
the children, the clergy, the villagers and perhaps even the
psychiatrists in the two cases, involving the whole community
in a public psychodrama?

Reflecting on the synchronized activities of the Illfurt lads,
the girls of Garabandal and the visionaries of Medjugorje, it
struck me that the significance of such patterned behaviour
was to give onlookers a dramatic – a theatrical – impression
of control from an outside power; the control might be evil, or
it might be good, but the importance of the pattern was the
impression of possession, manipulation, by a higher power.

This is to say nothing about how such things were achieved;
but it seemed to me important at this stage to acknowledge
that phenomena involving onlookers, audiences, should be
read, interpreted, in the light of their mimetic, their theatrical,
meaning, as much as their supposed paranormal potential. It
also seemed important to accept that although the paranormal
component might fade in the light of rational explanation, the
metaphorical, the symbolic significance would remain.

24   The Virgin of the Ukraine

As I was contemplating a visit to New York to attempt to find Conchita of Garabandal, an opportunity arose for me to cross the Atlantic to do a television interview with a man who claimed to have experienced a number of Marian visions in the Ukraine.

An independent producer of my acquaintance was making a film that would be shown as part of the 1990 'Soviet Spring' series on Channel Four in Britain; he had been intrigued by the claimed apparitions and the way in which they were contributing to the bid for religious freedom in the Ukraine.

The visionary was Josyp Terelya, the leader of the Ukrainian separatist movement, who had been expelled from the Soviet Union in the summer of 1987; his story seemed to complement the cases of Medjugorje and Garabandal. But this time the political overtones were not merely evident; they were overwhelming.

In the time-honoured tradition of rural sightings of the Virgin, the apparitions had begun with a twelve-year-old girl, Maria Kyzyn, who claimed that she had seen a Madonna and child hovering above the dome of the banned former Ukrainian Catholic Chapel of the Holy Trinity at Hrushiw, which lies a few miles from Poland's eastern border with western Ukraine.

The Virgin, dressed in black, looked down in silence.

According to Maria, 'She glowed in an unearthly light.' Within several days large groups of women had gathered outside the chapel. They confirmed that they, too, saw the image and that it was identical in every detail with the icon of Our Lady of Compassion, the famous Virgin and Child of Kiev given to Vladimir the Great by his wife Anna in 988 and dating back to the very origins of Christianity in ancient Russia. Within a week gatherings in Hrushiw of tens of thousands were reported on Soviet television and in *Pravda*. The apparitions were described in an editorial as a 'destabilizing miracle', the work of 'extremists attempting to undermine *perestroika* . . . a political provocation inspired by foreign clerical–nationalistic centres with the help of fanatics and extremists'.

But the first apparitions in April 1987 had occurred not only in the new atmosphere of *perestroika*, but against the background of the long struggle for freedom among the banned Churches of the Soviet Union. Those, moreover, with a taste for apocalyptic signals were not slow to see links with the anniversary of the catastrophe at the nuclear-power plant at Chernobyl just 300 kilometres distant. And 1988 was the millennium of the advent of Christianity in ancient Rus', to which the Ukrainians make exclusive claim against the rival 'pretensions' of the Russian Orthodox. The Virgin seemed to have arrived to demonstrate that history was on the side of the Ukrainian Catholics.

The historical origins of Ukrainian Catholicism, however, are far from straightforward. The Church is a curious blend of Eastern-rite Christianity with an ancient loyalty to Rome; it acknowledges the primacy of the Pope yet its liturgy and music are Byzantine; its bishops are in direct communion with Rome but its priests are allowed to marry. Its provenance is the subject of contention not only within the Ukraine but inside the Catholic Church itself. While it claims direct and unbroken descent from the ninth-century missionaries Cyril and Methodius, its local rivals, which include Russian Orthodox, Ukrainian Orthodox and even Latin-rite Christians, tell a different story, as do the Communists. The alternative view of Ukrainian Catholic history is that they are a seventeenth-century creation of Polish Jesuits, founded in order to undermine and annexe the region now known as western Ukraine.

The Communists claim, moreover, that all Ukrainian Catholics voluntarily joined the Ukrainian Orthodox Church at the Synod of Lvov at the end of the Second World War. For this reason the Communists refered to them pejoratively as 'Uniates'. There are rumours, too, originally put about by Stalin, that the Uniates had collaborated with the Nazis against the Jews. The official, Communist, view is that the Church simply does not now exist, since it disbanded itself and surrendered all its churches in 1946.

Despite the Ukrainian Catholics' loyalty to the Pope, even the Vatican's attitude towards them is equivocal; while Pope John Paul II professes his support for them, Cardinals Casaroli and Willibrands, who mastermind the Holy See's 'Ostpolitik', were known to be antagonistic. The Vatican diplomats believe that the Ukrainians could disturb the delicate politics of ecumenical dialogue with the Russian Orthodox Church and the desire to win freedoms for Latin-rite Catholicism, especially in the Baltic states.

Whatever the historical and political wrangles, Ukrainian Catholics patently do exist and have probably suffered as much as any Christian denomination in the long history of religious persecution in the Soviet Union. In the late 1940s eight bishops and almost 1,000 priests were executed; thousands of other priests were sent to the gulags and their churches closed or given over to the Ukrainian Orthodox.

But somehow the Church survived. In basements, in forest clearings, in abandoned chapels, the faithful continued to gather, despite fines and imprisonment. There are stories of groups that would regularly recite the words of the Mass up to the consecration before disbanding; on the altar they would place an item of the priest's liturgical vestments, symbolizing the absent celebrant.

To such a persecuted minority, news that they had been favoured with a series of apparitions would have seemed like a beacon of hope lighting up the Carpathian Mountains. And yet, such were the multiplicity of fierce political antagonisms, I suspected that things might be rather more complicated and ominous.

I flew out to Toronto to meet Terelya in what was described as a 'safehouse', situated in a leafy suburb of the city. There were extensive, well-patrolled grounds and an atmosphere of conspiratorial tension.

Before we started filming Terelya came out to talk to me in the shade of a coppice of maple trees. He was square, thick-set, with a wide Russian face and almond-shaped Slavonic eyes. His shock of hair was iron grey. He wore a sad, tense expression and I wondered whether he was unwell.

As soon as he sat down he told me that he was forty-three years old and had spent twenty-three of those years in prisons and concentration camps. He had been sentenced nine times. His brother had been killed in a terrorist action on behalf of a Ukrainian separatist group. 'I have been released,' he said, 'but not rehabilitated. Gorbachev has not rehabilitated a single political prisoner.'

He was eager to launch into a description of his visions and the background. 'She appeared,' he said, 'in a glow of orange and blue light. It was a band of light, that seemed to wave –

to ebb and flow. She held up a rosary: the Our Fathers were orange, and the Hail Marys were seeds of blue light. Her dress was made up of fiery rays.

'I had not long been out of prison,' he went on, 'when I heard that the Virgin was appearing near Lvov. I went there straight away; there were hundreds of militia all over the place. I was spotted and followed; they tried to stop me, but I gave them the slip and got into the churchyard. It was early evening and thousands of people were gathered there.

'All of us were blessed with the sight of the apparition. She did not move her lips, but each of us heard her speak privately.'

'And what did she say, to you specifically?' I asked.

Terelya was holding a rosary in his hand. He held it up in the gesture of a clenched fist.

'She told me not to be afraid. She said I must have courage to do what God had chosen me to do.'

'And what is that?'

Terelya leant forward earnestly, his massive shoulders squared. 'The Virgin told me that, because of their sufferings, the Ukrainian Church of Martyrdom would now come out of the catacombs. Because of our suffering we have been tried and strengthened, and specially chosen, We are the just remnant. She told me that through us the Ukrainian people would gain their freedom. We must be brave and prepared to shed our blood anew. In time we would convert Russia itself, bring Christianity to Russia.'

'But Josyp,' I said, 'there is already a Church in Russia, the Russian Orthodox – '

'They are puppets of the KGB,' he rasped with a dismissive gesture of his hand.

'Even though I was surrounded by KGB informers,' he continued, 'I stood up among the people and I preached to them for twelve hours after one vision. This is how it went on, day after day. People were coming in from all over the place, even from distant parts of the Soviet Union. There were car number-plates from the other side of the Urals, from Georgia . . . People came on horseback, on bicycle, on foot . . .

'The Queen of Ukraine begs and asks us to be penitent and to forgive sins and to be brothers to all Christians of the world – for only through our Ukrainian people will come the universal freedom from the Prince of Darkness.'

In the wake of the visions, said Terelya, there had been a spate of mass gatherings of Ukrainian Catholics. Some of their former churches had been taken back by force and there had been frequent clashes with the police. In the midst of this wave of militancy he had emerged as nationalist leader. Exile had only added to his authority.

He told me that he had continued to enter the Soviet Union in Scarlet Pimpernel fashion, and that he sent regular batches of propaganda material, and prayer books and Bibles, released from air-balloons dispatched across the Austrian border.

As he told me these things it occurred to me that he had also emerged not simply as a political figure, but as a holy man, a man of charisma, who would be followed for more reasons than his political and historical arguments.

'We are now 5 million strong in the western Ukraine,' said Terelya, 'and supported by loyal exiles here in Canada and in the United States.'

'Are you really in no doubt about your visions? Is it possible that you witnessed an optical illusion?'

He shook his head vehemently.

'Listen!' he said. 'A colonel in the Soviet militia pointed a gun at the vision. I was there, I saw this with my own eyes. As he went to press the trigger he dropped down in a faint. He had to be carried off to hospital. When he came round forty-eight hours later he was completely converted to the faith. He remembers nothing of his past life. He spends his time travelling around the villages relating what he saw.'

'So why did these things happen at Hrushiw?'

Terelya spread his arms expansively.

'She came in the nineteenth century, and during the First World War, when she gave a warning identical to that of Fatima: pray or Russia would be lost to God; pray or there will be a second, more terrible war. Again she is telling us that we must pray for the conversion of Russia, or there will be an even worse chastisement. Chernobyl was just a warning. She tells us that we Ukrainians will shortly obtain our own state, which will become the guardian of all those who have accepted Christ as their spiritual leader.'

All this time Terelya had been gazing fiercely into my eyes, his forehead creased with tension.

Suddenly I found his vehemence tedious. I had also remembered that orange and blue, the colours of his Virgin, were the Ukrainian national colours. I suspected that he was a man without a trace of irony.

I said to him, 'Josyp, you look very unhappy.'

It was, perhaps, an undiplomatic remark.

His response was explosive. 'Tell me something amusing,' he barked, 'and then I'll laugh.'

When we had finished filming I asked to be taken immediately to the airport to catch a plane to New York. I did not want to linger a moment longer with the visionary of Hrushiw.

By the end of the day I had found myself both suspicious and frightened of Josyp Terelya's brand of charisma. Quite apart from the question of the authenticity of the phenomena, his claimed visions seemed to me a highly combustible blend of dubious mysticism and fanaticism. I saw nothing wrong with the aspirations of the Ukrainians for independence; nor even with the Ukrainian Catholics making a bid for being the focus of that separatist goal – although there were other powerful claims from other religious and non-religious groups. The ominous element was the attempt to legitimize and bolster such a claim with a series of private revelations that were being spread, evangelistic style, as authentic revelations direct from the supernatural realms.

Against the background of burgeoning ethnic and religious rivalries in East Europe, Josyp Terelya seemed to me to be playing an extremely dangerous game, with all the violent potential of Beirut.

Pondering the peculiar nature of the visions (it was extraordinary for such large numbers of people to claim to have witnessed a Marian apparition), I recalled that there had been a parallel in Cairo in 1968. During the Egyptian phenomenon the Virgin, it was claimed, had appeared in the form of a light above the dome of a Coptic Orthodox church in the suburb of Zeitoun. The series of apparitions had started when some Muslim workmen say they saw a 'white lady' kneeling beside the cross at the top of the dome.

The phenomenon began to occur nightly, attracting, according to some newspapers, as many as 250,000 people at a time. On one occasion twelve people were crushed to death in the pressing crowds, which included both Muslims and Christians. There were reports of mysterious lights, canopies of shooting stars, luminous globes and blinding explosions of light. Witnesses say that the image shone with an overpowering splendour like the sun in human form; that the vision would glide across domes, bowing and greeting the throngs of people.

Police in Cairo insisted that the phenomenon was a result of a freak illusion created by the street lighting. This had been vociferously denied by a large number of witnesses who had written testimonies of what they thought they had seen.

The Virgin of the Ukraine

The parallels between Zeitoun and Hrushiw seemed to me too numerous to be coincidental: the proximity of the light phenomenon to the dome, the nightly appearances, the involvement of an ambivalent Christian denomination with Roman affiliations but Eastern cultural leanings. And there had been nothing quite like these two cases in the long history of Marian apparitions, which spanned almost sixteen centuries. Even at Fatima in 1916 the vast crowd, 100,000 strong, had witnessed only a solar phenomenon, and a handful of parishioners at Knock in Ireland in 1879 had seen static and silent visions of Mary and other biblical figures, suspiciously reminiscent of a lantern-slide show.

So what was one to make of the Egyptian and the Ukrainian parallels? Was the Hrushiw phenomenon a copy-cat instance of the Zeitoun visions? Was there some sort of stage-managed hoax involved, in which clever crowd psychology had been employed? Communist officials had been quick to suggest a contrived 'destabilizing miracle', yet nothing definite had been proved. And now that both sets of phenomena had ended it would be difficult to root out the truth.

One was left, for the time being, with the spectacle of powerful charisma in the making, a charisma emerging from the highly contagious attraction of a leader who was in receipt of divine messages and favours, and who exploited this situation without entertaining the possibility that he and his followers might be deluded or in error. In Josyp Terelya I had encountered, I felt, the dark face of popular mystical experience.

25   Joey Waits for a Miracle

In New York I made contact with Joey Lomangino, the blind millionaire who had dedicated his life to the promotion of the visions at Garabandal.

Joey runs a garbage-disposal company called Allied Sanitation. The offices are in Queens and I found him in a cabin out in the yard where he also runs his Charity House movement for the handicapped homeless. He was in conference with a group of hulking Italian-Americans; men in nylon suits were coming and going, shaking fat, ringed hands, being introduced – 'Hey! This is my nephew . . . kid brother . . . attorney . . . Meanwhile Joey was taking calls – 'Hi babe! . . . Hi honey! . . .'

Joey has the mighty frame of an all-in wrestler. His great head with a mop of white hair juts forward aggressively; his full lips seem to be formed in a permanent silent whistle. He peers forward intently when he speaks, as if screwing up his eyelids with intense concentration. But his eyes and brows and the upper area of his nose are entirely destroyed, as if he had been in a high-speed collision with a car bumper.

Eventually the men drifted from the room and Joey called me over. 'Never mind that, Johnny,' he said. 'These are just political people and stuff come to meet my family. You know, Johnny, we're the premier company in New York City when it comes to recycling the garbage. We're so far advanced, we're ten years ahead of the state ... Now we talk religion! I'm at your service, Johnny.'

He spoke in a marked Brooklyn accent, quick-fire, husky, impatient to get the words out. He did not wish to be interviewed. 'Let me share with you my testimony, Johnny, just as the Holy Spirit guides me,' he said.

Suddenly he delved into his pocket and brought out an ornate string of rosary beads made of rock crystal and silver; next to the crucifix hung a huge silver miraculous medal. Joey made the sign of the cross with the medal and kissed it. Now he was ready to launch forth.

'In the name of the Father, and of the Son, and of the Holy Spirit, Amen. We offer this conference, to the greater glory of God, and the destruction of sin, and the salvation of souls. Blessed Mother help us. Our lady of Mount Carmel, pray for us. OK, Johnny, here we go ...

'I was born in Brooklyn on 5 October 1930. My mother was immigrant Italian, my father was born in New York – but he himself was Italian-American. And when my father was a very young man he contracted spinal meningitis, and as a result my dad could look at you – and he knows that your name is John, and he knows that you're a writer – but he can't put anything else together. See? So as I started to come up at the age of eight I used to help my father on the ice truck and the coal truck, because that's what Italian immigrants did. They worked labour. And at the age of eleven I was already driving the ice truck to various houses to keep the food from going bad. My father had about 300 ice customers. My family was poor, but we always made things meet.

'When I was sixteen, on 27 June 1947, I came home on the last day of my third year at high school. I came round the back of the house and went up on the porch and looked through the screen door. And my mother was, like, ten feet in front of me, on her knees washing the floor with a scrub brush. And I said, "Mom, open the door!" And she looked up at me and said, "Joey, where'd you get that terrible mark across your face?" There weren't no mark there, but I thought that maybe there was a shadow over my face that would give her this here impression. Then she opened the door and she saw my face was normal. And she said, "Joey, don't go out there again because I know you're going to get hurt." Intuition, see? And I said, "Mom, give me a break, I've got to help Dad with the ice truck." So what happened, I went downstairs, sixteen years of age, dick-stupid, stubborn, a box of wrenches under my arm, and I went out. And I could hear my mother's voice crying, "Joey, you're going to break your mother's heart. I saw the mark on your face, you're going to get hurt . . ."

'I went down to where my father parked the truck and I saw that the back tyre was deflated. So I jacked up the truck, and I took the tyre off and I rolled it to a gas station. I was putting air in the truck tyre and my mind was telling me that it was going to explode. So I turned the tyre round so that if it did explode it would hit the ground. But the valve was too long because it was an inside tyre, so when I went to put the air hose on it I couldn't fit it under the tyre, so I turned it around the other way again, face up. As I put the air hose on to it – *Bam!* It blew – burying steel and rubber two inches into my eyes and forehead. It was 27 June. And I was in a coma until 16 July, the Feast of Our Lady of Mount Carmel. When I come out of the coma I had a whole new life. I was blind, I had no sense of smell – the olfactory nerves are completely destroyed. And I've wrecked my father's living because I can't work for him any more.

'I was back at home some weeks later, I'd gone to bed, and I woke with a start in the middle of the night. And I heard this voice of a woman, saying, "Joey, do you want your eyesight back? Then you pray," she says, "every day of your life." And I said, "When will you be back?" And she said "Soon." After that I fell asleep again. Next day I told my Mom what had happened, and she said, "What do I know? Maybe it was an angel." Anyway, after that I prayed those prayers every day of my life.

'In 1949, the priest from the parish took me to blind school. And the first thing they do is leave you in the infirmary for a week to check you out. I was very lonely there, it was the first time I'd been away from home. And the idea of being blind broke my heart. I laid down on the bed, I took out my rosary and I prayed. And I cried myself to sleep. And during the night I had a dream and what I saw was something that was equivalent to a golf course. Lush green rolling fields, and in the middle a clump of trees, and I was standing with my back to the trees. When I woke the next morning I had something that took over me, and the only way I could explain it is it was like a power coming into me; like a strength . . . When I got up I knew that I was going to be all right, but I knew that it was going to be a long haul.

'After I graduated from St John's a Jewish finance man, a philanthropist, lent me the money to buy my own business – a carting business. My three brothers came with me and my father, and we started to work. And we started to come up. That was 1954.

'By 1961 we were making a lot of money and I took a trip to Europe with my sister. We went to the Italian Riviera, down towards Rome, and south to Bari. I met my mother's people and stayed on. Now what happened. My Uncle Frank is a teacher of languages at the university, and one day he says to me, "Joey, we've got to go see Padre Pio." He tells me this priest has got the stigmata. I said, "Get away! Don't! Don't give me the story about priests and religion, I don't want to hear it. Every time I go near one they talk about miracles. Hey, look! It's got to be this way! Accept it."

'But Uncle Frank played it quiet, and kept on at me. Anyway, the night before I left Uncle Frank comes to me at three o'clock in the morning. He says, "Come on, Joey, we've got to see Padre Pio, it's on your way up in the car. Let's go."

'We got to Padre Pio's church at five o'clock and it was packed. I was at the back and the Mass begun, and I knew in my heart that there was something in his voice. At the end of the Mass we were all permitted to go upstairs. I was the last one up, standing in a corner. He comes in from a door and all of a sudden I hear the scuffling of knees, and everybody's whispering, and all of a sudden these arms are around my shoulders and he's kissing me on the forehead, hugging me, bringing me to his heart. "Joey, I'm so happy to see you." But I was in sin, Johnny, and I didn't know what to say.

'In 1963 I returned to Italy again, and when I was in Bari I decided I wanted to go to confession to Padre Pio. I made arrangements and at the appointed time I was taken into the church by the arm. I knelt down in front of him, close, face to face. And when I went face to face with Padre Pio I nearly *died*. I thought of all the crazy sins I'd committed in my whole life and I was speechless. So he touches me on the arm and he says, "Why don't you confess, Joey?" And I said, "Father, I can't speak." So he gets me by the arm and in perfect English he says, "Joey do you remember when you were in a bar with a girl named Barbara? Do you remember the sin you committed?" And he goes right on, Johnny, naming the people I was with, the places I was at, the sins I committed, *right down the line*.

'I was crying. I was sweating and nearly fainting. But I knew that if this was what I had to go through to come back to being happy it was worth it. At the end he put his hand to my lips so that I could kiss the stigmata, and he gives me a little slap round the cheek and says, "A bit of courage, and you'll be all right, Joey!"

'When I came away from that confessional I felt like a child again. I had a firm purpose of amendment, and I was sorry for every sin I'd committed in my life. I felt so good and so clean I didn't want to talk. And ever since then, 18 February 1963, the cross came off my shoulders. Ever since then I might be a little bit inconvenienced because I can't always do what I want to do, but I don't carry a cross. I don't suffer and I've been free.

'Two days later as I was kneeling down before Padre Pio in the corridor after Mass I got the fragrance of roses that comes from his hands. Now because I had lost my sense of smell, because my olfactory nerves had been destroyed, it came as such a shock I was thrown back against the wall as if I'd been hit by a bus. And Padre Pio touched me and said, "Don't be afraid, Joey!" And from that point on my sense of smell was restored after sixteen years, even though the doctor says that it's impossible for me to have a sense of smell; he says it's like getting electric light in a room without wires.

'The next day Padre Pio comes to me again, and he says, "Joey, I cannot give you physical sight to see with, but I will give you spiritual sight, for your soul. I will make you see things that your brothers will never see." That was 1963.

'Now, from there I was to go to Garabandal for the first time. I had this friend who said that the Blessed Virgin was appearing there. But because of these incredible gifts I received through Padre Pio I didn't want to go. So I asked Padre Pio personally whether it was true that the Blessed Mother was appearing there to these four little girls. And he said yes. And when I asked him if I should go there, he said, "Yes, why not?"

'So I went to Garabandal and I met Conchita, met the

whole thing. They described to me the whole village, the fields, the hill with the pines, all the messages from the Blessed Mother about the warning and the day of the great miracle. See this miraculous medal? Conchita gave it to me. It was kissed by Our Lady at Garabandal.

'In 1964 I was back home in my mother's house and I was lying on the couch saying my prayers and I started to fall asleep, and my mind starts to go like this: "Joey, at the blind school you had a dream – at the blind school, Joey, you had a dream. You saw something that looked like a golf course with trees at the back . . . you were looking at something up in the sky. Garabandal, Joey, Garabandal . . ." Maybe I was uptight; maybe I projected a voice. How do *I* know! But I'm looking for the truth anyway, and I realize for the first time that the scene of my dream all those years ago is one and the same as the descriptions that have been given to me of Garabandal, and I realize that I've been given in a dream a vision of the day of the great miracle.

'I believed in Conchita because Padre Pio told me it was all right. So I wrote to her. And Conchita wrote back to me on 19 March 1964, on St Joseph's day. Her letter said: "*Ave Maria.* Dear Joey, Today at the pines the Virgin Mary told me to tell you that the voice you heard was hers and that she will give you the new eyes she has promised on the day of the great miracle."

'Conchita came out here more than twenty years ago. She lives at Glendale, married with four children; she's a holy woman who suffers a great deal. I married a wonderful woman I met at Fatima ten years ago and we have two children.

'Conchita and I live waiting for the day of the great miracle, the day on which I will receive back my sight. On that day people all over the world will then have a permanent sign of the Blessed Mother's presence in the world. People will be converted the world over, and Russia will be converted.

'A year before the great miracle there will be a warning when everybody, irrespective of race, colour or creed, will see into their own hearts how they have offended God. Eight days before the great miracle, which will be a permanent sign over the pines at Garabandal, Conchita will announce the date. Then all of those who are convinced of the truth of Garabandal will make their way there. There will be hundreds of thousands, Johnny, because I've been busy all these years setting up Garabandal centres across the world. We'll be there in readiness. Now you have it all, Johnny. God bless you. In the name of the Father, and of the Son, and of the Holy Spirit, amen.'

All this time Joey had been leaning forward, making points by touching me on the arm with a huge hand; in the other hand he held his rosary. As he came to an end he stood up and pressed the medal on my forehead, then put it to my lips.

'And do you really have your sense of smell back?' I asked.

'Anything you put under my nose I can smell. It's a living daily miracle.'

'You smell cooking in the kitchen without seeing it?'

'Sure. My sense of smell is normal. In fact it's better than I ever remember it before the accident.'

As I shook Joey's hand he gave me Conchita's telephone number and address.

'It's the best I can do, Johnny. I can't arrange anything for you because Conchita does her own thing nowadays.' He guffawed breathily: 'I'm sure when she hears your accent she's gonna want to meet you, Johnny.'

As I drove in a cab back to Manhattan from Queens I wondered whether Joey's rebirth, the lifting of his suffering, had been a result of his firm trust in an eventual miracle cure, or whether it would have happened anyway. It seemed an extraordinary hope that he would one day receive a completely new set of eyes where he now had none. What was he going to do in the event of disappointment? Would it destroy his faith – both in the Garabandal apparitions and in Christianity? And as for the return of his sense of smell, I had heard of people hallucinating smells in the same way as amputees experience phantom pain.

Joey's story illustrated both the strength and the weakness of a literalist approach to supernatural expectations which carried specific promises, specific dates.

And what of Conchita? What must she now be feeling as she considered the trap she had constructed for herself, and Joey, and all the other hundreds of thousands of the devotees of the Garabandal cult who lived in expectation of the great sign? Had her visions not turned to a nightmare as the anticipated date drew nigh, threatening disillusion, disaster?

I had found Joey's story, and by association the Garabandal phenomenon, deeply affecting. The problem was now seeing how such phenomena could be understood within the framework of beneficent religious experience as opposed to the threat of despair.

26 Conchita, the Reluctant Prophetess

I called Conchita Gonzalez, now Mrs Conchita Keena, the seer of Garabandal, six times on the phone. Usually she remained silent for several moments after she had lifted the receiver. When she eventually spoke it was to refuse to see me. In the end, and somewhat against my inclination, I decided to make the journey to her home anyway.

Late on a summer evening I took a cab out to Queens via the 59th Street Bridge. We drove down Queens Boulevard to 69th Street, then along the flanks of Queens cemetery, and into the maze of streets in the district of Glendale. I was feeling uneasy and a little conscience-stricken, but I told myself that Conchita's story was in the public domain; if she was convinced that she was the vehicle for a message of supernatural warning to all humankind, she could hardly claim a private status.

The cab-driver left me in a narrow street lined with young plane trees. Children were playing out on the pavement. Her house was an anonymous-looking brick building with heavy iron grilles on the windows: it looked enclosed, shut up.

As I approached the front door I was suddenly seized with a sense of foreboding. Something about the house and the prospect of meeting this woman filled me with unease. I turned on

171

my heel and walked back down to the corner of the street. I must have gone up and down the street four or five times before I approached the door again.

I rang the bell. The house was silent. Almost with relief I was considering walking away when I cupped my hands and peered through the screen door into the darkened hallway and saw a figure standing motionless in the shadows, staring out at me.

'Hallo!' I said. 'I'm the English writer who called you. I just wanted to see you, shake your hand!' I was beginning to babble.

She did not move. In desperation I said, 'I bring greetings from Garabandal, from your brother Serafin and your sister-in-law Pacita.' I was speaking in broken Spanish.

With this she approached the first glass door and opened it a little. At last she said in English, 'I don't give interviews.' Her voice was deep, with a heavy Spanish accent.

'I know,' I blurted out. 'I just wanted to tell you how much I appreciate you.' It seemed a false and foolish thing to say.

'I'm nothing special,' she said.

'Nothing special! You spoke to Our Lady almost every day for four years and you think you're nothing special?'

She opened the door a little further. I could see her fully now. She was a woman of striking good looks, with high cheekbones and large dark eyes. She was elegantly dressed in a maroon silk blouse and a full black-and-white skirt. Her arms were bare and suntanned.

She gave a fleeting smile. 'Listen,' she said, 'when you die and go to heaven, you will see Our Lady too.'

It was as if she had spoken to a child.

'Can I come in?' I asked.

She hesitated a moment. Then she opened the screen door wide and let me through.

The hallway led into a sitting room with a dining area. The drapes were drawn. Two walls were covered with mirrors. On the other walls were icons, copies of Eastern originals. In the centre of the room was a low coffee table on a faded rug, faced by two white sofas covered in see-through plastic; she invited me to sit down, then she sat opposite me, resting her hands in her lap.

'How long have you lived in New York?' I asked her.

She told me that she had come to America aged sixteen. She was now thirty-eight. She had left Garabandal to escape an impossible dilemma. 'In Garabandal,' she said, 'nobody loved me for my own sake. They worshipped me because of the visions. I realized that nobody would ever love me or marry me who knew about the visions.'

'For a time,' I said, 'you dismissed your visions. Why did you do that?'

'I went to the Bishop of Santander, and after he had questioned me for hours on end I told him that I didn't believe in them any more. He gave me absolution and forbade me ever to talk of them again. Then when I got back to Garabandal I felt that I had betrayed the Blessed Mother. I believed in the visions, and yet I couldn't understand how they had occurred. I was torn in two.'

'So you came to New York?'

'I worked for a Spanish doctor in the city, and for a year I never spoke to anybody. He wanted to marry me; there were other people who wanted to marry me. In the end I married someone else.'

'Conchita,' I said, 'are you still expecting the *aviso*, the warning and the great miracle?'

'I'm not sure about anything anymore. I haven't even seen Joey for a long time now.'

'Are you saying you don't believe in your visions?'

173

'Everything is against Garabandal,' she said. 'The bishops, the Church; all sorts of people abuse me. They tell me I'm a liar and a fake.'

'So now you think that you were mistaken about your visions?'

'What I am telling you,' she said firmly, 'is that I saw a beautiful lady who told me she was the Blessed Mother. I saw her almost every day for four years. If this turns out to be false, then *nothing* is true. Do you understand what I'm saying? I mean that nothing whatsoever is true.'

Her face was sad. She fiddled with her rings.

'What makes you feel like this, Conchita?' I said.

She bit her lip and looked at me with angry eyes. 'How could the Blessed Mother come to me, give me all these signs and messages, and then abandon me? How can anything be true?'

She was looking at me challengingly, as if I could supply the answer. It was as if she were inviting me to offer her some sort of spiritual consolation to bolster her wavering faith.

'Do you ever wonder, Conchita,' I asked, 'whether you might not have been suffering delusions at the time?'

'We were tested by lots of psychiatrists and psychologists. They said we weren't sick or crazy or anything like that. I've never had any illness since. Anyway, if that was being crazy – I like to be crazy like that.' As she said this she managed a bleak smile.

'Conchita, would you mind my asking you a specific question?' I said. 'I've spoken to the old Guardia Civil, Brigadier Seco, in Garabandal, and he remembers you levitating in the kitchen of your house. Were you aware of doing that? Can you confirm that?'

'Look,' she said, 'when the Blessed Mother came she always appeared out of a bright light; I just wasn't aware of anything

174

else, or anybody else outside of the light. And I wasn't aware of the way I was behaving.'

'You know the date of the miracle, Conchita; and eight days before it you are going to travel to Garabandal?'

'That's right,' she said, with apparent reluctance.

'What will you do if the miracle doesn't happen?'

She sat in silence for a while wringing her hands. Then she said, 'That's what I'm telling you, Mister. If the miracle doesn't come, then *nothing* is true. What more can I say?'

She hung her head miserably for a while.

'Sometimes,' she said, 'I wish I'd never have to hear the word Garabandal again. I'm sorry!'

She stood up. 'Look, you'll have to go now,' she said.

As she went ahead of me to the door, she stopped and turned to me. 'Would you mind doing something for me?'

'Of course, Conchita.'

'Would you pray for me, please?'

27   Sacred Presences

The phenomenon of Garabandal had struck me as a dramatic religious mystery, rooted in local folk religion, unlike Medjugorje, which had been made insipid by extensive media promotion. Yet in the view of Catholic officialdom the cult of Garabandal had been an eccentric weed in the flower-garden of approved mysticism.

Conchita's temporary denial of her visions before the Bishop of Santander, her sudden lapse of memory when it came to divulging the prophetic secrets, and her later decision to marry rather than enter a convent had put her beyond the ecclesiastical pale. In common with similar phenomena down the centuries, in common with Marija of Medjugorje, her visions had outflanked the role of the male-dominated clergy in a peasant region where women are traditionally disadvantaged, disenfranchised. She had become a seer, a prophetess, a priestess, shaping and controlling her own liturgy; she was the focus of a strong religious experience unmediated by the clergy. But she had broken the expected pattern of final submission to the clergy by failing to take the veil and disappear into a convent.

Two of the girl seers at Medjugorje had now married, and I found it significant that Father Svet had accordingly criticized them for failing the challenge of their visions. The failure, ironically, had been to submit themselves to the Franciscans

The author (*back row, fourth from left*) as a student at Oscott College, 1958. (*John Cornwell*)

The children - (*left to right*) Ivan, Jakov and Marija - receive a vision at the parish house in Medjugorje. (*Medjugorje*)

The children of Medjugorje were submitted to numerous medical tests: Ivanka wears an EEG harness during a vision, while (*background*) an opaque screen is held in Marija's field of vision. (*Medjugorje Messenger*)

Two of the Garabandal visionaries in ecstasy.
(*Fr A. Combe, Notre Dame du Mt Carmel*)

Joey Lomangino, who hopes to regain his sight on the day of the promised Garabandal miracle. (*Garabandal*)

A photograph 'captures' the apparition of the Virgin at Zeitoun, in Cairo, 1968. (*Mary Evans Picture Library*)

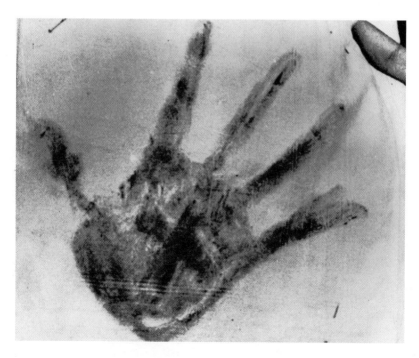

After the apparition, a handkerchief that purports to show a handprint in blood made by the Virgin Mary was displayed to the pilgrims who had flocked to the Egyptian suburb. Note the cross on the palm. (*Popperfoto*)

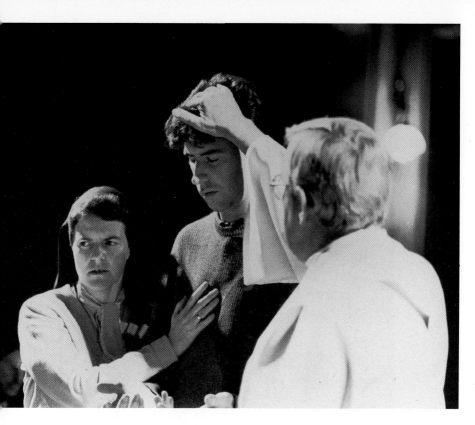

Sister Briege McKenna. (*Jane Bown/Observer*)

(Left) Georgette Faniel, the stigmatic of Montreal, and her spiritual directors, the twin priests Fathers Armand and Guy Girard.
(*Medjugorje Messenger*)

The head of the Shroud Man, as it is seen by the naked eye (*left*), and as a photographic negative (*right*). (*Popperfoto*)

(Left) A full-length negative image of the Turin Shroud. (*Popperfoto*)

Padre Pio the stigmatic says Mass at San Giovanni Rotondo, 1955.
(*Popperfoto*)

(Right) Elizabeth K., bleeding from the eyes after being hypnotized.
(*Dr Alfred Lechler, courtesy of Dr Theodor Stockle, from the
collection of Iain Wilson*)

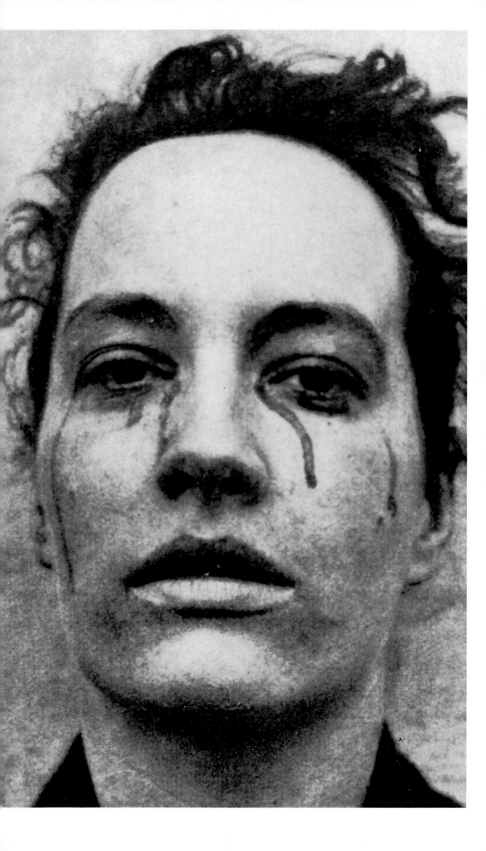

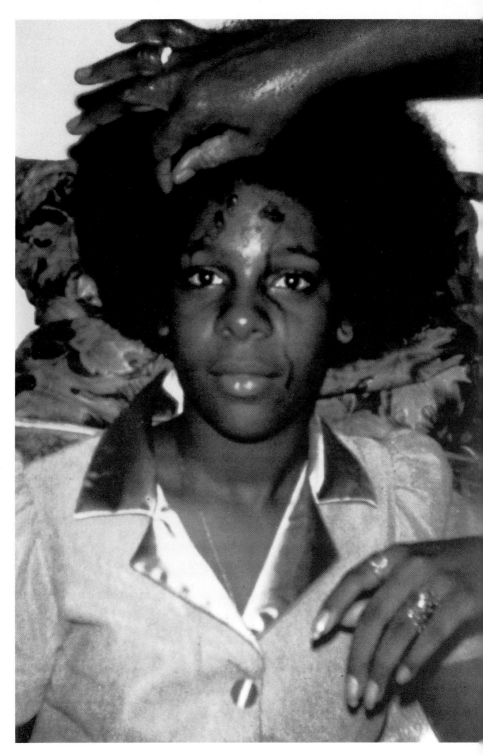

The stigmatic Cloretta Robinson, who developed wounds consistent with the crown of thorns, Easter 1972. (*Rev. Anthony Burrus, from the collection of Iain Wilson*)

Joseph of Copertino levitates while in ecstasy; eighteenth-century engraving. (*Mary Evans Picture Library*)

The liquefaction of the blood of St Januarius, Naples Cathedral.
(*Dario Mitidieri/Select*)

(Left) 26 September 1951: the priests hand out to the pilgrims
wads of cotton that have been soaked in the tears of the weeping
Madonna of Syracuse. (*Topham Picture Library*)

Archbishop Milingo at a service of healing in 1985. (*Rex Features*)

and the discipline of the religious life. Now the promotors were evidently pinning all their hopes on Marija entering a convent, as if this were the final hurdle before official acceptance of the cult could take place.

As it was, Conchita had exiled herself both from the protective custody of the Church and from her country. She had travelled to America, where she knew no one except Joey Lomangino, to escape notoriety in the vast anonymity of New York. Yet as long as she lived she would never escape the burden of her visions nor the implications of having involved herself in the promise of a great visible sign.

I found it moving that she had fled Garabandal and rejected the role of idolized *spirituelle* precisely because she wanted to be loved not for her visions but for her own sake. It argued considerable strength of character that she had been determined to define herself according to her human relationships rather than the shadows of pietistic adulation, thus escaping the predicament of the Lady of Shallot: 'I am half sick of shadows.'

Entering a convent, of course, would have been no guarantee of psychological and spiritual security: 150 years before Garabandal, the seer Melanie Mathieu of Salette in Alpine France had taken the veil, but ended her life as an alcoholic, wandering from convent to convent throughout France and England.

Yet it seemed to me that Conchita was suffering because the Church had failed to comprehend her experiences. Her predicament underlined the absence of a coherent theology of popular forms of mystical phenomena.

What was the status of Conchita's visions? I do not believe that Conchita was sick, nor do I believe that she was a liar. Her ecstasies, like those of the leading seers at Medjugorje, struck me as something primitive, sacred and real. But did the strange physical feats by themselves indicate the involvement of an alternative supranatural world? In the absence of in-controvertible evidence under proper test conditions, I was not inclined to entertain the idea. In any case, the question seemed to be missing the main point. The visions, the strange physical feats, were a group experience intended to be observed by the local community in much the same way as an audience witnesses a play, or a congregation the liturgy. Hysteria might well have been involved and some form of kinetic force as yet poorly understood, but the phenomena taken as a whole seemed analagous to an art form, displaying special aptitude, inspiration, dance and choreography, the exercise of imagination and deep emotion.

The physical feats – the strange backward marches, the apparent levitations – lent legitimacy to the central contention that the girls were aware of a sacred, immensely powerful yet benign presence in their midst. The phenomena required to be *read*. The 'magic flights', the pine trees, the promise of the great miracle sign created a sense of unique focus. It told the participants and spectators that Garabandal could become the centre of the universe – a place where a higher power had chosen to make its sacred presence felt among human kind.

The imponderable question was the extent to which the folk religion of the region, the prevailing established religion of Spain, brought this sacred presence into the ambit of official religious belief and iconography. How much collusion had taken place between Conchita and the women of the village, before the precise identities of the apparitions had been announced? In the case of Lourdes the apparition was initially referred to in dialect by Bernadette as *acquerro*, 'that thing', until extensive conversations had taken place with the pious ladies of the locality.

These reflections by no means indicate a reductive attitude towards the Christian content of the phenomena. I see no necessary contradiction between a primitive awareness of sacred presence and a Christian's notion of God's, or Mary's, real presence. Might they not converge towards the same point? The important question for Conchita, however, was this: what happened when these two notions of transcendent presence and power found themselves in conflict as a result of the dogmatic strictures of Church officialdom? For her it had resulted in a life of inner torment. A naturally devout person, with an outstanding loyalty to her faith, she was now riven with doubt to the point of speculating whether her private revelations should become a test of her wider sense of faith. Her predicament illustrated the insidious potential of paranormal religious experience.

As it is, Conchita still awaits the warning, the miracle and possible chastisement. And if, as I now believe she suspects will happen, the warning and miracle fail to materialize, she not only will become a laughing-stock but will risk losing her faith in her visions as well as her faith in God.

And yet something continued to nag me. How special, how unique was the Marian visionary experience? And to what extent was it exclusive to a particular culture and religion?

28   White Ladies

B etween interviews I had been spending many hours in the
New York Public Library, which was just a short walk
from my hotel. Browsing through a stack of psychology publications I found what I had been seeking for days: confirmation that apparitions of 'beautiful ladies' bathed in white light
were by no means the preserve of Christian visions, even in
the west.

In 1954 the popular Swiss fortnightly newspaper, the *Schweiz-
erischer Beobachter*, had conducted a survey amongst its
readers about paranormal experiences. Some 1,500 responses
came in and the material was passed to Aniela Jaffé, the Swiss
psychologist and associate of Carl Jung. Encouraged by a
New York psychologist, Martin Ebon, she had published a
paper in 1978 that established the leading categories of the
experiences. One of her categories was entitled: *Apparitions of
the 'woman in white'*.

Without giving precise numbers, Dr Jaffé reported that a
significant number of correspondents had witnessed the apparition of a beautiful lady in a white light who conveyed a
warning of danger. Invariably the visionaries were girls and
boys, and there had been no specifically religious context
attached to the experience.

Among the samples she quotes are the following.

A man wrote that in his boyhood he and his brother had

woken to their father's calls. They went out on to the veranda and in the light of a full moon they saw leaning against an apple tree 'a woman in white with her hair hanging down in plaits'. They jumped down into the orchard and ran towards her. When the correspondent was a few feet away from the apparition he asked what she was doing there. She stared back in silence. 'Two dark eyes were fixed on me, imploring me, with sadness and reproach, not to disturb her.' He tried to grab hold of her, but his hand remained empty. With a gentle, apologetic smile she glided away. They ran after her. 'Then the miracle happened. As if borne by an unseen power, she glided swiftly away from us, and the next moment had vanished.'

In another submission a woman wrote that in her childhood she had once gone to meet her mother, who was returning from work. At a lonely spot on the road she saw a 'beautiful lady' before her – 'not very tall and snow-white'. The apparition was wearing a long dress and veil and floated along a little way behind her, hovering just above the ground. 'I stopped again and again to look back at the wonderful figure.' When her mother eventually approached, the apparition disappeared.

A woman recollected that in her childhood she woke during the night plagued with thirst. She called out for a glass of water and waited for her mother to come, raising herself in the bed in anticipation. At that moment a figure of a woman appeared at the bedroom door. 'It was a completely strange figure, a woman, tall, beautiful, in a flowing white robe, with long black curls hanging down.' The apparition approached the bed and stood for several seconds gazing at her before returning slowly to the door. At that moment her mother appeared with a glass of water. 'I saw the two figures quite distinctly side by side – my tall mother looked small beside the apparition – then suddenly it vanished as if dissolved in air.'

Another woman wrote that when she was aged about ten she was walking with her mother on a lonely footpath next to a wood when they saw a woman 'dressed all in white walking slowly along'. As they gazed at the figure it suddenly vanished.

In her analysis Dr Jaffé attempts to relate these contemporary experiences with a wide range of parallels in what she calls the 'old texts', notably with the *femina alba* – Venus or Aphrodite, the Goddess of Love. Why, though, she asks, does the White Lady so often seem a harbinger of misfortune?

Her suggestion is typically Jungian: 'If we are to understand such a strange contradiction,' she writes,

> we must bear in mind that, as long as they are unconscious, all archetypal contents are twofold and ambiguous. In the unconscious the opposites are not yet separated; an unconscious content becomes conscious only through discrimination of its latent opposites. When the two sides stand face to face they can be comprehended and the conscious mind can grasp them.

Aphrodite, Jaffé points out, is not only the goddess of love; she is also the queen of the underworld or of death. In Germanic mythology, moreover, the corresponding goddess is Frigg or Freya, who is both radiant goddess of love and the goddess of the dead known as Hel. In an alternative pantheon, Jaffé goes on, there is a still more powerful manifestation known as Erda or Hertha, encompassing both the great powers of light and darkness. 'This goddess of earth, or the archetypal figure of the "Great Mother",' she says, 'has to be understood as a personification of the unconscious. The unconscious is the maternal, instinctive foundation of man as a living creature, it is the "mother" of his mind and consciousness as well.'

While her interpretation struck me as rather woolly, the ambivalence of the archetypal figure suggested a great many echoes, from Isis through to Keats's *La Belle Dame Sans Merci*, the loving harbinger of his own fatal disease. And this more poetic approach, it struck me, found echoes in the rich materials gathered by Robert Graves in his book *The White Goddess*.

Graves points out that in medieval Irish literature the Virgin Mary is identified with Brigit, the goddess of poetry, and Brigit, the patroness of healing. Brigit was also known as the White Swan, as the Bride of the White Hills and the Bride of the Golden Hair. Brigit, or Mary, had a variety of mythic proto-types, he claims: in the Aegean, she was Brizo of Delos – a moon goddess – and she was associated with healing incanta-tions at sacred wells in Roman Britain and Gaul.

Jaffé remarks in conclusion that the White Lady appears invariably to girls at the point when they are becoming con-scious of their femininity. The female principle, says Jaffé, is their future fate, and the divine or mysterious phantom is like an intimation of what they have yet to become. This does not imply, however, that the child has grasped its meaning. 'Nature is lavish and reveals herself to the blind as well as to the seeing eye . . . Nature, or the unconscious, presents itself, and leaves it to consciousness to ask questions or seek for a mean-ing.'

Like dreams? Like poetry and mythology? Like theatre?

Jaffé comments that visions of the White Lady are frequently encountered more than once by the seer. And she suggests that questions raised by such impressive dreams or childhood ex-periences are only asked later, in adult life.

Throughout the discussion she is not in the least concerned with the status of the phenomenon: that is, with accounting for the apparition in terms of imagination, dream or hallucination. She is more interested in the timeless, archetypal, constants. But what was one to make of this evidence in relation to the seers of Medjugorje and Garabandal, or any of the other 230 recorded series of major sightings of the Virgin Mary throughout the twentieth century?

Jaffé's material, it occurred to me, complemented the fascinating work done by the social scientist Michael Carrol in the University of Western Ontario, published at the time of my visit to New York. Carrol had put the details of many hundreds of apparitions of the Virgin into his computer in order to discover an empirical pattern. Among the most constant features were these:

1 The Virgin appears to girls at about puberty.
2 The favoured seer usually colludes with the local community before announcing the Virgin's identity.
3 The seers are normally working children, who are out looking for lost cattle or sheep at the time of the first phenomenon, which usually occurs as a light.
4 The seer has lost a mother, or a mother figure (with Bernadette of Lourdes it was her elder sister) in the previous eight weeks. (As exact as that!)
5 The Virgin imparts secrets and warnings of doom if certain religious formulas are not adhered to.

There was clearly an interesting overlap between Jaffé's and Carrol's work; yet did this indicate a reductive conclusion as far as religious faith was concerned?

It seemed to me that the White Lady phenomenon might even add depth to the significance of Marian apparitions provided one was not looking for specific and literal quantities and values. At the heart of the experience was the impression of encounter with a supernatural presence that was not so

184

much the procuring of a state of feeling, or the apprehension of an object (such as might be acquired by drugs, or techniques of meditation), as a meeting of two presences, the supernatural personality having *chosen* to manifest itself, or herself, to the mortal.

The paradigm of gift and response in the suggested relationship between a human being and an awareness of a sacred presence seemed to me far more potent than a highly specific and literalist approach, that asks questions such as: How was she dressed? Was she three-dimensional? What specific instructions did she give? What is the precise date of the chastisement? and so forth. How much are these sorts of questions, in any case, the result of collusion with those eager for precise eschatological answers?

The mysterious, poetical context, suggested in particular by Garabandal (and by inference Medjugorje), did not preclude a spiritual, a Christian interpretation. On the other hand I was finding it increasingly difficult to fit Conchita into a clinical or pathological pattern. Two recent psychiatric studies have attempted to link the incidence of hallucinatory experiences in non-psychotic children with specific mood problems and family circumstances. In the first, published in 1987, psychiatrists at the Royal Ottawa Hospital assessed eleven children who had experienced spontaneous hallucinations without any evident signs of mental illness. In ten of the cases the content of the hallucinations was frightening or threatening and involved male or 'monstrous' figments or presences. In only one case was there a female presence, described as a 'white woman', who urged the child to do 'good things'. According to the authors, 'most children presented mood disturbance, mainly anxiety . . . The children were socially inept or withdrawn.'

In another relevant study, 'Grief and Hallucinations', published in 1988, the authors propose that non-psychotic hallucinations arise from 'incomplete mourning within a closely bonded mother and child dyad'. These hallucinations, say the authors, represent a 'reassuring companion and ego-support, an inclination of a family-systemic need, and a cognitive-emotion repression in the service of defence and of ego-mastery striving'.

The picture of typical 'mood disturbance' and social ineptness observed in the Ottawa study, and the bereavement process hypothesis of Yates *et al* in the 'Grief and Hallucinations' study, clearly had no bearing (as far as I could ascertain) on Conchita's personality and circumstances, and from this point of view a psychiatric, a clinical, diagnosis or solution seemed unhelpful.

Reflecting once more on my conversation with Conchita, her diary and the village testimonies, her story conveyed above all a conviction that she had encountered the real presence of a beautiful lady. The reality of her experience, the reality of the relationship, was impervious to any sort of rationalization or contradiction.

Conchita had been able to identify her vision with the Virgin Mary without doing violence to the reality of the encounter. She was not, however, prepared to sacrifice her vision in the interests of Church doctrine and discipline that repudiated the reality of her experience.

Even if the Church, even if the Pope himself, were to tell her that the Virgin Mary had not appeared to her, even if she were to be betrayed by the non-fulfilment of the secrets, she would continue to believe in the reality of her beautiful lady. This suggested to me an impression of presence more profound and striking than anything encountered in neurotic states or, indeed, in religious conviction based on faith. Perhaps this gave new meaning to the Jungian term 'archetype' and the significance of a primitive religious experience. Perhaps it was a clue to the powers of religious imagination, little acknowledged and seldom understood.

PART FOUR

Wounds and Healing

29   Briege's Gift

Towards the end of my stay in New York I came in from the library one evening to find a phone message to call Sister Briege McKenna on a Long Island number.

When I got through to her I was reassured to learn that she had not been indulging in ESP. Father Foley, with whom I had been in contact, had told her of my whereabouts when he discovered that she was coming through New York.

'I wanted to ask how your work is getting on,' she said cheerily. 'You've been in my thoughts and prayers . . . Come and have lunch tomorrow.' She gave directions and rang off.

So I found myself next day riding the Long Island Railroad out through Woodside, Flushing, Douglaston, to Manhasset. Passing through the pleasant wooded suburbs I thought of Thomas Merton, the Trappist monk and writer, who had described this journey in his autobiography *The Seven-Storied Mountain*. He was riding this very train the afternoon war was declared in Europe, and came up with the extraordinary thought that one mortal sin might have been responsible for the outbreak of the Second World War.

At Manhasset a man was waiting for me outside the station. He held up a card with my name on it. We drove in silence along Rock Shelter Road and eventually turned off and through a gateway, where two men scrutinized me and waved at the driver. There was a track through thick woods of beech and maple, then another gate with more guards. At length a rambling country mansion came into view. There were half a dozen black labrador dogs lounging around on the terrace. I gasped. What sort of convent was this?

The driver heard me. 'This,' he said with evident pride, 'is the home of Mr and Mrs Peter Grace.'

I knew only one thing about Mr Peter Grace: he was one of the richest men in America.

At the front door I was greeted by a secretary, who ushered me into an elegant drawing room. Sister Briege would be down directly, she said. Suddenly a figure swept through a doorway – a youngish-looking woman in a turquoise silk gown and white high-heeled shoes. Her hair was well-coiffed and she was wearing a string of pearls. She was laughing pleasantly as she came towards me. It was Sister Briege McKenna.

'Don't worry about this,' she said, patting her hair. 'I'm on my holidays. How are you, John?' With this she gave me a hug and a kiss on the cheek. With her freckles and gappy grin, she looked like a mischievous urchin who had been delving in the dressing-up box.

She led me through to another drawing room resplendent with Victorian furniture and family portraits and sat me down on a sofa. She explained that her work had been sponsored by the Grace Foundation so as to relieve the burden on Third World missions that were keen for her ministry.

'I come here for a few days every year to unwind.' she said. 'Now, John, I just wanted to check up on you, to see how you are. We've a few minutes before we go in to lunch. Is there anything you'd like to talk to me about? How is the miracle hunt?'

I was speechless.

She touched me on the arm and laughed teasingly, and I

realized at that moment that I felt attracted to her more than was good for me, and despite my better judgement.

I noticed that she had been holding her right hand clenched all this time, and slightly extended towards me. She now opened it to reveal a small black Celtic cross with a thin leather string to go around the neck.

'I want to give this to you,' she said. 'It's made of compressed Irish peat.' She stood up and came around behind me. Before I could protest she had placed the cross on my chest and put the loop over my head.

'There. Put it inside your shirt.'

As I did so the cross felt uncomfortably cold next to my skin. I felt embarrassed, imposed upon, and it must have shown in my face. Briege looked at me for a moment, then laughed happily and tapped me on the cheek with two fingers. The blow was strong enough to hurt a little. She was looking directly at me, and her eyes were filled with tenderness. I felt as if I had known and loved her all my life.

She sat down again and took my hands in hers. She had guessed that I was upset.

'Take it off later,' she said, 'it's not important to wear it . . . but keep it; you might want it one day.'

Then she said with feeling: 'I love you, John. I really love you.' She was looking into my eyes with an amused and quizzical expression. With this she took me in her arms, and kissed me on the forehead and on the cheek.

As we went into lunch I was conscious that my face was burning.

Before I left for the station to return to New York Sister Briege gave me a picture of the alleged face of Christ on the Turin Shroud; there was an address on the back.

'Here's another little present for you,' she said. 'There's a convent in the Bronx where some Carmelite nuns claim miraculous occurrences. I wonder what you'll make of it. Tell them I told you to call.'

As I got into the car, she said, 'I've a feeling we'll see each other again before too long.'

She stood at the doorway waving. As soon as she was out of sight I took the crucifix from around my neck and put it in my pocket.

I looked at the 'face' of Christ. It conveyed an impression of deep sadness and resignation. I put it in my wallet, with my plastic credit cards.

30   Bleeding Host in the Bronx

When I called the convent of St Joseph on the telephone, a woman's voice said, 'Praised be to Christ!'

Sister Mari sounded dubious about receiving me; but she relented when I mentioned Briege's name.

I was driven from midtown Manhattan by a Bengali cabdriver who got us lost for one and a half hours. When we finally arrived at our destination in one of the poorest parts of the Bronx I wondered whether I had made a mistake about the address. I had been expecting a Gothic building with a chapel. The driver left me outside a dingy apartment block.

A young man opened the door and directed me up a stairway smelling of cabbage to the apartment above. At the top was a statue of St Michael the Archangel, doughty champion against the snares of the Devil. I was surveyed through a grille by a pair of eyes, then a door opened and a nun greeted me. She was small and plump with a bright red face and dressed in the full habit of the Carmelite order – brown robe with a scapular back and front, a white wimple and a black veil. This was Sister Mari; another nun, tall, stooped and pale, stood beyond her: she was introduced as Sister Gertrude.

The nuns' habits were so voluminous that they could hardly move in the narrow confines of the apartment. The floors were covered in linoleum and the walls painted an institutional green. The place was spotlessly clean but smelled of damp.

Sister Mari invited me to sit down in a sort of kitchen area, comprising a sink and a gas cooker, but it was merely part of a corridor. She pointed to a glass door beyond which I imagined there might once have been a proper kitchen or bathroom.

'That's our chapel,' she whispered. 'We have perpetual adoration of the real presence. We maintain silence within the convent, it's our Rule, but I can talk in special circumstances.' The rest of our conversation was continued in a stage whisper, as if this somehow mitigated the breaking of the vow of silence.

Sister Mari told me that she was the superior of this convent, which numbered just three nuns. The third nun was resting. For ten years they had been running an experiment in conventual living in inner-city areas.

'We were part of a regular convent in upstate New York, but we're bringing the contemplative life into the heart of the city,' she said.

They had no money, no back-up resources. Neither did they beg. They waited for gifts of food and donations. Whenever they had an excess beyond their needs for a day or two, they gave it away. They fasted continuously and they were vegetarians. They believed in the power of prayer and encouraged local people to come and join them in silent contemplation and adoration.

'We make ourselves free to pray for those who cannot pray for themselves,' she said.

All this was said with a directness and simplicity that belied any sense of spiritual pride or religiosity.

Their lives were not without anxiety. Several times they had been turned out of rented apartments. 'This usually happens,' she said, 'after we have cleaned and renovated the place. The landlord sees that we have made it more commercially valuable and puts up the rent.'

Then she told me how the miracles began.

On the previous Christmas the nuns had entered the chapel for the third Mass of Christmas Day and noticed that something strange had happened to the child Jesus in the crib. There had appeared on both sides of the hand of the twelve-inch-high wax statue the likeness of a wound. Then, on the Feast of the Holy Innocents, the statue shed tears on two different occasions. Still during the Christmas period, on the octave of the feast, the left foot began to swell. Gradually another wound showed itself, and a red substance looking like blood flowed from it.

'It took some time before we realized that this was the sign of the stigmata,' said Sister Mari. 'We had to mop up the substance with a napkin.'

'What was your first reaction?' I asked.

'We were cautious,' she said. 'But it's difficult to know how it might have happened naturally. Nobody has access to the chapel except us. We know each other well, and it's inconceivable that any of us would have engaged in a deceit. And what would be our motive? We don't look for miracles. We're not mystics; our spiritual life is based on faith and prayer.'

'What happened next?'

'Six months later, on the Feast of Corpus Christi and the Precious Blood – the two feasts are now combined – we noticed that the host that was being used for the exposition was oozing red drops; in a matter of hours it had darkened in just the way that blood is affected by contact with the air.'

The nun took me through into the chapel, where there was barely enough room for more than eight people standing. It was simple, austere. She opened the tabernacle behind the altar, genuflected and opened the door with a tasseled key. There on a gold mount was the subject of the claimed miracle – a circular wafer of unleavened bread, about an inch in diameter. Most of the surface of the wafer was a dark-brown colour, exactly the colour of a bandage that has been stained with blood for a day or so before.

I asked Sister Mari if I could take a photograph, but she signalled that this was not allowed.

Next she took me into a small room, no more than a cubicle, which served as a vestry or sacristy. On a chest of drawers was the effigy of the child Jesus in its crib. The brown stains were still clearly visible on one palm and one foot.

'Has the substance been analysed, both from the host and the effigy?' I asked.

'A bishop came, and several scientists; everything has been taken to Rome. They say the liquid isn't blood, but there is a mystery substance they cannot identify. It could be years before anything is decided.'

We fell silent for a moment. I was wondering whether the nun would offer me a cup of tea or coffee.

Then she said, 'Excuse me, sir, but if that is all – we have a life of prayer to get on with.'

I felt suitably rebuked. I had somehow assumed that these nuns, with their prayer life, were nevertheless ladies of endless leisure.

'One more question, Sister,' I asked. 'Why do *you* think that this miracle happened here in this little community in the Bronx?'

'I've no doubt whatsoever why it happened,' she said promptly. She fixed me with a look of complete frankness.

'A few days before the phenomenon somebody had placed a human foetus in our garbage and we found it. We saw in that dead little creature the image of the crucified Christ. Somehow the effigy with its stigmata was pleading for that link to be made more firmly, perhaps, and for prayers of reparation to be said . . .'

'So it's a sort of political statement,' I said.

'I don't know about politics, Mr Cornwell,' she said. 'I see only the facts. There are 5 million unborn children aborted every year in the United States. That's the equivalent of the Jewish holocaust once a year in this society. And the products of this carnage assist in the manufacture of lipstick . . .'

'Nevertheless,' I went on, 'the occurrence of a miracle here would support the anti-abortion lobby.'

The nun smiled. 'I don't know . . . We've made no attempts to publicize it. We simply reported it to the bishop. You are the first writer to come here and observe the phenomenon. We didn't ask you to come.'

The nun's coolness impressed me. I wondered, though, whether she was aware of the precedents of Eucharistic miracles and whipped and bleeding statues which had been prolific during the Middle Ages and which had widely supported the grotesque blood libels against the Jews – reports that Jews routinely desecrated the sacred host and crucifixes and shed the blood of Christian babies for sacrifices.

As she was walking me to the door of the apartment I asked her whether she had studied in a university.

'I was at Fordham in New York, and a post-graduate student at Freiburg University, where I took a doctorate in mystical theology.'

As I descended the staircase with its smell of boiled cabbage I decided that Sister Mari was probably better aware of the precedents than I.

I took the subway back to Manhattan, all the way mulling over the strange experience of the afternoon. I could not discount the notion that the stains on the wafer had been caused by a species of mould. And yet that would not have accounted for the prior phenomenon of the stigmata on the effigy.

The simplest explanation, then, was fraud. But why should they do this and keep quiet about it? Surely the only motive for perpetrating a hoax would have been to create publicity for themselves. I was thinking of a case in the town of Entrevaux in France in the fifties, when blood appeared on a broken finger of a statue of the Virgin in the church; it was tested and found to be human blood. After 2 million pilgrims had flocked there, and many miracles had been reported, a local man confessed that he had devised the 'miracle' in order to put the church 'on the map'.

In another case in my files, at Stockport in England a man had recently confessed a holy hoax involving flowers forty years earlier. In 1947 the roses on the head of the statue of the Madonna failed to fade or shed their petals during a period of three years. The miracle of the 'eternal roses', which drew hundreds of thousands of pilgrims from all over England, was a trick devised by the parish priest and a local florist.

It seemed to me that the Eucharistic miracle of the Bronx had the unmistakable characteristics of a hoax, and yet I found it difficult to believe that the nuns themselves would have perpetrated it.

There was an element of mystery, then, closer to Agatha Christie than to genuine mysticism. But what did it matter? The prayer lives of these heroic women, who had chosen to accept the drawbacks of the religious life with few of its consolations, would impress me for a lot longer than their 'miracle'.

Back in midtown Manhattan I went into a shop that sold religious publications and found on the shelves a book containing some thirty accounts of Eucharistic miracles – spanning the eighth to the twentieth centuries; it had been published in Rockford, Illinois in 1987, with the imprimatur of the Archbishop of New Orleans, Philip M. Hannan. I bought it and took it off to read over dinner.

The majority of the accounts occurred in Italy, Spain and France. Most involved priests who had suffered doubt and whose faith had been restored by the miracle of a bleeding or fleshly host. There were other sorts of unbelievers, Saracens and French revolutionaries and Republicans in the Spanish Civil War, whose attempted depredations of tabernacles had been foiled by dramatic prodigies of flying and disappearing hosts. And there were instances in which a miracle had occurred to expose the use of the consecrated host in acts of sorcery, like the woman of Altari in Italy who had removed the Eucharist from her tongue, and then later returned it to her mouth again in order to captivate a young man in a kiss; or the housewife of Santarem in Portugal who stole and ground down a host to make a love potion to win back her philandering husband. Sacrilege had been revealed by the appearance of a telltale sign: the host would 'bleed', or go dark brown. But how often, I wondered, did the discovery of a moulding host lead to the search for a fantastic cause?

Then, to my dismay, I came across a type of Eucharistic tale that I had hoped had been long expunged from modern hagiographical collections. But here it was, written up in this recently published paperback: a repetition of the Jewish blood libel.

The story was entitled 'The Miracle of Brussels', and I recount it here in outline, as it reveals that evil element of the 'miraculous' that once raged through Christian Europe and clearly smoulders still in contemporary pietistic literature.

A Jewish resident of Enghien named Jonathan, the tale goes, purchased from a Christian some sixteen consecrated hosts for 62 gold coins. The hosts eventually ended up in the synagogue in Brussels on 4 April 1370. 'After laying the sacred hosts out on a table,' the author relates, 'they inflicted upon them both verbal and physical abuse. At some point during the sacrilege, knives were drawn and the Hosts were stabbed.'

201

Then the miracle happened. Before the 'stunned' eyes of the Jews, blood gushed from the stab wounds. Terror-stricken, the perpetrators fell to the ground.

According to the legend, an accomplice of the thief reported the crime to the curate of the local bishop and the Jews were rounded up and imprisoned. The modern author tells us that there are alternative endings to this story: in one version, they are banished from Belgium by the Jewish community; in the other, they confess their crime and are burned at the stake.

Commenting on the guide-book to St Michael's Cathedral, where the remnants of the hosts are kept to this day, and where the story is depicted in stained glass, the author, Joan Carroll Cruz, refers with complacent naïvety to 'a very surprising notice': 'On 30 December 1968 the diocesan authorities of Maline-Brussels Archdiocese declared the charges of theft and sacrilege of the Blessed Sacrament in 1369–70 which were brought against the Jewish community of Brussels were unfounded.' The author is clearly irritated by the disclaimer and assures the reader that 'tourists and the faithful of Brussels still honour the miracle by visiting the chapel where the miraculous Hosts were kept'.

Pondering this story, and the scholarly explication of the Jewish blood-libel myth by historians like Po-chia Hsia and Norman Cohn, it struck me that there was a deep irony in the survival of this powerful relic of suffering. At a deeper, more powerful level, it was a commemoration of the prejudice against the Jews as Christ-killers – not only as they are remembered in Christian scripture and passion plays such as that at Oberammergau, but in those vicious eras when they were tortured and murdered in the name of Eucharistic miracles. The Eucharistic miracle of Brussels is surely a relic of astounding irony, for it perpetuates unwittingly the agony of innocent medieval Jews who might otherwise have been forgotten.

31 Sacred Wounds

The Eucharistic miracle of the Bronx reminded me that supernatural phenomena in the Western Christian tradition tend to alternate between Marian presences on the one hand and the stark images of Christ's blood and wounds on the other. Marian apparitions were recently depicted by Pope John Paul II (in his encyclical *Mater Redemptoris*) as signifying the Virgin's journey through time and space on a pilgrimage towards the Second Coming and the final victory over Satan. Her appearances in different locations can be explained in the light of popular folk religion in a tradition that goes back to pre-Christian times in Mediterranean communities, but the Church amplifies these specific occurrences so as to fit them into a pattern that coincides with universal doctrine: Mary is the second Eve, the woman who cooperated in our redemption by becoming the Mother of God. She is the Immaculate Conception, the mediatrix of all graces, and she has a major apocalyptic role yet to come – to foil Satan in the last days of the world.

Like the rosary itself, which exemplifies the story of Mary's joyful, and sorrowful, journey on earth as well as her glorious status as Queen of Heaven, there are periodic pauses in which the devotee dwells on Christ and particularly his Passion and death. Physically this is illustrated by the dominant image of the crucifix that hangs from every set of rosary beads. The

203

emphasis on Mary, as a regular heavenly visitor, rather than Christ, is possibly explained by the dominance of the divine male, real presence in the Eucharist.

Paranormal manifestations of Christ invariably emphasize suffering, pain, sacrifice, wounds, blood, the Cross and the instruments of Christ's passion, the veil of Veronica, and the holy shroud.

Mary on the other hand exemplifies birth, gentleness, motherhood, mediation, consolation. The contrasting figures of Mary and Christ can perhaps be most strikingly illustrated by the depiction of the Virgin suckling St Bernard at her breast, while Christ inflicts the stigmata on St Francis of Assisi.

In the varied storehouse of Catholic tradition there are countless instances of the physical manifestations of Christ's passion on favoured persons. One sixteenth-century example involves the Blessed Clare of the Cross. After her death the sisters opened her heart with a razor and found, fashioned out of muscle and tissue, not only the image of the Cross, but representations of 'the whip, or scourge with which Christ was beaten . . . the pillar, the crown of thorns, the nails, the spear and the pole with the sponge . . .'

But the most dramatic representation of the Passion of Christ consistently manifested since early medieval times is the phenomenon of the stigmata – the appearance of Christ's wounds on the appropriate part of the hands, feet and side of a 'servant of God'.

The very first recorded 'authentic' instance of stigmatization is believed to be that of St Francis of Assisi in September 1224. Thurston, however, cites the curious story of an Englishman who in 1222 allowed himself to be crucified and thus bore the wounds of Christ by artificial means. The unfortunate fellow was either imprisoned at Banbury or burnt to death, possibly both, his self-crucifixion being judged a blasphemy. (In a more recent case, in which two labourers crucified a man on Hampstead Heath in London, it was the crucifiers who were charged and fined, even though their victim admitted that he had requested the treatment.)

Imbert-Gourbeyre, author of *La Stigmatisation* (1894), reckoned that of the 300 and more stigmatics (deemed authentic or otherwise), 280 were female and only 41 were male. Italy has been most favoured with stigmatas, but the phenomenon has also occurred in France, Spain, the Netherlands and the United States. At the time of writing current cases involve an Australian (a nurse who believed that she was in need of expiation) and an Anglican Englishwoman in Derbyshire called Jane Hunt, the wife of a bus driver.

A typical stigmatic, according to clinical descriptions, is a single woman, invariably a Catholic and a member of a religious order, who shows an excess of religious fervour in youth, including excessive self-denial. Before the onset of symptoms she will have suffered prolonged physical and psychological illnesses necessitating invalid status and long periods of confinement in bed. In nearly all cases the stigmatic will have experienced trances, visions and raptures, and intense contemplation of the crucified Christ. The stigmatization involves great pain at the site of the wounds.

I was very keen indeed to meet a 'genuine' case.

32   *The Stigmatic of Montreal*

I had asked my guide, Father Foley, if he knew of a current stigmatic and he readily recommended a seventy-four-year-old woman in Montreal called Georgette Faniel, who, he said, was probably the most authentic living example in the world today. On the way back to Europe I took a side trip to Canada to meet her.

It was arranged that I should go straight from the airport to the headquarters of the Society of the Holy Apostles, near the Olympic Stadium, where I was to meet my contact. It was an imposing brick house next to a concrete church. As I rang the bell the door opened immediately to reveal the astonishing spectacle of identical middle-aged twins; the fact that they were both priests made the phenomenon all the more strange. The brothers were Father Guy and Father Armand Girard, one Georgette's spiritual director, the other her spiritual adviser. They were dressed in pale-blue clerical shirts with Roman collars, identical grey pants, identical moccasin shoes and identical spectacles. They had open, grinning, child-like faces and wore their hair in straight fringes, monk-style.

Father Guy was deputed to take me in his car to Georgette's. On the way he filled me in on her story. Georgette was the daughter of a modest painter of religious murals. At the age of six she had begun to experience inner-locutions, voices that 'resounded in the depths of her heart'. She believed that Christ

206

and Mary spoke to her. Often she heard the voice of Satan, too, telling her that she was deluded and damned. Eventually her most constant voice was to be that of the Eternal Father, the first person of the Holy Trinity.

She had trained to be a pianist as a girl, although her family did not possess a piano. She practised at home on a cardboard keyboard; nevertheless, she took the gold medal in her final year at the Montreal conservatoire. But at the age of twenty she fell ill with inexplicable paralysis and pain. She became a chronic invalid. Her suspected illnesses were legion – everything from cancer to rare forms of bone disease; the doctors never reached a definitive diagnosis. For the next half-century she was to be virtually bedridden, spending her life in constant pain and prayer. She lived an intensely private, reclusive existence, although stories of her peculiar life and powers reached the outside world from time to time. Nowadays she never leaves her apartment in downtown Montreal.

She says that she suffers the pains of Christ's wounds, and that she bears the vestigial signs of stigmata. She sleeps no more than an hour or two each night as this is the time, she says, when she travels spiritually throughout the world tending the needy through prayer and her suffering.

She started at an early stage to commit her inner-locutions to paper; her writings fill many volumes in manuscript.

In her late twenties she met a Jesuit, Father Joseph Gamache, who believed that she was a genuine mystic; he became her spiritual director, seeing her daily until his death twenty years later. He encouraged her to take vows of poverty, chastity and obedience.

Another Jesuit, Father Paul Mayer, then came on the scene and advised her for the next seventeen years, until his retirement. And now the Girard twins had been looking after her spiritual life for the preceding six years.

Wounds and Healing

This is how Guy Girard came to hear of her. 'One day a friend told me that a sixty-two-year-old holy woman had become pregnant,' said Father Guy. 'Naturally I didn't believe it; but I was fascinated and wanted to meet her. It turned out to be Georgette. She had a young, non-Catholic friend who was pregnant and wanted an abortion for fear of the pains of childbirth. Georgette offered to take upon herself all the discomforts of the pregnancy if the woman would have the baby. From that time Georgette developed the symptoms of pregnancy. On the day of the birth Georgette suffered the pain of the delivery, while the young woman did not have the slightest discomfort in giving birth.'

Though Father Guy related his story in a calm, matter-of-fact manner, the story of the phantom pregnancy did not encourage me to believe that all was well with Georgette.

We eventually drew up in front of a modest clapboard apartment block with staircases on the outside of the building. He let himself in through a door on the first floor and we mounted a staircase painted emerald-green and pink. At the top we were admitted by an elderly housekeeper called Régine. Behind her, standing still and silent, was a small figure in pale-blue pyjamas and a dressing-gown. It was Georgette.

The moment I set eyes on her I knew that there was something unusual about her. Although she was elderly and pallid with evident pain and illness she had the pure and youthful eyes of a very young child. She looked straight at me with a curious gaze of affection and innocence. I found her captivating from that very first moment; yet it did not stop me wondering if she were a lunatic or a fraud.

She led the way through a door across the lobby. One half of the room was a simple sitting area decorated with a few items of cheap furniture. There were two love-birds fidgeting in a cage. In the second half of the room was a double bed covered in imitation satin. The bedroom area had been constructed as a shrine, with the bed as the centrepiece; there were some plastic Doric pillars, festoons of dried flowers, votive lamps and holy pictures. The scene made me feel uneasy.

Georgette sat down and talked for a while in French with Father Guy. She said that she was not happy about having an interview as she did not want publicity. But Father Guy persuaded her that it was all for the good. At last she turned her attention to me and smiled apologetically. I felt embarrassed.

She asked me how I would like to begin.

I had been looking at her limbs to see if she was showing any signs of the stigmata. Her fore-wrists were monstrously swollen, with rounded protuberances the size of tennis balls, but there was no sign of bloody wounds. She was wearing woollen socks and bedroom slippers on her feet.

'Jesus has talked with you?' I asked.

'Yes.'

'How does he address you?'

'He calls me beloved. He calls me his little bride, his little victim of love.'

I felt as if I were talking to a sick child.

'Was anybody cruel to you when you were young?' I asked.

She thought for a moment. 'There was a nun,' she said. 'I was looking up adoringly at the host during Mass when I was six years of age. She slapped me around the face and told me that I would be seized by the Devil to show such lack of respect in the presence of God.' She continued to smile in a self-deprecating manner.

'Father Guy was telling me that you had a spiritual director from a young age . . .'

'Father Gamache.'

'Can you tell me something about him?'

'He was sometimes strict.'

'For example?'

'When I first met him I was very young and a pianist. I told him that I had a licence in music. He said to me, "So what? Even dogs have licences!"' Georgette's eyes lit up and she laughed gently.

'When did you begin your prayer life?'

'From the age of four. Throughout my childhood I prayed at least one hour each day. I thought it quite normal to hear the voice of Jesus. I thought this happened to everybody.'

'When did Jesus begin to tell you that you were his bride?'

'On 22 February 1953. He told me that he was everything and I was nothing. He asked me to wear a ring and have it blessed by my spiritual director.'

'Was your life filled with happiness after this?'

'No. I got tired and disgusted with the demands his love put on me. I threw away the ring. I went through a period of dryness. There were struggles and attacks from Satan, who wanted me dead. The sacraments were disgusting to me and I couldn't even stand the presence of my spiritual director. I did not believe him any more, or the purification he was demanding of me. One day Father Gamache told me that his direction of me was costing him much in prayer, self-denial and fasting. He said that he was trying to liberate my soul.'

'How did you come out of this?'

'He persuaded me to write the story of my spiritual life.'

'Anything else?'

'I committed myself to greater denial. I severed myself from my family, my friends, my inclinations and possessions.'

'And the stigmata? When did that begin?'

'That began earlier, in 1950.'

'You have the wounds?'

'Yes. In my wrists and on my feet. Also in my heart. And I

received the crown of thorns on 25 April 1953. I was not worthy, but it was God's will. I also have a sixth wound, which is the pain that Christ bore from carrying his cross. This wound was revealed to St Bernard of Clairvaux. Christ told him that while carrying his cross he had a wound three fingers deep and the bone was laid bare on his shoulder.'

'Do these wounds give you a great deal of pain?'

'It's always worse on Fridays and during Mass,' she said, 'especially at the consecration. But the inner sufferings of Jesus were much greater than his physical sufferings. He died of too much love.'

'Are your wounds visible?' I asked.

'For many years there was no sign,' she said, 'even though the pains were real and intense. But in more recent years there have been clear signs, although they do not bleed. And in 1982, on the Feast of the Precious Blood, God manifested himself with a terrible pain and by leaving a sign in my flesh in the shape of the figure two.'

This item of information surprised me; it was certainly an unfamiliar emblem in the long history of physical phenomena of mysticism.

'Does this number have a special significance?' I asked.

'The sign indicates that God and I are two in one same flesh.'

'Have you had these marks checked by a doctor?'

'Oh, yes,' she said. 'The doctor examined it with a magnifying glass and said that it was unbelievable.' She smiled and seemed to look pleased with herself. 'It looks like luminous neon, and the blood can be seen circulating. He also said that the number was made up of seven dots, which Jesus has told me indicate the seven gifts of the Holy Spirit. Jesus also said that the name of this sign should be known as the Alliance, indicating the intimacy of God with the soul and a greater identification with the suffering of the crucified Christ.'

211

'As you get older, Georgette, do your pains decrease?'

'No, they're worse. Much worse. I frequently have a pain like a burning arrow in my heart.' Her face clouded as if with memory of the pain. 'The pain is even more intense when the arrow is withdrawn. But at that moment I experience great joy in my soul. I offer up this suffering to God for the whole Church.'

'Do you take pain-killers?'

'No,' she said promptly.

'As we were coming along,' I said, 'Father Guy told me that you had heard the voice of Satan. What sort of thing did he say to you?'

She sighed. Again she looked like a little child. A seventy-four-year-old child.

'Satan told me,' she said, 'even when I was a child that I was going to hell because I had made bad confessions and committed sacrileges. Now he comes to me and tells me that my whole life has been wasted in spiritual pride and that I am his, and damned. He plays tricks on me.'

'How is that?'

'He distorts the way I say my prayers. He makes me say, "Thank you Jesus for allowing Satan to wander throughout the world for the good of souls," or, "I hail myself Mary, Satan is with me."'

'Anything else?'

'Sometimes he attacks me physically. He has tried to strangle me. Father Guy will confirm that the bruises of his fingers have been left on my neck.'

Father Guy now suddenly intervened to say that he was going to prepare to say Mass and that Georgette would attend the service in bed, because her pains would become so severe.

I remained sitting in an armchair while the priest vested and prepared the Mass receptacles on a table at the foot of the bed. Georgette in the meantime went through into the bed-room area, took off her dressing-gown and got beneath the sheets.

Before he began the Mass the priest said: 'Mr John, you will notice that at the consecration the birds will begin to sing.'

It was a short service, and I remained sitting.

Just as Father Guy had said, at the words of the consecration the birds began to sing in extraordinary cadences. At the same time I could hear Georgette gasping and moaning as if wracked with pain. But I did not dare look at her.

When the Mass was ended she came out slowly into the sitting area again, holding on to the furniture as she moved. She was deathly pale and seemed exhausted. She was breathing with difficulty and making little sighing noises. She sat down and whispered to Father Guy, then turned to smile at me.

The priest said: 'Georgette says that she had an inner-locution about you from the Eternal Father during the Mass.'

Georgette smiled. 'The Eternal Father hovered over you,' she said. 'I saw him as I sometimes do in the form of protective hands. He gave me a message for you. I feel so happy, because I have had no messages for three months. The Eternal Father said this – "Mary and I were overjoyed to see our son bowing before the real presence of Jesus. And I have put my hand on him to bless him in a special manner, giving to him all graces that he needs in his work and upon those whom he has in his heart and in his prayer. All those things he asks for will be given to him in accordance with his faith and trust. He will live happy days."'

It was nicely put, I thought, and it would have been lovely to believe. It made me feel cosy, despite my natural scepticism, but a little voice inside my head was saying, 'Quel bullshit!'

In the mood of new contentment that now seemed to fill the

room I took advantage of the situation to ask if I could examine Georgette's wounds.

She smiled, saying that there was not much to see that day. She would show me, however, her feet. With this she beckoned me over to the sofa where she was sitting and began to take off her slippers and socks.

She allowed me to hold both of her feet one by one and to examine them closely. Her feet and ankles were very badly swollen and in the centre of each foot was a distinct deep-purplish mark, red and angry at the edges. The skin of the whole foot looked extremely tender and inflamed, but it was neither broken nor showed any signs of blood. It was as if the wounds had been painted on. But scrutinizing the marks very closely, the images seemed to be composed of broken or dis-tended capillaries as a result of some trauma below the skin's surface. Both feet looked extremely painful.

Next I looked at her wrists. There were no similar vivid signs, but instead monstrous swellings that had the appearance of an unusual kind of arthritis. The skin was drawn taut almost to breaking point and although I touched the pressure area very gently she shut her eyes and gasped as if in agonizing pain.

'And what of the sign that you call the Alliance?' I asked.

After a short whispered conversation between the priest and Georgette it was agreed that I would be shown this final sign.

'Georgette will show you that mark only in her little chapel,' said Father Guy.

The chapel was a tiny adjacent room with just enough space for the three of us to stand side by side. There was an altar and a statue of the Sacred Heart and the Virgin. Georgette and Father Guy faced the altar and began to sing a hymn. When they had finished Father Guy asked me to go down on my knees and face Georgette.

Then she raised her dressing-gown and pulled down her pyjama trousers a little so that I could see her bare hip. The sign of the number two was distinctly visible, apparently composed of seven bright-scarlet spots. It was strangely impressive, and yet I could hardly restrain myself from laughing. What on earth was I doing here in Montreal, in the middle of a working day, kneeling before an old lady who was pulling down her pyjama bottoms to show me her spots?

After the exhibition of Georgette's Alliance it was time to go. At the door she asked if she could kiss me. She touched the back of the nape of my neck with her hand and kissed me gently on the cheek. As I was about to go out of the door I paused and came back.

'Georgette,' I said, 'why do you have all this physical suffering? What is it for?'

She smiled. It was as if I had at last asked the one question that really mattered. 'My wounds,' she said, 'are a great grace. It is by Christ's wounds that we are healed. I share my wounds of the heart with the souls God entrusts to me, especially those of priests. There is a prayer of St John of the Cross: "Lord wound me with a wound of love, which may be healed only by being wounded again."'

Georgette's life seemed morbid, unhealthy and self-absorbed. But how much of this was her fault? I was wondering about her first spiritual director, Father Gamache. Was it possible that he had been a manipulative fanatic, dominating and shaping the young Georgette? What hidden layers of self-interest and vicarious satisfaction may not have lurked beneath the story of that first spiritual relationship?

Then, looked at in a clinical light, the characteristics of Georgette's symptoms were distinctive, and obvious even to a lay person. Episodes of depressive guilt; periods of elation; the hearing of voices, often conflicting; the experience of multifarious and excessive pain with no very clear diagnosis; susceptibility to suggestion; phantom pregnancy; dramatic dermatological signs; years of self-absorbed chronic ailments requiring invalid status. Was she not a classic hysteric?

But what did that mean?

Hysteria, as far as I knew, was an extraordinarily vague and outmoded diagnosis. Deriving from the Greek word for womb, the condition focused on the idea of unbridled, neurotic female emotion, revealing itself in 'imaginary' illnesses. Then there was Freud's more specific conversion hysteria, the notion that repressed sexual conflicts were manifested in physical symptoms precisely symbolizing stifled wishes and desires. Having met Georgette I was eager to study the link between hysteria and stigmatism more closely.

Yet even at this first acquaintance with the phenomenon of stigmata I was reluctant to accept that Georgette could be dismissed entirely by psychological or neurological explanations. She was clearly a talented and sensitive woman, imaginative and affectionate. Her personality did not strike me as altogether neurotic, even though she was highly strung and had suffered traumas in her childhood and youth.

Above all it seemed to me that the dedication of her life to prayer and contemplation was genuine. What if one accepted for a moment the idea of the efficacy of prayer and sacrifice? Was she not pursuing an unusual interior vocation of great courage and nobility?

I was far from satisfied that I had completely grasped the character of Georgette Faniel, and my perplexity had much to do with the mystery of suffering, so central to the Christian idea of the Passion and Crucifixion. A positive vocation to suffering and solitude seemed an alien and a neurotic thing from the perspective of a busy and healthy twentieth-century life.

33 *The Shroud Mystery*

In Montreal I decided to fly on to Italy to take a closer look at the life of the most famous stigmatic of the century, Padre Pio. But before heading for San Giovanni Rotondo in the Gargano Peninsula, I planned to linger in Rome for a while. Among other things I wanted at this point to explore the significance of one of the most mysterious and yet contentious paranormal manifestations of Christ's wounds in history, the Shroud of Turin, believed by many to be Christ's winding-sheet.

Ever since my visit to Briege I had occasionally taken out the picture of the Turin Shroud face and pondered its haunting expression, finding it difficult not to believe that this was the face of an actual person. As a student I had spent several summers working as a hospital porter on geriatric wards; I had consequently seen a great many faces in death. Whatever else it might be, the face on the shroud seemed to me unquestionably a highly accurate representation of a real *dead* person.

The shroud is a fourteen-foot piece of linen showing a full-sized back and front image of a crucified man. Pathologists examining the full-length image have identified a large number of 'particularities' consistent with the marks of scourging wounds, the crown of thorns, the signs of crucifixion.

There had been a variety of tests performed since the Second World War, most of them pointing to the conclusion that the shroud might well date from the beginning of the Christian era. Some thirty scientists had concluded, as a result of tests conducted on sticky-tape-lift samples, that the image had been formed by blood and other bodily secretions. STURP, a Shroud of Turin symposium of researchers, had declared in 1982: 'We can conclude for now that the shroud image is that of a real human form of a scourged, crucified man. It is not the product of an artist. The blood stains are composed of haemoglobin, and also give a positive test for serum albumin.'

Pollen tests, moreover, seemed to demonstrate that the material had originated in Palestine, and laser technology indicated sophisticated techniques of image-forming quite beyond the scope of pre-1980s science.

It seemed that the shroud had revealed more and more of itself at each stage of the century's technological advances. The negative image, of course, had remained hidden until 1898, when the first photograph of the shroud was taken. Was it possible that the shroud was a fifth Gospel? The Sign of Jonas for an unbelieving age? Was it a unique example of God's revelation discovered through science and technology?

Despite the excitement generated by the indications of authenticity, the evidence had never altogether pointed one way. There were some nagging problems. The earliest surviving record of its existence, for example, was ominous. We first learn of the shroud as a fake relic contrived in order to extort money from the unsuspecting faithful. The evidence centres on a memorandum sent to Pope Clement VII in 1389 by Pierre d'Acis, Bishop of Troyes. Referring to the shroud, he writes: 'Eventually, after diligent inquiry and examination, he [Bishop Henri of Poitiers] discovered the fraud and how the said cloth had been cunningly painted, the truth being attested by the artist who had painted it, to wit, that it was a work of human skill and not miraculously wrought and bestowed.'

Nor had the scientific evidence remained entirely undisputed. Between 1978 and 1979 an American microscopist, W. W. McCrone, was involved for a whole year on a set of spectroscopic tests on sticky-tape-lift samples from thirty-two spots of representative image and non-image areas of the shroud. He examined some 40,000 linen fibres and other loose particles and concluded that the marks were made by paint pigment – red ochre, an iron oxide of variable degrees of hydration. McCrone claimed that thin-paint-layer paintings were known in Europe only from between 1275 and 1425; taking all the other evidence into account, in 1980 he put the shroud's date at 1356 or very slightly earlier. In subsequent debates with the pro-authenticity lobby, he frequently pointed out that the thirty scientists who disagreed with him on the sticky-tape tests were neither analytical chemists nor microscopists.

The dispute, however, had now been conclusively resolved.

Before I arrived in Rome, scientists in Arizona, Zurich and Oxford had completed carbon-dating tests on samples of the shroud and found that the cloth was mid-fourteenth century. The implications of the exercise, conducted in the full glare of media publicity and reputedly under meticulous test conditions, had caught the imagination of the world. The main question about the shroud's provenance had been settled once and for all. The image of the cloth could not be that of Christ.

But did it matter? What had been at stake?

It was nonsense to suggest, as did some commentators, that the faith of many millions of relic-loving Catholics had now been undermined. Nevertheless, it was clear that an unfavourable result was a severe blow to those who were hoping that in this instance science would act as a prop to religious belief.

From my own point of view I was particularly intrigued by

the reactions of the losers in the argument. The exercise was about to reveal much about the psychology of scientific evidence in support of cherished belief, or unbelief, and therefore the extent to which tangible phenomena really do aid faith or the lack of it.

First indications were that the believers had by no means braced themselves for a climb-down. Fierce champions of the shroud's authenticity had already fired their first shots from what looked like a precarious fall-back position. They had claimed in the Catholic press that anything from bucketfuls of water used to douse a fire in 1532, to a hypothetical release of ionizing radiation from Jesus's body when forming the mysterious imprint, could have affected the carbon-dating reading.

Other shroud believers, like Leonard Cheshire, the famous wartime RAF bomber pilot, had commented on the search for the truth, in the expectation of bad news, 'I do not believe you can prove it scientifically or logically, any more than you can give a man faith through rational argument.'

There were still others who were capable of sitting comfortably on the fence. Gerald O'Collins, a Jesuit professor of theology at the Gregorian University in Rome, had described the shroud as a 'both/and, rather than an either/or', meaning that even if the shroud were not first-century in origin it might be regarded as a spectacular icon and revered like any other holy and mysterious artefact: a sort of cake-and-eat-it solution.

The most ingenious suggestion from the believers, however, came from those who argued that the image was indeed an authentic apparition, but one that had appeared during medieval times, and on a medieval piece of cloth. The exponents of this view pointed to the sixteenth-century apparition of Our Lady of Guadaloupe on an Indian peasant's garment outside

Mexico City, which was to become the focus of the shrine of Our Lady of the Americas, currently visited by some 16 million pilgrims a year. They also cited numerous instances of miraculously formed icons in the Eastern Church, and, above all, the reputed appearance of the Virgin on an airborne shroud to save the Greeks of Constantinople from an Arab invasion in 910.

The shroud is kept safely wrapped and secure in a casket in Turin and only rarely taken out for public view; the last occasion was in 1978 when some 3 million pilgrims, among them Pope John Paul II, were allowed to see the object. Those wishing to examine a full display of the shroud in photographic form, along with an array of other evidence relating to its significance and authenticity, must go to the Centro Romano di Sindonologia in Via Pio XII near the Vatican City. The centre is directed by eighty-year-old Monsignor Giulio Ricci, who has spent forty years studying the shroud in minute detail.

I visited the centre shortly after my arrival in Rome and found Monsignor Ricci weary and ailing in the midst of his gruesome exhibits, which included plaster models dripping with blood, reproductions of the crown of thorns, the scourge and the nails, and hundreds of blown-up colour photographs of details of the shroud. The place had the chilly, blood-stained atmosphere of a butcher's shop.

The centrepiece was a life-sized model of Christ crucified, a monstrous spectacle of explicit cruelty quite unlike any depiction of the Crucifixion I had ever seen. It was minutely based on the evidence of the shroud, and one look at it convinced me once and for all that the Turin burial-cloth had not been a work of imagination. But if the 'model', the victim, was not Christ, then who was it?'

I asked Monsignor Ricci how he thought the image had

been created. Was it blood? Was a miracle involved? What did he think of the popular sci-fi theory going the rounds that Christ's body had emitted a radioactive flash at the resurrection, thus causing the image?

'No, it's certainly not a miracle,' insisted the monsignor. 'Everything about the shroud is natural. The marks are composed of the natural secretions from the Shroud Man's body and the myrrh and aloes that were used for embalming. No miracle. No radiation flash.'

I was intrigued by his reference to the 'Shroud Man', as if he were prepared to leave room for an area of doubt. Such historical courtesy seemed admirable in a Roman monsignor.

Forty years was a long time, I said, to devote to studying one relic.

'A very *short* time,' he replied, 'to meditate on the conclusions.'

The monsignor drew my attention to a blow-up photograph in which the supposed marks of scourging could be traced.

'We are not simply engaged on cold research,' he said in a mournful voice. 'One is overcome by deep emotion when one attempts an accurate analysis of the numerous whip-strokes.'

'And how accurate is that analysis?'

'The shroud tells us the precise nature of the flagellum,' went on the monsignor; 'the number of soldiers inflicting the strokes; the number of strokes; the direction of the strokes. Teams of pathologists have confirmed the very precise geometrical implications of the marks on the shroud. Is it possible to believe that a forger would have known all this?'

Unless, I thought, the forger had used a human guinea pig.

'After considering all the scientific evidence we are virtually certain that the scourge was composed of three thongs; and at the end of those three thongs were five further strands, each weighted with two pieces of lead or heavy bone.

'The Shroud Man received his whipping while bent over a post – 120 strokes at the very least, from two distinct directions. We can trace every mark in the throbbing flesh.' The priest gazed at me with tears welling into his eyes. He seemed to be carrying a huge burden of sadness.

'How can we imagine such a punishment?' he went on. 'His scourged body – from the soles of his feet to the top of his head – must have looked like the body of a leper.' He fell silent for a few moments.

'When they untied him,' he continued, 'he must have fallen exhausted into a pool of blood. He would have pondered the words of Isaiah: "I have trodden the winepress alone; of my people, not one was with me."'

The monsignor seemed to groan inwardly and hung his head a little to one side. At last he said, 'Look, I am very tired.'

I bade him farewell quietly, and left him pale and exhausted among his terrible mementoes.

As I walked back to my lodging I kept thinking about the arresting face of the Shroud Man. Devout Christians had spoken of its majesty and peace; I had read a remark by a theologian to the effect: 'What kind of man can it be who, after such torturing, can show serenity in death?'

What kind of man indeed. For if the image on the shroud is *not* Christ's, then whose is it? And how was it produced? And can the faithful continue to venerate the image with an easy conscience?

It is here that those impressive particularities of the wounds present a chilling prospect in the light of the carbon-dating tests. The remarkably accurate pathological details of the scourging wounds, the crown of thorns, the signs of crucifixion, including the accurate effects of the severing of the median nerves, have always suggested the presence of an actual human being, a man who had endured these appalling torments and death in order to make the image possible. As for the image's special quality of serenity, it is only in fiction that dead faces are frozen in horror, suffering or beatific smiles. In reality facial muscles, be they of saints or sinners, ultimately relax into a semblance of peace whatever the expression at the moment of death.

An icon is an idealized image produced in circumstances of prayer and devotion as an object of veneration. It would be consoling to think that the shroud was reproduced by an artist of preternatural visionary and mystical powers; but, as we have seen, the first mention of the shroud, in 1389, seems to endorse its status as a bogus relic. The auspices of its provenance, then, do not encourage one to believe that a mystic was on hand in its making. But such is its awful sense of visual authenticity that we are forced at least to speculate that a human victim was involved, and that the man was almost certainly a Jew since, according to experts like Professor Carlton S. Coon, his facial characteristics correspond exactly with the 'Sephardic Jew or noble Arab' type.

While the possibility existed that the image was first-century, it seemed to me that Christians were justified in hoping against hope that they were gazing on an image of the body and face of Christ. But now that the carbon test points to a medieval date, we can longer postpone reflecting on the likelihood that the image is an unspeakable anti-Semitic product of barbarism manufactured in the interests of ecclesiastical commerce.

But even as I write, shroud believers, I understand, have announced that the carbon-dating process was not fairly conducted and that its findings are therefore false.

34   The Power of Relics

I went to visit Santa Croce de Gerusalemme, the church in Rome which houses, it is claimed, the True Cross of Christ.

There I saw within a protective glass case the wooden placard on which is carved in Greek, Aramaic and Latin the inscription, 'This is Jesus the Nazarene, King of the Jews'. As I gazed on the object I found it difficult to summon anything but a mild sense of historical interest, not unmixed with cynicism. There were dark spiky things behind the glass, that purported to be the nails that had pinned Christ to the cross; the finger-bone of Doubting Thomas (that, of course, which he had placed in Christ's side); two needles from the crown of thorns; a fragment of the column on which Christ was bound during the scourging; a piece of the tomb in which he had been buried . . .

As I looked on these things I felt troubled. There were pilgrims passing to and fro among the relic cases, whispering in pious awe, and others kneeling at prayer in an ante-chapel. It was not for me with my phlegmatic English sensibilities to pass judgement, but I wondered whether the archaeology of science was going to stop at the Turin Shroud. How long would it be before the carbon-dating experts put these instruments of the Passion to the test, and then on and on through Rome's leading relics?

To the modern mind these tarnished impedimenta, of

dubious spiritual resonance, let alone provenance, smack of superstition and simony – the sin of making profit out of holy objects. Perhaps there are some strong arguments to enlist science to sweep it all away. And yet how would the Christian Church have fared had the cult of relics never existed? There is a theory, eloquently argued by the scholar of Christian antiquity, Peter Brown, that without them, and the spread of their unique sense of holy presence in the early Church, Christianity might never have become a universal religion. If the spread of relics had not established a major place in Christian piety, Brown argues, the spiritual landscape of the Christian Mediterranean might have been very different. It might have been more like that of the later Islamic world: the holy place might have been permanently restricted to a few privileged areas, such as the Holy Land, and cities where the saints are buried, such as Rome. There might have been a Christian Mecca or a Christian Kaaba, but not the spread of the sense of *presence* of the major saints, such as Peter and Paul, far beyond the ancient frontiers of the Roman world.

But the spread and the practice of relics eventually brought commercial exploitation in its trail; by the Middle Ages it had become a widespread trade, involving lies, fraud, fakery, theft; and the attendant scandals echo to this day.

The reliquaries jealously guarded in Rome's hundreds of churches are an intrinsic part of the attraction of the Eternal City; but they linger in an uneasy limbo of authenticity, from which they could soon be expelled into oblivion by the scientists. The extremes of picturesque fakery satirized by Boccaccio and Chaucer have long gone: the feather from the wings of the Angel Gabriel, the receptacle preserving the breath of the ox in the stable at Bethlehem ... But with three rival heads of John the Baptist, and seventeen arms of St Andrew, and five breasts of Saint Agatha, there are still a great many fakes around, and the scientists could make short work of proving them so.

With these thoughts revolving in my mind, I called in later that afternoon at the medieval convent of Santa Lucia, the only place in the world where Catholics may acquire relics that carry a stamp of authenticity. The religious house and church, which is the official repository of relics in Rome, is situated in Via Selci, a quiet street near the Colosseum. You enter the principal door by a steep flight of steps; to the right is a grille and an electric bell. Above is a piece of card with the legend '*Ho Sete*' ('I thirst'), Christ's cry from the cross.

A diminutive nun with a shiny, dark, rounded face peered through the iron bars. When she had ascertained that I was in the business of acquiring relics she disappeared, then reappeared quickly at a side door to admit me into the convent.

I entered a vast and lofty whitewashed parlour with another huge iron grille set in the wall. She seated me at a plastic table, then popped through another door to reappear on the other side of this second grille.

She announced herself as Sister Cathy and asked me which saint's relic I required.

'Would it be possible,' I asked her, 'to acquire a relic of the True Cross?'

She looked at me askance.

'For you personally? Or for a church? Are you a priest? No, you are not a priest!'

Sister Cathy told me that a splinter of the Holy Cross was a very major relic, available only for churches or religious institutions, it required an application from a bishop. Seeing me crestfallen, she asked whether I would like another sort of relic.

I told her that I had as a boy possessed a relic of Thérèse of Lisieux, which I had lost. Would it be possible to have another.

'Of course,' she said with a smile. 'But I'm sorry to hear that you were so careless as to lose the first.'

We talked for a little.

The monastery of Santa Lucia, she told me, had a special relationship with the 'Vicariate' in Rome, the office that dispenses the licences for relics. There were forty nuns in the community, and the majority of them were, like Sister Cathy, Filipinos.

'We have deposits of 2,000 relics,' she said. 'These are of three different classes. First-class relics are actual pieces of the bone of the saint; second-class are items of clothing; and third-class are pieces of the saints' tombs.'

'Are some relics more popular than others?' I asked

'Oh yes . . . St Rita of Cassia, St Benedict, St Lucy . . . and, of course, St Thérèse.'

'So what happens,' I asked, 'if you run out of a popular relic?'

'We tell the Vicariate, and they find us some more,' she said simply.

'And what about the Virgin Mary, could I have a relic of hers? I believe you have a bit of her veil?' I said, teasing her.

Sister Cathy suddenly burst out laughing.

'Who told you that? That isn't true,' she cried. 'There *are* relics of Our Blessed Lady,' she went on, 'but they are third-class, because Our Lady was assumed into heaven without corruption. It's possible to have a relic of the rock of the assumption, or an item of her tomb, or a piece of the Holy House at Loreto.' She was referring to the extraordinary proposition, widely credited by Italian Catholics, that angels had transported the house of the Virgin from Nazareth via Yugoslavia to the Italian marches, where it arrived in 1294, to become one of the greatest shrines of Europe. Not surprisingly Our Lady of Loreto was to become in the twentieth century the patroness of air pilots.

Sister Cathy, whose order was permanently enclosed and imposed vows of silence, seemed to have enjoyed our little colloquy, but she now urged me to the business in hand. What kind of reliquary would I like to purchase for my relic? With this she produced a display case with some twenty or thirty different glass and metal receptacles, ranging from objects the size of a coffee cup to tiny lockets to be hung around the neck. The prices, which were written on labels next to each sample, ranged from 10,000 up to 70,000 lira. I chose one at 13,000 lira.

'There is an extra charge for postage,' said Sister Cathy. 'Five thousand lira to send your relic to England when it is ready; and then there is a 5,000-lira charge for administration, that goes to the Vicariate.' As I searched for the money in my wallet, Sister Cathy reassured me, 'Of course, there is no charge for the relic itself, which is free.'

We said farewell, and I passed a small donation through the grille to the smiling little nun.

'Allow eight weeks for delivery,' she said.

35   Dinner with Briege

I'd heard it said that people who experience a spiritual awakening often encounter a proliferation of coincidences. Jung and Koestler were so astonished by the incontrovertible proliferation of such synchronicities in some people's lives that they speculated that there might be some sort of quantum-theory explanation. Whatever the case, walking across Piazza Farnese the next day I ran into a coincidence that seemed too extraordinary for comfort. Bustling towards me came Sister Briege McKenna, with a broad smile and a look that said, 'Here we are again!'

She was back in her religious habit and wearing a short veil.

'I was just thinking about you,' she shouted.

'I think you're following me, Sister,' I said. 'How come you nuns manage to gad about the world like this?'

'This is nothing,' she said, giving me a resounding kiss. 'The day after tomorrow I'll be in Papua New Guinea . . . but I've got to dash now, I've got a meeting with some people. Have dinner with me tonight?'

I felt suspiciously privileged. People travelled halfway across the world to spend a few minutes in private with this woman, and I couldn't get away from her.

We agreed to meet that evening in a trattoria near the Gregorian University.

*

Throughout the rest of the day I could not get the coincidence out of my mind: I had heard from so many people that Briege McKenna's life buzzed with non-stop paranormal happenings – all of which she accepted as perfectly normal; added to which, I had been sensing the beginnings of a serious infatuation with her, not so much overtly sexual, perhaps, as an obsessive inclination to think about her.

As I set off to walk from the Via di Monserrato to the restaurant that evening I had a feeling that our assignation was 'meant' in some way.

It was a modest restaurant, and empty. Sister Briege was sitting in a back room and jumped up to embrace me.

She looked tired. Grumbling about keeping her weight down, she ordered some fish and accepted a glass of white wine.

During the meal we talked about our families, about the troubles in Northern Ireland, about her frequent journeys in South America and Africa. As we talked I had to keep reminding myself that this was a woman who spent, so I had been reliably informed, several hours in silent prayer each day.

Did it show?

She was warm, affectionate, humorous, deeply human: these were common qualities of natural goodness. But there was a difference in her sort of goodness that was hard to define; it had something to do with an impression that in everything she said, in every gesture and nuance of her physical presence, there was a quality I can only describe as purity of heart; and she had the capacity to speak, constantly and directly, from her heart.

And while she spoke I kept wondering what it would be like to be married to such a person.

When the dishes were cleared and the waiter had left us to ourselves, I said, 'Do you mind if I ask you some straight questions about yourself? And do you mind if I take a record of it?'

'That's OK,' she said. Then she punched me playfully on the arm. 'But don't expect too much at this time of the evening.'

'I want to try to understand your healing gift. You talked about it briefly in Dublin, and I wanted to ask you more, but I got itchy feet . . .'

She was silent for a while, as if putting her thoughts together. She fiddled with the gold ring she wore on the third finger of her right hand. 'I was born on Pentecost,' she began, 'and Pentecost has always been a special time for me. In 1971, on the eve of Pentecost Sunday, when I was twenty-four years old, I was praying in our oratory in the convent in Tampa. I was just sitting there, saying, "Jesus, here I am."

'After about five minutes I sensed an extraordinary stillness in the chapel – it was like a cloud descending. I heard a voice say, "Briege." I turned round to look towards the door, thinking that somebody had come in. There was no one there, yet I was conscious of a presence. As I looked towards the tabernacle again, I heard the voice saying, "You have my gift of healing. Go and use it."

'I felt a burning sensation going through my body. It was as if my hands had touched a live electrical current. The burning sensation went through and out of me. Then the sense of stillness seemed to lift.

'On Pentecost morning I woke up to a voice roaring in my head: "You have the gift of healing. Go and use it."

'That day I was invited to pray with a sick child. I only learnt years later that the child had been healed after that prayer.

'I told no one about my voices, but in the next week or two several people came to me to say that they were convinced that I had a gift of healing. I ignored them. I rejected it. I think I rejected it because I didn't trust it, and I didn't want people to think I was some kind of religious maniac.

'Then things came to a head in my life. It was the early 1970s; everybody seemed to be looking for a mystical key to everything. I heard that a group of women were going to see a guru who claimed to be a sort of prophet. I got the idea in my head that he could help me.

'This so-called prophet turned out to be dangerous. He fixed me with his eyes and asked all sorts of questions. Then he said, "Have you had a man?" I thought that was a strange question to ask a nun. He said all sorts of things, but nothing that I didn't already know.

'A couple of weeks later a nun I knew came to stay and I told her about my visit to the prophet. "I want to see him too," she said. I thought that maybe it would do her some good. So I went again.

'As soon as he saw me, he said: "Have you been with a man?" I said he wasn't much of a prophet if he didn't know that I hadn't. Then he said to me, "You need your head cut off," and he traced his finger along the back of my neck and around to the front. He kept saying that I shouldn't be a nun, that I was wasting my young life.

'I was arguing with him, and he was gazing into my eyes. After half an hour I felt as if I was in pieces. Nobody was any good or worth anything, and I was wasting my time thinking I could be any good either. I had never questioned the existence of God in my entire life and now I was riven with doubt. I came away weeping and distraught.

'That night in bed I felt as if I were being choked where the man had touched my neck. I couldn't even cry out for help. It was like a dark power over me, tempting me to deny Christ and stop serving him. I tried to pray and I couldn't. Somehow, though, I managed to utter the name Jesus, and the choking stopped.

'For days I was in a state of misery, convinced that I was going to leave the religious life. I went on a trip to a convent in San Francisco, and all the way I kept saying, "God please help me." When I got there I just stayed in my room. I took the Bible and said, "Jesus, I know this is your living work. Please tell me what I am to do, and where I should be."

'I opened my Bible and the words leapt out of the page at me. It was the passage in the first letter of St Paul to the Corinthians, about committing yourself to the single life for the Lord. I was filled with peace and joy. I also knew that God had work for me to do.

'After that the opportunities kept arising in which I prayed over people and they were healed. It even happened over the telephone. People came to me and said that I had appeared by their bedsides when I was 200 miles distant. For the first six months I was very sceptical. People were healed; I saw it again and again with my own eyes, but I still wouldn't believe Jesus would work through me. It didn't seem possible that I could be of any use until I was changed and perfect.

'But I knew very little in those days about real sickness. One day at a prayer meeting a woman stood up and asked me to pray for a friend who was blind and paralysed. I was convinced that this was far too big an order for me, but I went to see her anyway.

'I found that she was very bitter, angry, and had given up on God. I put my hand on her paralysed arm and prayed with her, and as I did so I felt the sensation of needles, just as I had in the chapel when I had been given the gift of healing. But I wasn't confident that I could do anything for her.

'A few days later she asked to see me. She had received her sight, and the power had come back in her arm. But as we talked later I realized that it was the woman's spiritual attitude that had totally changed. The woman's inner healing, spiritual healing, was more important. It also enabled me to see that psychological healing and physical healing often follow in a natural way from spiritual healing.

'If you believe, as I do, that our bodies, our minds, our souls, are one entity, it stands to reason that the healing of the body might follow from spiritual healing.'

For the space of an hour Sister Briege related stories of healings, of prophecies, of amazing coincidences, of miracles major and minor. She talked of voices and visions and divine interventions as if they were normal daily occurrences. And the more she talked the more exasperated I became, not so much with the woman herself, but because she seemed to inhabit a world in which God behaved like a fixer, favouring some more than others, with no very good reason. It wasn't Briege McKenna that annoyed me so much as her God.

'Briege,' I said eventually, 'I need to ask you something. I've no doubt that all these things happened just as you've described them, but what puzzles me is why on earth God should favour one person with healing rather than another. What sort of God is this that goes around allowing one person to suffer in agony, and another to escape? And why does he answer your prayers rather than mine?'

Sister Briege leant forward; her face was kind, gentle, without a trace of sanctimonious zeal.

'During the first few months of the healing ministry,' she said, 'I had those thoughts myself. I asked that question all the time. I got all sorts of books on healing written by recognized experts. On the first day I read a chapter in one of these books, and the next morning I couldn't remember a thing I'd read. I was on retreat at the time in a Franciscan convent in Birmingham, Alabama, where Mother Angelica runs a

Catholic satellite-television network. Finally Mother Angelica took me into the chapel. She pointed up at the altar to the real presence of Jesus, and she said, "Let Jesus teach you."

'That day I made a commitment to spend at least two or three hours a day in personal prayer. And the Lord started to teach me that I didn't have to answer all these questions. Not everybody is going to be healed physically, and that isn't my problem. Nor do I need to defend God, or apologize for the way in which he works; my job is to proclaim him, not defend him.'

I felt myself smiling inwardly at this cop-out, and yet it seemed an ingenuous answer and true to her character. I was glad that she had not given me some complicated theological rationalization, and yet I realized that all debate, argument, probing, would be useless.

She was looking at me, as if wondering how I had taken her answer. Then she said, 'Jesus has a way of healing that is tied in with his teaching. Every healing in Scripture is an opportunity to teach. Through prayer I began to learn about his healing in the same way. And so he enabled me to be more effective in letting him work through me.'

She fell silent for a moment, as if waiting for this to sink in.

'I am not the healer,' she went on. 'Jesus is the healer. And we shouldn't be surprised when he answers prayer by suffering, and even by taking someone we love back to himself.'

She stopped, as if uncomfortable with the didactic way in which she was talking. Then she went on: 'Some years ago the father of a little girl came to see me. She was dying of leukaemia. He had heard that I had been instrumental in the healing of many children with leukaemia. I went to the hospital with him. The child was in terrible suffering and obviously dying. As I knelt down and took her hand I felt as if she were saying to me, "I don't need healing, but my father does. I'm happy to go."

'Outside the ward I spoke with the father and mother; I took their hands and said, "I'd like to be able to tell you that Mary is going to be healed the way you want, but I have no idea how she is to be healed. I just know that Jesus will not disappoint you." As I spoke to them they couldn't accept what I was saying. They were distraught.

'We often act as if we can manipulate God into doing what we want him to do – by saying the right words, or making promises, or having sufficient faith. But God teaches us through prayer that he doesn't do anything to suit us. In prayer and through prayer we change to fit into God's will.

'About three days after my visit to the hospital, the parents phoned to say that Mary had died. I went to see them at once, thinking they would be badly in need of comfort. The father came up to me and embraced me and said, "I realize that healing doesn't mean getting my own way, but getting the strength and the grace to say yes to God's way. Mary wasn't mine; she didn't belong to me. I didn't have the strength to accept that until the moment she died." You see, John, whenever we can say yes to God, we will never be hurt. He is a God of love and you should never put limitations on him. It is only in our resistance and pulling away and saying no to God that we get hurt.'

Briege was talking rapidly and earnestly. I could see that we could never have a discussion about any of these matters; she had only one role – which was as explicator and mentor. It was clear from what she told me that there had been doubts in the early days, but her world picture was based on an extraordinary act of continuing faith. She was consequently impervious to anything I, or anybody else, might say to challenge her.

And yet I felt she was both sane and sound, and she radiated a sense of love and warmth. There was not the slightest hint of mania, or pride, or eccentricity. Nor did she strike me as sentimental or pietistic. Her mission and her beliefs had a sort of bracing purity, like mountain air. The problem was, how on earth could one live in the real everyday world and cope with such beliefs?

'Have you kept records, Sister, of the various miracles you have performed? Have they been properly recorded and vetted by medical experts? Can I see some tangible evidence?' I was conscious that in attributing the miracles to her and not to God I had invited her to make a pietistic disclaimer.

She ignored the invitation, and said, 'I'm not really interested in doing that. You'll get that sort of thing at Lourdes. In any case, people who have faith don't need that sort of proof; and those who are without faith won't be impressed by any kind of evidence . . . even priests.'

I wanted to ask a final question, one that contained a bit of a mean performance test. It was the question of the Fourth Tempter in T. S. Eliot's *Murder in the Cathedral*. Even as I framed it I felt ashamed. Nevertheless, 'Are you never worried, Sister,' I began, 'by the idea of spiritual pride? There are a lot of people who think you are a saint. Are you a saint? And do you behave in the way you do so that you will achieve sainthood?'

'Listen, John,' she said, 'the most important thing to be in life, the most beautiful thing, is to be human. Never mind being a saint, whatever that means. And if you're asking whether I have normal human weaknesses – of course I have plenty of them. And self-indulgences. I like going to the beach, and going out to dinner with friends, which a lot of nuns would think outrageous.'

With this she looked at her watch, and sighed, 'Talking of which,' she said, 'I must be off.' And she stood up at once to go.

On the way back to her convent lodging she put her arm in mine. 'You know,' she said, 'belief in miracles is an unpredictable business. A priest once came to my retreat with a gangrenous leg; there was talk of having it amputated. He said to me, "Briege, just cure this foot and my faith will know no bounds." I prayed over him that night and asked God for healing. The next morning he appeared at breakfast all red in the face. His trouser was rolled up as he walked into the refectory. The leg was completely healed. He just sat there staring at it, but he looked unhappy. "I don't know, Briege," he said, "it might have cured itself."'

As we embraced at the door of her convent, she said, 'I might send you a miracle tomorrow. I wonder what you'll make of it.'

36   The Healthy Oesophagus

I was staying in Rome at the Venerable English College near the Piazza Farnese. In the middle of the morning on the day following my dinner with Briege I was reading in the college library when a message was sent up from the porter's lodge that I had a visitor.

The visitor turned out to be a Sister Margaret Scully from Sydney, Australia, a very tall nun dressed all in blue, clutching a document file.

'I'm your miracle,' she said with a loud laugh. 'Got any coffee in this place?'

She was a rangy, raw-boned woman with high colouring and swift movements. In her plain spectacles and uniform she looked rather severe, but she had an open, expressive face, and a ready wit.

We repaired to the college staff kitchen and she explained that she was a friend of Briege's and studying on a course in Rome for the year.

'Briege McKenna healed me of a very nasty, chronic disease in 1986,' she explained. 'So I've brought along my papers to show you, although Briege says it won't make any difference to a hard-headed chap like you!'

With this she began her story. She said that she was fifty-six and that she had been a Sister of Charity since the age of eighteen. From early childhood she had suffered a digestive problem, which became progressively worse as she got older. In 1979 she began to experience severe abdominal pain and vomiting. She was admitted to hospital and a test revealed that she had an 'utterly abnormal oesophagus'. But too little was known about the condition to provide any help other than a diet of soft food and liquids.

At this point in her tale Sister Scully delved into her file and brought out a sheaf of letters with impressive notepaper headings from consultant physicians in Australia. They referred to matters such as 'oesophageal motility', 'diffuse spasms', 'peristalses' – all of which I took on trust. The main point of the correspondence was that Sister Scully appeared by all expert medical opinion to have had a clinically abnormal oesophagus back in 1979, and the view was that she had had it all her life:

> She really is a very difficult problem. She has a very long history of post-prandial vomiting, intermittently, losing a lot of weight ... Her attacks have occurred since childhood and she is no different now at forty-three than she had been for the last twenty-five years, I think ... I don't think there is any doubt that Sister Scully has a congenital motility disorder involving essentially the oesophagus.

Thus wrote a Dr N. A. Talley, her consultant physician, on 21 March 1979.

'Now,' she said, 'this is where Briege McKenna comes in. In 1986 Briege was doing a tour of Australia and I attended one of her retreats. I was sitting in the kitchen of the convent and Briege came through and saw me consuming my usual diet, which was a soupy mess from the blender. She said to me: "Sister, why are you eating that muck?" When I told her about my trouble, she said, "We'll have to do something about you." At the next healing session in the convent chapel Briege laid her hands on me and prayed for healing. After I returned home I was preparing some food in the usual way with the blender when I had the most incredible desire, for the first time in my life, to have a lamb chop. I cooked a couple of chops and boiled potatoes and I ate them and enjoyed it! And I've been eating normal meals ever since. A few weeks later I went to the same specialist and he confirmed the complete cure.'

The nun now handed over a second sheaf of letters, dated the spring of 1986. According to state-of-the-art tests it seemed that she was now completely normal. The same Dr Talley could say that according to his examination she had now 'normal oesophageal motility'. Writing to her general physician, he also commented, in relation to the possibility that she had responded to 'faith healing', that he was 'quite prepared to have some faith in this sort of cure in certain circumstances'.

Having made her point Sister Scully jumped up from her seat and said, 'I'm going to get out of your hair now, Mr Cornwell. But never let it be said that Sister Briege's successes could not produce proper documentation. You can keep all that stuff, they're copies.'

As I showed Sister Scully to the door, she said, 'My doctor said an interesting thing to me after my healing. He said he believed that when something like that happened to someone it was not just for that person's sake, but so that it could be shared with others.'

As I returned up the stairs I found myself wondering about the implications of her last remark.

Sitting in the library I went through her batch of letters more carefully. In the midst of them I found at least one sceptical testimony. It was from a second opinion, based at St

George's Hospital in the University of New South Wales, although Sister Scully appeared to have excised (unwittingly, I am sure) part of the letter and the consultant's name and status. It was dated 10 March 1986 and addressed to Dr Talley:

> Thank you for asking me to see Sister Scully again. She gives a fascinating story . . . In reviewing the tracing from 1979 we were unable to demonstrate a sphincter but at that time I was not using a sleeve catheter. In addition we saw several synchronous contractions consistent with an abnormal oesophageal motility pattern. In retrospect the tracing is not characteristic of scleroderma, diffuse oesophageal spasm or any other specific motor disorder. The current tracing does not have any of the abnormalities noted on an earlier tracing but the changes are not dramatic. I told Sister Scully that there had been some improvement and she was very excited about this. To a sceptic such as I am dramatic changes would have been very exciting and would have deserved reporting, but this is not the case!

At this point the remainder of the letter had been excised.

Should I have been impressed by the fact that Sister Scully had included this opinion, and the doubts expressed? Did it matter that her 'miracle' was not so dramatic after all?

Reflecting on the nun's visit, I had to admit that her claims, and the manner in which she had presented them, made me uncomfortable. But why? Hadn't I set out to find the sort of evidence she was giving me? I was glad for Sister Scully's sake that she felt better, and I had no doubt that Briege McKenna's intervention (mediation) had something to do with the improvement in her health. But Sister Scully's approach to her miracle

243

exemplified an antagonistic divide that seemed characteristic of most claims for miraculous healing.

There is obviously a widespread hunger among religious believers for evidence that their faith is justified, and in this context the phenomena of sudden, inexplicable cures associated with divine healing can be dramatic and demonstrable. After all, this is an opportunity to enlist science in favour of the divine. If the doctors say it's true, it *must* be true! On the other hand, such evidence can be extremely annoying for those who have set their minds against the possibility of divine intervention of this sort and who associate such proofs with crude attempts to force the sceptical into submission.

For my own part I was not inclined to take up a position on either side of this divide. If there was such a thing as a miracle of healing, it seemed to me that something more gentle and subtle was at work than counters to be used in religious polemic. But was it possible to believe in such miracles? And if one did, what on earth did they mean?

37   Miracles at Lourdes

At the outset of my inquiry I had opened a file on miracles of healing with a view to collecting some current case histories supported by evidence and opinions from specialists. After my conversation with Briege McKenna and Sister Scully's visit it seemed a good time to review some of the significant items in my file, including the most recent material on cures at Lourdes.

There is a common scepticism towards miraculous healings which focuses on the evident fact that, outside Scripture and medieval hagiography, it is difficult to find a real miracle: for example, the appearance of a new eye or a new leg. For the most part, miracles of healing tend to involve illnesses that may well have had a psychosomatic cause and are therefore amenable to psychological suggestion. At very best, they appear to involve inexplicable remissions of diseases as opposed to the growth of new organs or new limbs. Healing therefore involves a dramatic process of nature, a return to wholeness, rather than a display of magic – now you see it, now you don't.

The problem for the sceptic is therefore a simple one: do not dramatic remissions occur as often in non-religious contexts as they do in the milieu of divine healing?

In my file I had reports of two recent cases of startling remissions of terminal cancers, taken from *The Times* of London:

Mrs Kathleen Matthews, aged 45, was told she had cancer of the pancreas and would survive another 12 months after an operation last December at Queen Alexandra Hospital in Portsmouth . . . [reported the newspaper on 24 August 1988]
Mrs Matthews made a will and settled all her affairs before leaving on holiday for Australia . . . While in Perth she visited a hospital and showed doctors a letter she carried from Portsmouth explaining what was wrong with her. When doctors in Perth put her through a scanner they told her they could see no sign of cancer.

Mrs Matthews returned to England in perfect health. The responsible consultant in Portsmouth declined to comment.

The second story, published on 6 April in the same year, involved a cinema projectionist who twelve months previously had been given a 1 per cent chance of living longer than six months.

Three separate medical tests all concluded that Mr Albert Oxley, a widower aged 52, from Stockton, Cleveland, had cancer of the stomach which was spreading to his liver. Doctors told him that the condition was both inoperable and terminal . . .
Seven months after the original diagnosis, he returned to North Tees General Hospital for a further blood test, which showed that his liver was functioning perfectly . . . Last month further tests revealed that there were no longer any traces of cancer. A stomach tumour had also disappeared . . .

Dr Tanner, Mr Oxley's consultant gastroenterologist, had commented that 'although it's possible for some malignant tumours to disappear it is virtually unheard of when they are located in the stomach'.

There was no question of divine healing in either case, nor were the cures referred to as miraculous even in a metaphorical sense. So what is the difference between the merely inexplicable and the miraculous? Would the International Medical Committee (CMIL) at Lourdes have declared such incidents miraculous?

I discovered that few medical bodies are as painstaking and cautious over the term 'inexplicable' as the CMIL. The Council, which convenes once a year, is composed of twenty-five members, mostly from West European countries, the majority of them being French. There is a wide spread of specialities and at least ten of the panel hold chairs in major medical schools.

An exhaustive report on each potential miracle is drawn up for the scrutiny of the members. The original diagnosis must be proven correct with all the appropriate evidence of laboratory investigations, X-rays, endoscopies, biopsies and so forth. The committee must be convinced that the disease was organic rather than psychological, and that the natural history of the disease precluded the possibility of spontaneous remission. Nor will the committee accept cures that might have been effected by medical treatment.

The cure must be 'sudden' and 'complete'. In the case of multiple sclerosis, for example, it would be normal for the committee to wait up to six years before making a final declaration of a cure. Even so, the CMIL does not announce a miracle as such. The members are posed the following question: 'Does the cure of this person constitute a phenomenon which is contrary to the observations and expectations of the medical knowledge and scientifically inexplicable?' The final decision is made on the basis of a simple majority. It is then the

Catholic Church that declares whether or not the cure was of supernatural origin and therefore a miracle.

In a rare medical presentation by an English member of the CMIL, Dr St John Dowling, MB, MRCGP, has described the relevant details of the latest Lourdes cure in the *Journal of the Royal Society of Medicine* of August 1984. The cure involves a girl called Delizia Cirollie, who lives in a village on the slopes of Mt Etna in Sicily. [At the time of going to press, January 1991, the case is still the most recent to be approved as a miracle by the Catholic Church.]

In 1976 when she was 12 years old she presented with a painful swollen right knee [writes Dr Dowling]. An X-ray showed bone change, so she was referred to Professor Mollica at the orthopaedic clinic of the University of Catania. After further X-rays he did a biopsy, which Professor Cordaro reported as showing a bony metastasis of neuroblastoma. The surgeon advised amputation; the family refused. He then advised cobalt irradiation and she was transferred to the radiotherapy unit, where she was so unhappy that her parents took her home the next day, before she had had any treatment.

Her teacher suggested that Delizia be taken to Lourdes, and a collection made locally enabled her to go with her mother in August 1976. There she spent four days attending the ceremonies, praying at the Grotto and bathing in the water. There was no improvement and X-rays in September showed extension of the growth.

The child went downhill and her mother began to prepare for her funeral. None the less, the villagers continued to pray to Our Lady of Lourdes for her cure and her mother regularly gave her Lourdes water.

Shortly before Christmas she suddenly said that she

wanted to get up and go out, which she did without pain, but she was not able to get very far owing to weakness; at this time she weighed only 22 kg. Her knee swelling disappeared, leaving her with a degree of genu valgum, and her general condition returned to normal. X-rays showed repair of the bone. The following July she returned to Lourdes to present herself to the Medical Bureau and did so again in 1978/79/80. X-rays of the thorax and abdomen showed no sign of the calcification often seen in neuroblastoma.

There was no doubt that she had been cured, but the exact diagnosis proved more difficult. The histological opinion of Professor Cordaro of Catania was a metastasis from a neuroblastoma. He sent the biopsy slides to the Lourdes Medical Bureau and they were submitted to French histologists eminent in the field of bone tumours. Professor Payan of Marseilles gave his opinion that it was a Ewing's tumour. Professor Nezelof of Paris agreed that the diagnosis of a metastasis from a neuroblastoma could not be absolutely excluded, but concluded that Ewing's tumour was the most likely diagnosis. Dr Mazabraud and his colleagues at the Curie Institute reached the same conclusion. Spontaneous remission of neuroblastoma has been reported but very rarely and never after the age of 5 years. Spontaneous remission of Ewing's tumour has not been recorded.

The CMIL studied the case in 1980 and 1981 and at their meeting in 1982 they decided that Ewing's tumour was the correct diagnosis and concluded that the cure was scientifically inexplicable. The fact that the moment of the cure was at home in Sicily and not in Lourdes was irrelevant to the work of the committee.

*

Wounds and Healing

The difference between a report of an inexplicable cure at Lourdes and any other claimed cure, then, is clearly the wealth of painstaking detail and the cooperation between a very large number of doctors, albeit Catholic doctors. The Lourdes assessment leaves little area for doubt as to the original diagnosis; in fact, it probably errs on the side of caution and for this reason official Lourdes cures are few and far between. In the absence of such stringent criteria we shall never know whether the case of Mr Oxley of Stockton and the 'virtually unheard of' disappearance of his stomach cancer constitutes a cure just as inexplicable as that of Delizia's.

All the same, it is worth emphasizing the little-known fact that of the estimated 2 million sick pilgrims who have visited Lourdes since 1858 (nowadays there are an estimated 65,000 seriously ill persons each year out of a total of 4 million annual visitors) only sixty-five cures have been accepted as miraculous by the Catholic Church. That is an extraordinarily small number, roughly one person in 130,000 every other year. There are medical statisticians who acknowledge that on the basis of the figures the statistical link between Lourdes and cures is therefore utterly insignificant.

Naturally these figures have little bearing on the enormous number of people who claim to have benefited spiritually and psychologically as a result of making the Lourdes pilgrimage; nor do they reflect those sick people who have experienced an alleviation of their physical symptoms, but without official recognition. That number is estimated to be in the region of 2,000 since 1858; but it is doubtful whether the figure is any better than the number of cures at any of Europe's famous secular spas.

The paucity of cures at Lourdes, and indeed at other centres (such as the Anglican healing centre at Burswood in Sussex), is unlikely to disappoint mainstream Christians who regard divine healing as a means of teaching or re-emphasizing religious truths. In this sense modern claims of miracle healing can echo the significance of miracles in Scripture.

On leaving Medjugorje I had promised myself that I would read the Gospels; something I had not done for almost twenty-five years. I had been as good as my word, and I had rediscovered the multi-layered, symbolic nature of the miracle narratives as expressions of the story of Redemption, indeed that Christ repudiated the notion of performing miracles merely as a display of power: 'It is an evil and unfaithful generation that asks for a sign! The only sign it will be given is the sign of the prophet Jonah.'

Christ's miracles are in no sense magical: there is no hint that he is engaging in a formula or ritual technique. His healings and exorcisms are invariably performed in a context in which he challenges the Jewish rules of separation, the divide between the clean and the unclean. He heals on the Sabbath and he cures people who were considered beyond the pale of Jewish piety – lepers, tax-collectors, a woman with a menstrual flow. And his healing contains clues and foretastes of Salvation.

In the case of the raising of Lazarus from the dead (John 11), Christ deliberately delays his arrival at Bethany so that he might 'waken him out of his sleep'. Martha rebukes Christ for coming too late, and Christ replies that he is the resurrection and the life, and that those who believe in him, if they die will live forever. The story is clearly more than the mere raising of a corpse. The miracle anticipates the promise of eternal life, and conveys a clear signal that out of those who respond in faith to Christ will come a new covenant people, 'to gather together into one the scattered children of God'. The raising of Lazarus, like other miracles in Luke and John, is symbolic of the promise of a new people of God and of eternal life.

251

Wounds and Healing

I had been intrigued by Briege McKenna's assertion that there was always something to be learned through praying for miracles, whether the results were successful or not, for it carried the implication that the lessons were not always obvious. Before they can be fully understood, miracles of healing, perhaps like apparitions, must be read, almost as one would ponder the meaning of a poem, a narrative or a play. The more one concentrates merely on the power, the proof, manipulation and magic, the more one scrutinizes the purely medical and scientific data, the less one is capable of understanding the spiritual implications.

And if one were to accept that there is such a thing as spiritual healing, in the sense of discovering faith and confidence in a power beyond oneself, is it so very difficult to accept that such a renewal might culminate in psychological and even physical benefits?

Our understanding of the operation of the autonomic and immune systems on the control of pain and spontaneous remissions is still rudimentary, but the gathering evidence looks incontrovertible. It is certainly clear that what people call faith and hope can elicit both subjective and objective changes in the body – involving psychological and physiological effects that are measurable. And why should this be surprising? Whatever a person's philosophy of the relationship between mind, body and soul, our thoughts are incontestably, if not merely, electrochemical events which can bring about other physical events.

Advances in our understanding of the effect of endorphins, opioids and other neurone transmitters on pain and illness may soon threaten the assumptions of the Lourdes criteria for miracles, to the point where the notion of the inexplicable may disappear altogether. To invoke the notion of the inexplicable is to appeal to a temporary state of affairs; is to put the phenomenon of divine healing at the mercy of scientific progress.

Is this to veer, once again, towards reductionism? It is common nowadays for historians of medicine to harp on the gap between medical knowledge and superficial symptoms that so easily led to miraculous conclusions in the past. During the Middle Ages, for example, only the very learned had guessed that the pulse might be a sign of life in a body; people relied mostly on skin colour, body temperature and lack of obvious breathing and, as a result, miracles of revival from the dead – as with Lazarus – were not uncommon. As I scanned contemporary commentaries on miracles, however, I could take little comfort from the idea that most miracles of the past could be dismissed as inaccurate diagnoses.

In a revealing article in the *British Medical Journal* (24–31 December 1983) Dr Rex Gardner, a consultant obstetrician and gynaecologist at Sunderland General Hospital, draws parallels between miracles of healing in Anglo-Celtic Northumbria and some contemporary cures associated with religious auspices in the same district.

One example of the seven cases he cites should suffice. In his homily on Luke, the Venerable Bede tells the story of a woman suffering from hideous ulcers who was healed by prayers and the application of salt and holy oil. As a modern parallel Dr Gardner cites the case of a young woman in Monkwearmouth, Northumbria, who had a 'deterioration in a large varicose ulcer of the leg which had been troubling her for many years ... She asked for prayer at the monthly charismatic prayer meeting. A general practitioner present examined the leg and judged that even were the ulcer to heal, it would require skin grafting.' By the next morning the ulcer had almost healed, and after a second prayer meeting a week later the cure was complete. Dr Gardner comments: 'This story is so bizarre that it would not have been included were I not one of the doctors who examined the patient's leg.'

But the crucial point he wishes to make involves the relationship between expectation of miracles and their fulfilment. Bede's stories of miracles and especially those of St Cuthbert, says Gardner, have up to now been discarded as mere copies of New Testament incidents written for hagiographical purposes. Indeed, he says, there is evidence that during his own lifetime Bede himself believed (probably encouraged by Pope Gregory the Great) that the age of miracles had passed. Gardner's study is a salutary warning both against seeing miracles purely as a metaphorical or hagiographical device, and against assuming that they arose out of our ancestors' ignorance of medical matters.

On reflection, and paradoxically – considering my starting point – what worried me most about miracles, as defined by the Churches (and especially the Catholic Church), was their attempt to institutionalize the quality of inexplicability. The notion smacked too much of magic as opposed to mystery. Isn't it enough that the cure should be unusual, surprising, or mysterious? Surely the crucial factor should be that the cure follows prayer or religious ritual; it is the context, the narrative, of the cure that matters. In other words, as with apparitions or visions or stigmata, I could not see, from a believer's point of view, why there should be any contradiction involved in grace or spirituality building on natural processes. But this does not satisfy the literalists, who condemn such an approach as subjectivist and rationalist.

Pondering the case of Delizia of Catania, I had to admit that there seemed to be more than a purely coincidental link between Lourdes and her cure. But by the same token, I was equally impressed by the alteration in a terminally sick friend of mine whose pilgrimage to Lourdes earlier in the year resulted in the overcoming of bitterness and depression and a sense of renewal and hope, despite the absence of a physical cure.

The more one attaches limits and rigorous criteria to the meaning of miracles, or apparitions, or any of the other physical phenomena of mysticism, the more, it seemed to me, the value-laden, non-materialistic significance of these events seems to recede and elude us.

The best illustration I can offer is a strange miracle-in-reverse that I had first heard on my journey through America after my dream. It occurred to my friend Tobias Wolff, the American writer, and I quote it in full, for it illustrates, as can no amount of discussion or ratiocination, the insights, the ironies, the potential for growth and self-understanding that can arise in a place like Lourdes. It says something too, I think, about the role of imagination, irony and narrative, in the most humble of religious experiences.

I don't see well. It's a condition I've always resented. As a boy I wouldn't even admit to it until I began to suffer from headaches, and could no longer read the blackboards at school. I hated my glasses and wore them only upon necessity, walking around most of the time in a blur, as if underwater. Later I tried contact lenses but my eyes wouldn't tolerate them. Anyway, they made me feel like a fraud. What I really wanted was perfect vision.

I mention this by way of preamble to a story about something that happened to me in the summer of 1972, during a pilgrimage to Lourdes. But first I should explain how I got there.

At my mother's wish I was baptized a Catholic at the age of ten, but faith, conscious faith, played no part in my life until I was in my twenties.

That's not true. It did play a part in my life, an active part, because I was vigilantly suspicious of it, under-standing instinctively that it would subvert the plans I had for myself, mercenary, vainglorious as most of those plans were. And I believed that faith would somehow blind me, keep me from seeing things clearly. Certainly it would change me. I was afraid of it. I went on being afraid of it, go on being afraid of it even now, years after it entered my life irrevocably.

In my twenties, as I said, faith became a possibility for me. Why then? I can think of reasons. But reasons don't, in the end, explain faith any more than they can create it. Something happened, an inward turning, a sense of being both cornered and upheld. But even in this turning I felt a sense of reluctance and doubt.

In the summer of 1972 I went to Lourdes for a week. I lived in a barracks with other men. We weren't there very much – only to eat and sleep. The rest of our time was given over to performing different services for the sick, to whom Lourdes is dedicated. We worked in the dining halls, in the hospitals, in the baths – wherever we were needed. I worked mostly at the baths, volunteering again and again because the experience was strange, and harrowing, and therefore, I thought, good for me.

Good health makes provincials of us; we take the border between ourselves and the unhealthy as ordained, fitting, and eternal, and do not give much thought to what lies on the other side. At the baths I was, at least for a time, shaken out of this provincialism. There were four of us in each bathing pool. Our task was to receive the men and boys who were brought in to us and to separate them from their wheelchairs and braces and walkers, then undress them and carry them into the water, where we prayed over them. I saw the human body under every kind of attack. It was good to recognize that hope and faith and even joy could live on in such ruins. But the experience also appalled me, and I was not displeased to be taken out of the baths one afternoon and driven with some other volunteers to the local airport, where we were to help a group of disabled Italian pilgrims embark for the plane-ride home. It was a hot, muggy day. The heat hung over the tarmac in a haze that made the light harsh, almost blinding. At first things went smoothly. We wheeled a number of people out to the plane, where they were taken up a ramp by crews of nurses and medics. Then there was a mix-up. They told us to wait at the bottom of the ramp. We waited for a time, and then, outrageously, someone shut the airplane door.

I was with a little girl about two years old. She was completely paralyzed, and had tubes in her nostrils that drained into bags under the sheet that covered her. She looked up at me calmly, too calmly somehow; I couldn't tell whether she heard me or not when I murmured to her in what I hoped was an encouraging tone. I moved her gurney into the shade of the fuselage and fanned her face with my hand. Still they kept us waiting. Then the flies discovered her. I couldn't keep them off, no matter how hard I tried. They swarmed on her face, over her lips, around her eyes. I kept brushing at them but they came right back, humming, persistent. I became desperate with anger. My anger went beyond the situation. It was fundamental, unreasonable; it had to do with the scheme of things. By the time they opened the airplane door again I was weeping, though only I knew it – by now all our faces were flushed and glistening with sweat.

The little girl was with the last group of passengers.

After the plane took off I got on a bus back to Lourdes, and it came to me along the way that something peculiar was happening. I had taken my glasses off earlier in the afternoon because they kept slipping down. They were still in my pocket, but I could see as well as if I had them on, could read license plates and make out the features of people we passed, see sheep grazing in distant fields. I couldn't understand it. I squinted and blinked and rubbed my eyes, thinking it must be a lens formed by sweat and tears, but it didn't go away. I felt giddy and restless, happy but uncomfortable, not myself at all. Then I had the distinct thought that when we got back to Lourdes I should go to the grotto and pray. That was all. Go to the grotto and pray.

But I didn't do that. The bus let me off at the barracks and I went inside for a moment to cool off, and fell into conversation with an Irishman I'd gotten to know. He was sharp and honest and very funny. We sat down on his cot and talked, and all the while I was aware of what I wasn't doing and what I wasn't telling him. I had no reason not to mention what had happened – he would have been keenly interested, not at all derisive – but I didn't say a thing about it. We talked and laughed for a couple of hours, then went to dinner, and I never made it to the grotto that day. Next morning I was wearing my glasses again.

Later I told this story to a priest I knew, Father Michael Hollings, and he said, 'O ye of little faith.' He said it with a smile, but he meant it.

What happened? Possibly it was, as I first suspected, a film on my eyes. Possibly it was an illusion – I only *thought* I was seeing clearly. It would seem ungenerous, un-Godly, to make such a gift conditional, and to take it back. Of course there's no way of knowing what really happened, or what would have happened if I'd gone to the grotto that afternoon.

What interests me now is why I didn't go. I felt, to be sure, some incredulity. But this wasn't the reason. I have a weakness for good company, good talk, but that wasn't it either. That was only a convenient distraction. At heart, I must not have wanted this thing to happen. I don't know why, but I have suspicions. I suspect that I considered myself unworthy of such a gift. And if I had secured it, what then? I would have had to give up those doubts by which I defined myself, in the world's terms, as a free man. By giving up doubt, I would have lost that measure of pure self-interest to which I felt myself entitled by doubt. Doubt was my connection to the world, to the faithless self in whom I took refuge when faith got hard. Imagine the responsibility of losing it. What then? No wonder I was afraid of this gift, afraid of seeing so well.

PART FIVE

Saints, Angels and Prodigies

38   *In the Gargano*

Throughout my journey I had been constantly reminded of the reputation of the astonishing stigmatic, Padre Pio, and of his legendary powers – which, by all accounts, he had continued to exert beyond the grave.

The time had come for me to gain an impression of the life and influence of this great recent 'saint' by visiting his shrine and by talking with the man who was urging his canonization. Would I feel that sense of *potentia* which, according to Catholic tradition, is exerted at the tombs of those of outstanding holiness through the special presence of God, from whom all miracles and wonders spring? Or would I, on taking a closer look at the phenomenon of his stigmata, decide that he was a neurotic fraud – a creation of primitive Italian superstition?

I hired a car in Rome and drove across Italy to San Giovanni Rotondo in the Gargano Peninsula, the site of the monastery where Padre Pio lies awaiting the deliberations of his Church on whether or not he is to join the calendar of the saints.

In the early Middle Ages there were three great pilgrimages in Europe, known as the journey to the Man, to the God, and to the Angel – to Rome and Saint Peter; to Jerusalem and the Son of God; and to Gargano and the shrine of St Michael.

The Gargano Massif, the spur on the boot of Italy, is an

austere high tableland of rock and forest jutting out into the Adriatic sea. Isolated, harsh, poverty-stricken, it was for centuries a haunt of mystics and pilgrims. Monte Sant' Angelo, on a beetling peak dominating the peninsula, is the site of the cave where, according to legend, Michael the Archangel – the champion of the Powers of Light against Satan – appeared three times to shepherds in 491. It is a windswept, melancholy place, of vast skies and arid landscapes.

Pope Gelasio I and the local Bishop of Manfredio were quick to confirm and authenticate the visions, and before long a trail of kings and princes, bishops and priests, and armies of the faithful were making the arduous journey to this mountain fastness to encounter a unique token of holy presence. It was popular, too, among saints: St Bernard, St Anselm, St Bridget, St Alphonsus, came to fast and pray; St Francis of Assisi received the stigmata shortly after completing his pilgrimage there.

From the end of the Middle Ages until recent times the place fell into neglect; but it had enjoyed a revival by association with the man known as Padre Pio of Pietrelcina, who lived for most of his religious life in a monastery in the small town of San Giovanni Rotondo just a few miles below the old shrine. For fifty years or more people trekked to Gargano to catch a glimpse of this man, who seemed to rival the greatest saints of old, both in his evident heroism and in his extraordinary paranormal powers. Padre Pio died in 1968, but the faithful have not ceased to journey there.

I arrived late in the afternoon at the Monastery of Our Lady of Grace after driving across a featureless plain from Foggia, the largest city of the region, some forty miles distant to the west.

There is a square with a modern, barn-like church to the side of the monastery; but Padre Pio's vast hospital, set back a little to the right of the church, dominates everything. The hospital is one of the great ironies of the place: for this man who was famed for his gifts of divine healing, and who lived in retirement under a vow of poverty, established before his death one of the biggest, best-endowed, best-equipped hospitals in the south of Italy.

From the outside the church looked like a political convention hall: there were posters of Padre Pio stuck all over the façade. Middle-aged Italian women were barging their way through the main doors like beefy heifers; many of them were dressed in black; they were squat, energetic, formidable.

Inside, the church was light and airy and free of ornament save for a mosaic mural behind the high altar, a crowned Madonna and Child surrounded by pink and pastel-green angels. There were a few pilgrims kneeling in prayer, but the majority of people were coming and going down a flight of steps that led to a crypt. I followed the flow.

The crypt was cold and smelt of damp plaster, like an underground shelter. But the principal and most startling impression was the echoing sound of droning, crooning, humming women, circulating in swarms around a grey slab of marble situated behind a steel grille. This was the tomb of Padre Pio, the goal of their pilgrimage.

There were two prominent signs on placards attached to the grille. One depicted a recommendation of the shrine by Karol Wojtyła in 1974, when he was cardinal in Krakow; two years after his ordination the future John Paul II had visited Padre Pio, and the living saint had prophesied, according to reasonable evidence, that the young priest would one day be Pope. The second notice warned: '*Non gettare monete sulla tomba.*' ('Don't throw money at the tomb.')

There were capacious collection strong-boxes situated around the walls, announcing: '*Offerte per la causa di beatificazione di Padre Pio.*' ('Offerings for the cause of the beatification of Padre Pio.') Canonization costs money.

The vast basement was heavy with an atmosphere of primitive belief in the power, the efficaciousness of the presence of the 'saint' who lay within the tomb. Part of me was repelled by the crude irrationality on display. But part of me felt glad, in a way that I could only dimly understand, that there were places like this in the world, where men and women could find solidarity, reassurance, by standing in the presence of the spirit of a fellow human who had been transformed in life by a heroic imitation of Christ.

I found the office of the Vice-Postulator behind an electronically-operated steel gate surmounted by spikes. No women could penetrate this sanctuary. A rascally looking monk of immense girth took me through a modern office complex to my appointed meeting.

It is the job of the Vice-Postulator (he is the key person in the operation, the Postulator himself being a bureaucrat in Rome) to act as impresario in the long, expensive and difficult task of persuading the Church to accept a 'servant of God' as a candidate for sainthood. In the case of Padre Pio the Vice-Postulator is a Franciscan called Father Gerardo di Flumine. He greeted me at the door of his room, yet another rotund friar with a polished bald pate and the enigmatic, lineless face of a Buddha. He seemed to narrow his eyes with suspicion as he shook my hand. In the business of sainthood, publicity counts for much.

He glanced down at my shoes, which were black. Suddenly he was smiling. 'Are you a priest?' he asked.

'No,' I said. At which the smile came down like a well-oiled trap.

'It's so difficult,' he murmured, 'to tell the difference nowadays between the clergy and the laity . . . But never mind.'

He invited me to sit, while he placed himself at a vast desk. Behind him, and all around the room, were shelves of box-files and weighty-looking theological tomes; in the offices on the way I had gained a fleeting impression of blinking computer terminals, banks of filing cabinets, documents by the ton.

'It would take me several lifetimes to tell you about Padre Pio,' he began. 'I will give you some books, and you can do your own homework. There's no other way.' With this he began to take books out of a drawer in his desk and bang them on the table in front of me.

'But Father,' I asked, 'how are saints made?'

I had a second question too: what are they *for*? But that could wait for the time being.

The priest blew a silent whistle and raised his eyes to the ceiling.

'Many years. Much expense. And much patience,' he said shaking his head. 'There are three stages towards canonization,' he went on, 'Venerable, Beatus and finally Saint. We only started working towards the venerable status of Padre Pio in 1983.

'You see, although he died in 1968, for a number of years you are not allowed to do anything. We gathered together eighty major testimonies to present to the tribunal, which has two branches – the president on the one hand, and the lawyer on the other, known in popular parlance as the Devil's Advocate. The second stage is what we call a historical commission, in which we collate all the letters, journals, memoranda, books – edited and unedited – documents – official and unofficial . . .' The priest droned on and on, describing the proliferation of depositions, the weighing, the sifting, the difficulties, the hurdles, the obstacles, the sheer time-consuming drudgery, stage after stage.

'*Finalmente!*' he said. 'If all is OK, the responsible cardinal goes to the Pope and presents the evidence to await his verdict. And if he says yes, then the candidate becomes Beatus, and the process starts all over again as we present his case for sainthood. It can take another fifty, sixty years ... and even then that would be fast.'

'So what is your biggest headache, Father?'

The priest smiled. 'Every year when I think I have completed the collection of Padre Pio's correspondence, something new turns up.'

I picked up the pile of books that he had given me. 'Tell me something,' I said, 'do you believe in the Holy Shroud of Turin?'

He looked at me quizzically. 'Of course I believe in it.'

'Now. On the shroud, Christ is pierced in the wrists. So, if Padre Pio received the genuine marks of the Crucifixion from God, why are his wounds in the palms of his hands?'

The priest narrowed his eyes. 'How interesting,' he said. 'We had a congress on the stigmata and Padre Pio just last September and this question came up.' Father di Flumine stroked his well-trimmed beard. 'The answer, my friend, is very obvious when you think about it,' he said. 'Listen. If God speaks to you, does he speak in Italian, English or Chinese? Do you get my meaning? If God did not operate for the benefit of the receiver he would have to perform *two* miracles; he would have to enable you to speak a language you did not understand. Now are you with me?'

I nodded, eager to move on from these casuistic quibbles, which were, after all, of my own making.

'In any case,' said Father di Flumine with finality, 'the important thing is that he lived for more than fifty years as a living crucifix. The wounds, the sufferings, were intensely real ...'

As I rose to go with my stock of books, the priest shook my hand. 'Make up your mind after you've acquainted yourself with his life,' he said.

39   *The Life of Padre Pio*

Padre Pio's real name was Francesco Forgione and he was born, one of five children, at Pietrelcina near Naples. His father, a migrant worker, twice made the voyage to the United States to earn money to support his family.

At the age of eight Padre Pio witnessed a miraculous event that was to have a profound effect on the course of his life. In August 1895 he accompanied his father to the shrine of San Pellegrino. A statue of the saint stood on the high altar before a great crush of pilgrims who had come to attend the ceremonies associated with miraculous healings.

In the midst of the ritual, a 'raging, dishevelled' woman started to scream. She pushed her way to the front until she stood before the statue. In her arms she held a child with a huge, hydrocephalic head and shrunken, paralysed limbs. Unable to talk, the child made a horrifying squawk 'like a crow'. The woman cried out ceaselessly for a miracle; in the end she threw herself on the ground before the statue. Next she began to abuse the saint, screaming and cursing the statue. At this point Pio's father decided that it was time to be gone, but Pio refused to budge. He stayed on, earnestly praying for a miracle.

Suddenly the woman let out a final scream and hurled the child at the statue. 'Why don't you cure him?' she yelled. 'Well, keep him! He's all yours!' The child bounced off the statue and fell to the floor of the sanctuary, hitting his head on the marble with a loud thud. The people surged forward to restrain her, but the child stood on its feet, completely healed, and ran towards her, calling out, 'Mother, mother!'

It is clear that Pio associated the healing with his own prayer, rather than the efficacy of the saint, and he saw the defiance of his father's wishes as an important element in the story: he was already about his *real* father's business.

The incident, whatever its retrospective accretions and exaggerations, anticipates the central significance of his life: more than any holy man in Christendom this century he was to provide proof, according to his countless devotees, that God intervenes in direct and observable ways in human affairs.

Pio grew up in a region that outstrips even the rest of Italy in its manifestations of popular folk religion. Towards the end of the nineteenth century there were estimated to be as many as 10,000 churches, chapels and shrines in the region of Naples. The proliferating legends of its saints featured heroic self-denials and extravagant paranormal behaviour, including levitation, flying and bilocation. Its local Virgins, its relics and its ubiquitous incorrupt bodies of saints provided a complete and alternative world of the sacred. Ritualized miracles were a familiar part of people's lives.

As a child Pio was deeply religious; even allowing for the hagiographical excesses that surround his memory, it is clear that he believed he enjoyed visionary experiences of angels and conversations with Mary and Christ. He heard celestial choirs and bells, and was aware of holy odours, and he believed he was harassed by 'assaults of the devil'. It comes as no surprise to learn that his hobby was making statues, his favourite figure being Michael the Archangel.

Pio grew up with the single-minded ambition to be a Franciscan priest, and after a haphazard education entered a seminary at the age of fifteen. He was ordained eight years later. From the very start his superiors found him a problem. He went in for excessive self-denial, fasting, long hours in private prayer. He was frequently ill, running phenomenally high temperatures and prone to migraines, constipation, vomiting. He often slipped into ecstasies, and took nearly two hours over a Mass service that normally takes thirty minutes.

The solitude and inactivity occasioned by his frequent illnesses created further opportunities to pursue his intense interior life. In the early years of his priesthood he spent months on end living alone in a tower at Pietrelcina. We hear of demonic and poltergeist activity. Neighbours talked of crashes, bangs and shouts, like 'drunken brawls'. Pio was to confirm later that he had been locked in dire struggles with demons. 'They hurled themselves upon me,' he wrote, 'threw me on the floor, struck me violently and threw pillows, books and chairs through the air and cursed me with exceedingly filthy words'.

He was called up for army service in the First World War, but simply went absent without leave and never returned to duty. In desperation his spiritual director had him removed to the remote monastery of Our Lady of Grace at San Giovanni Rotondo.

There his mystical life deepened. And its focus was a powerful dedication of himself as victim, to suffer with Christ on behalf of others: 'Deep down in my soul,' he wrote, 'it seems to me God has poured out many graces of compassion for the sufferings of others. When I know that a person is afflicted in soul or body, what would I not do to have the Lord relieve him of his sufferings! Willingly would I take upon myself all his sufferings to see him saved.' At times this vocation for self-sacrifice seemed to go beyond the norms of even the most radical expressions of spirituality: 'Punish me and not others. Even send me to hell, provided that I can still love You and everyone else is saved.'

His visions, his voices, his insights in prayer, seemed to be of two kinds: on the one hand, they fell within a rigorous peasant folk tradition; on the other, they approached the classic high mysticism of Teresa of Avila and John of the Cross.

He has left accounts of jocular, scolding, Browningesque conversations with his 'guardian angel', whom he referred to as 'my boy': 'Angel of God, my angel – aren't you my guardian? God gave you to me. Are you a creature or are you a creator? You're a creator? No! Then you are a creature and you have a law and you have to obey – you must stay close to me whether you want to or not. You're laughing! What is there to laugh about?'

At the same time he was engaged in that long and arduous climb through the 'dark night of the soul' to the pure, airy summits of unitive prayer: 'My ordinary way of praying is this: hardly do I begin to pray than at once I feel my soul begin to recollect itself in a peace and tranquillity that I cannot express in words. The senses remain suspended.' He writes of being 'forever lost in that immense ocean of good ... and enjoying that by which He Himself is blessed'. Again, he describes a vision of Christ in which 'The Lord immersed my soul in such peace and contentment, that all the sweetest delights of this world, even if they were doubled, pale in comparison to even a drop of this blessedness.'

In Padre Pio, the peasant piety of southern Italy seems to meet and blend with the higher reaches of spirituality and prayer, suggesting that the rituals and images of Mediterranean folk religion, commonly regarded as uncouth, superstitious, even pagan, have immense potential for powerful spiritual insights.

Pio's spiritual life was by no means exclusivley sweet and ineffable. It seems that for the most part he was subject to a long chain of afflictions, both physical and psychological.

His spiritual director was convinced that Pio had been specially chosen as a 'co-redemptor and victim' by God, and an indication of his special status was an experience referred to by mystics as 'the Assault of the Seraphim', in which he was struck in a vision by a fiery weapon that delivered a 'mortal wound in the depths of my soul, a wound that is always open and which causes me continual agony'.

Nothing could have illustrated better the marriage of vivid traditional iconography and the deeper implications of Pio's self-immolation than the phenomenon of the stigmata. He had gradual warnings of its arrival, with incipient pains and visible symptoms over several years. Then, at the age of thirty-one, things came to a crisis. On 20 September 1918, after eight years of intermittent pain in his hands, feet and side, he received the stigmata proper. The five wounds opened up fully and poured with blood. He was to become the most famous male stigmatic since St Francis in the thirteenth century.

He wrote to his spiritual director: 'After I had celebrated Mass I was suddenly filled with great peace and abandonment which effaced everything else and caused a lull in the turmoil. While this was taking place I saw before me a mysterious person . . . his hands and feet and side were dripping with blood. The vision disappeared and I became aware that my hands, feet and side were dripping blood. Imagine the agony I experienced and continue to experience almost every day. The heart wound bleeds continually, especially from Thursday evening until Saturday. I am dying of pain because of the wounds and the resulting embarrassment . . .'

The phenomenon of the stigmata in Padre Pio was to last for fifty years; in addition to the pain he would suffer both unwelcome adulation and aggressive scepticism.

A succession of psychiatrists and physicians trooped to San Giovanni Rotondo over the years. Some marvelled at the fact that they could make their fingers meet through the wounds in his hands and that the blood, which remained constantly fresh, seemed perfumed. Many declared themselves to be baffled and proclaimed that here was a genuine mystery to science. But others accused him of fraud, hysteria, self-hypnosis and even of being in league with the devil. An archbishop set spies on him and asserted that the phenomenon was perpetrated with the aid of eau-de-Cologne and carbolic acid, which he claimed had been found under the monk's bed. The archbishop was in time discredited; but the rumours and accusations persisted until Pio's death.

His life was fraught with paradox and controversy. Many hours of his day were spent in contemplative prayer, and yet he conducted an outward-going, energetic ministry right up to his death, spending as long as twelve hours a day in the confessional and performing a host of good works. His spirituality seemed 'private', elevated, unattainable, and yet his attachment to familiar pieties kept him in touch with the people. All spoke of his evident saintliness, and yet he could be irreverent, brusque, sharp-tongued and comic. He lived a life of retirement enclosed in his monastery, and yet he had an impressive grasp of what was happening in the local community, in Italy and around the world. Italian Communists scoffed, calling him 'the richest monk in the world'. His hospital was free to the poor, and yet he was criticized for his insistence that it should be built with the finest materials; there was too much marble in it, they said. There were wrangles over the building contracts, rumours of financial scandals. Rome was suspicious of all this, and of his popularity; people flocked to him by the hundreds of thousands.

The attraction was undoubtedly the curiosity of his stigmata, and there was an abundance of miraculous and paranormal occurrences associated with the cult of his personality.

The number of miracles of healing claimed in his name would run into many thousands. It was believed that he regularly bilocated; in the books that Father di Flumine lent me there were scores of testimonies from people who claimed that on meeting Padre Pio they realized that they had encountered him before – on a sickbed, on a battlefield, in a church confessional, in a dream. There were even accounts of airmen who had seen his bearded figure over the skies of Italy. Invariably these experiences were accompanied by an arresting perfume. When he was challenged as to his awareness of these episodes he would invariably wink and quip cryptically, 'Oh, these little visions and voices!'

A brother monk claimed that Padre Pio had come to him while in hospital and healed him of a fatal illness, although it was known that Pio had not been out of the monastery. When his superior asked him whether he had bilocated, Pio said, 'Is there any doubt about it? Yes, I went, but do not say anything to anyone.'

His long struggles with demon presences had given him, it was believed, unparalleled efficacy as an exorcist, and in confession he was credited with a discernment tantamount to clairvoyance. People would say that he 'saw the whole of one's life at a glance'. It was in confession that he was most often angry, especially if he detected pride or mere curiosity in a penitent; or worse still if a person came to him who was living in sin, with no evident purpose of amendment. He could send people away with an earful of abuse and without absolution, and he was known to slap faces and box ears. Many people quaked at the idea of confronting him in the confessional; many funked it at the last moment.

But the high point of the day at San Giovanni was Padre Pio's Mass. He would rise at 2.30 in the morning to prepare himself in prayer and meditation. The people would be let in at five, and there would be a race for the best places. A party of local women would always be to the fore, and there were stories of uninitiated pilgrims being bitten, knocked to the ground and trampled in the rush to the altar rails.

Once started, though, the silence and concentration during every moment of the Mass became an unforgettable experience for the congregation. As a fellow monk wrote; 'His Mass produced such an impression that time and space between the altar and Calvary disappeared. The Divine Host, raised by those pierced hands, made the faithful more aware of the mystical union between the offering priest and the eternal priest.' He seemed to struggle with waves of emotion, trembling and weeping as he passed through fear, joy, sadness, anguish and pain. From the expression on his face the people could follow his interior meditations. Often his whole body would be shaken by sobs.

Padre Pio wrote: 'When I celebrate holy Mass I am not standing, but hanging on the Cross together with Jesus, and I suffer inadequately all that Jesus suffered on the Cross, as much as is possible for a human creature. The Lord has deigned to associate me with the great work of human redemption, and this despite my every demerit, and only because of his supreme goodness.'

As he grew older his physical suffering increased, he was confined to a wheelchair and seemed prematurely aged. The monks prepared a tomb fit for a saint in the crypt of the new modern church. In the final year of his life the stigmata began to disappear. When he died on 23 September 1968 there was no sign of the wounds. Hundreds of thousands flocked to his requiem Mass, which was celebrated in the presence of cardinals and bishops. The famous perfume filled the church where he had lain in state.

40   *Physical Phenomena of Mysticism*

I had a disturbed night. Whenever I slept I dreamt vividly about Padre Pio; he seemed to be hovering in the room, a powerful, ambivalent, haunting presence, demanding to be understood. I had acquainted myself with his personality merely through spoken and written testimonies and photographs, but here in San Giovanni Rotondo I could sense something of his immense charisma, as if I had known him intimately.

What did I believe about Padre Pio? Was I convinced that his stigmata offered irrefutable evidence of supernatural intervention? In preparation for this trip to Italy I had studied, among other things, the relevant chapters on his case in Herbert Thurston's *Physical Phenomena of Mysticism*, to discover that the Church had seriously wavered on the question of the significance of his stigmata.

In 1923 the Holy Office in Rome had declared, after 'due investigation', that his stigmata was definitely not of supernatural origin, and that pilgrims should not visit him or correspond with him. Although the official attitude softened in later years the early investigations are of great interest, especially the medical reports that Thurston managed to secure for inclusion in his study; for these were thorough and im-

278

partial, from the days before Padre Pio's widespread adulation began.

One of these investigations, conducted in 1919 by a Professor A. Bignani, an agnostic pathologist of Rome University, confirmed the existence of 'superficial scars' on the hands and feet, and the form of a cross on the left breast. He commented that the 'wounds' were marked by extreme sensitiveness (hyperaesthesia), and he was quite convinced that they had not been artificially produced. Professor Bignani's verdict was, nevertheless, that they were of 'neurotic origin' and that their symmetrical arrangement indicated 'unconscious suggestion'.

Another distinguished physician, a Dr George Festa of Rome, who was a Catholic, examined Padre Pio four months after Bignani. He saw drops of blood trickling from the scar on the breast, although he commented that the 'wound' was not 'open' in the sense that there was no rift in the flesh with 'open lips'. He also found drops of blood oozing from the scab on one of the hands. Both doctors remarked on the exacerbating effect of iodine and carbolic acid that Pio used to cleanse the wounds and prevent infection.

There nevertheless seems to have been serious disagreement as to whether the 'lesions' really were superficial or not. Padre Pio's physician, Dr Andrea Cordone, and Dr Luigi Romanelli of Barletta, insisted that the wounds were deep; Cordone reckoned that he could 'see light' through them, as did members of the monastic community who cared for Pio every day of his life.

The disagreement is important, as superficial bleeding, even in the apparent form of stigmata, has come to be related in recent times with a condition called psychogenic purpura, in which spontaneous haemorrhages can occur with no current physical trauma. In my researches after meeting Georgette Faniel I had unearthed a description of this phenomenon in a paper published in 1969, in *Archives of Internal Medicine*, by Drs D. P. Agle and O. D. Ratnoff. According to the study, the phenomenon of painful spontaneous bleeding can follow trauma such as an automobile accident, but not occur until months or even years later, during times of emotional stress. It occurs in people of 'hysterical predisposition' and may be reproduced with a hypnotic procedure. Their work was remembered in 1972 in Oakland, California, when a ten-year-old black Baptist girl, Cloretta Robinson, experienced the stigmata during the Easter season, apparently influenced by a book – John Webster's *Crossroads*. During subsequent examinations the girl's 'wounds' were scrutinized with five- and ten-power magnifying lenses, and showed no skin abnormality or lesions. During the fourth examination investigators 'observed the blood to increase in volume fourfold, welling up in the centre of the palm and spreading over the palmar creases. After wiping the wet blood away, no lesions were present with the exception of pea-size bluish discoloration remaining in the palm of her left hand for approximately three minutes.' The phenomenon was considered to be in all respects similar to psychogenic purpura.

Yet even if Padre Pio's wounds had indeed presented more than purely superficial lesions, there is still evidence that his stigmata was psychological rather than supernatural. Father Thurston's book contained a reference to a remarkable although little-known pamphlet by Dr Alfred Lechler entitled *Das Rattsel von Konnersreuth in Lichte eines neuer Falles von Stigmatisation*, published in 1933 in Germany. The pamphlet is still to be found in the Jesuit house at Farm Street, London, where Thurston lived for most of his life.

In 1928 Dr Lechler, a psychiatrist, took on an Austrian Lutheran patient, Elizabeth K. She was highly neurotic and hypochondriacal and had been in and out of a number of psychiatric clinics without avail. One of her principal problems was that she manifested the symptoms of any illness she heard about. Her sufferings seemed real enough, to her at least, and she had attempted suicide on several occasions. Lechler was interested in her case and decided to take her into his house as a domestic so that he could study her at close quarters.

On Good Friday, 1932, Elizabeth K. went to a cinema to see a slide-show of the Passion realistically depicted. When she returned home Lechler saw that she was upset and complaining of pains in her hands and feet. The idea then occurred to him of hypnotizing the girl and suggesting that she, like Christ, had been pierced with nails in her hands and feet. He renewed the suggestion under hypnosis several times and the appropriate wounds accordingly appeared. With subsequent suggestions he induced tears of blood to flow freely from her eyes and bleeding punctures to appear on her forehead representing the crowning of thorns. Photographs of the wounds are reproduced in the pamphlet. According to the text the wounds are 'open', and the flesh 'torn'. In subsequent sessions Lechler succeeded not only in healing the wounds by the same hypnotic process but in bringing them back once more by non-hypnotic suggestion.

While some doubt must remain, then, as to whether an auto-hypnotic process can bring about wounds through which the light appears, there is sufficient disagreement about the actual depth of Padre Pio's stigmata to suggest that the phenomenon might owe as much to the psychological as to the supernatural, in the case both of the monk himself and of those who observed the phenomenon. It is surely significant that only those who knew him well and came from the locality spoke of drastic fissures.

And yet, even though the evidence might suggest an explanation based on hypnosis and hysteria, I was not inclined to minimize an element of essential mystery in his stigmata, although that sense of mystery had less to do with miracles than a rare combination of poetic and spiritual aptitudes.

The more I pondered Padre Pio's stigmata against the background of his life and character, the more I was reminded of that powerful eighth-century Anglo-Saxon poem known as *The Dream of the Rood*. The dreamer had a vision of the Rood, the tree of the Cross that bore Christ. The Rood addresses the Dreamer, telling of its humiliation at the hands of those who made it an instrument of torture for criminals, its sense of unworthiness when the hero Christ mounts it, and its joy as it is restored thereby to glory. Throughout the story the tree's meditation is related to the sadness and loneliness of the sin-stained Dreamer. What is most striking, however, is the powerful sense of empathy and identity with the wounds of Christ that reveal the spiritual and poetic potential of the state of stigmata:

> The young hero stripped himself – he who was God almighty – strong and stouthearted. he climbed upon the high gallows, valiant, in the sight of many, for he would redeem mankind. I shook when the warrior embraced me, yet I dared not bow to earth, fall to the ground's surface: I must stand fast. A cross was I raised; I lifted up the Mighty King, Lord of the Heavens; I dared not bend. They pierced me with dark nails – on me are the wounds seen, open hateful gashes. Nor did I dare do harm to any of them. They mocked us both together. I was all wet with blood shed from the sides of that man by the time that he had sent forth his spirit. Many bitter things I had endured on the hill. I saw the God of Hosts cruelly racked. Darkness had covered with its mists the Ruler's body, the bright splendour. Shadow came forth, dark

under the clouds. All creation wept, bewailed the King's fall: Christ was on the Cross.

Padre Pio was apparently not neurotic, nor self-absorbed, nor in any sense egotistical. His holiness was of a selfless, humble kind, that proclaimed the invitation to imitate Christ in a radical and heroic manner. His way of life was essentially simple: he said the Mass with deep and sincere feeling; he spent his entire day in prayer and ministering to souls; he meditated ceaselessly on Christ's passion. More than this, he was a down-to-earth, loving member of his community, and he built before he died one of the largest hospitals in the south of Italy.

Wordsworth and Coleridge, in the Preface to the *Lyrical Ballads*, describe good poetry as 'the spontaneous overflow of powerful feelings', and a poet as one 'who, being possessed of more than usual organic sensibility, had also thought long and deeply'. It seems to me that Padre Pio was a holy man who combined the sensibilities and powerful feelings of a poet with an unusually sensitive psychosomatic disposition (clearly capable of non-pathological hysteria and self-hypnosis) that enabled him to make a poem of his own body. Was this a miracle? In the sense in which most of us understand that word, the answer must be no. If there was a miracle in his story, it surely consists in the fact that he lived the life of Christ without compromise, and yet managed to keep both feet more or less firmly on the ground.

In the morning I went up to the monastery to return the books. An American priest called Father Bill came to greet me, as Father di Flumine was saying Mass. Father Bill had been very close to Padre Pio, and had cared for him physically in his declining years.

He took me through the building to see Padre Pio's room, which is preserved exactly as it was at the time of his death. It was a simple cell, about ten feet by seven, with an iron bedstead, a prie-dieu and a wash basin. There were some blood-stained bandages behind glass.

'It was all in his eyes,' said Father Bill. 'Right up to the day he died he had the eyes of a young child. The whites were astoundingly clear, and they gave the impression of the most extraordinary innocence and love . . . You just could not resist those eyes.'

As he said this I remembered the strange child-like gaze of Georgette Faniel in Montreal.

Father Bill led me back to the door of the monastery. I said, 'You lived with him for many years here in this monastery; what was he like as a fellow monk? Were you in awe of him, or was he genuinely a friend?'

Father Bill stopped in his tracks. 'I'll tell you what he was like. Towards the end of his life, when he could move only with difficulty and great pain, I got up on the morning of my saint's feast day; I could hear somebody fiddling at the lock. I was a bit startled and called out, but nobody replied. When I opened the door I found a flower had been stuck in the keyhole, and I saw the figure of Padre Pio slowly disappearing down the end of the corridor . . . He loved each one of us in a very individual way. That was how he was, and how I always remember him.'

41   Michael the Archangel

On my way home from San Giovanni Rotondo I went up to Monte Sant' Angelo to visit the site of the Archangel's fifth-century apparition. The day was bleak and windy and a funeral was passing silently through the town.

Over the façade of the church that houses the shrine is the legend: *'Terribilis est locus iste hic domus Dei est et porta coeli.'* (Terrible is this place: this is the house of God and the Gate of Heaven.) The vestibule was decayed, weed-ridden, abandoned. There was no sign of human life save for two Italian youths practising karate kicks beneath the portico. Five great flights of stairs plunged down into the bowels of the mountain. In the final cavern brimstone exuded from the living rock, as if the visitation of the angel had gouged and scorched the interior like a white-hot meteorite. A ridiculous fifteenth-century hermaphrodite of a statue representing the mighty Archangel Michael was sited for veneration in a grotto, watched over by a squinting monk in a soiled white habit.

The place was dark, humid, and there was indeed, I felt, a sense of something truly terrible having occurred which would leave its stench in mortal nostrils till the end of time. But was it Christian? This damp cleft, this sticky inner sanctum at the end of the labyrinthine flights of marble steps was reminiscent of those womb-like Cretan sanctuaries of the Mother Goddess, who belonged to both the mountain and the cave; who fostered dream incubation and miracles of healing, and who, according to legend, had given birth to Zeus. Was Michael a mutant figment of that ancient cave goddess? Or of Apollo? Or Hermes? Or Mercury? The greatest enigma of angels is surely the elusiveness of their evolution; even within the history of Christianity.

When I was a child we said a morning prayer: 'Oh my good Angel, whom God has appointed to be my guardian, enlighten and protect me, direct and govern me during this day.' The angels of my childhood were protectors, companions, ministers. Several times in my life I have shared memories with people who as children saw angels, often as pillars of light; and I carry in my mind a powerful description of a supernatural presence recollected by the naturalist W. H. Hudson. It would appear, said Hudson, at a distance of three or four feet from the head of his bed, in the form of a column five feet high and about four feet in circumference. It was blue in colour, and varied in depth and intensity; sometimes it was sky-blue, but usually a 'deeper shade, a pure, soft, beautiful blue like that of the morning-glory or wild geranium'.

In the 1940s my boyhood was filled with stories of sightings of angels. As young men and women went off to war, as London crumbled in the blitz, there was a burgeoning of interest in the protective power of angels. During the Battle of Britain there were strange tales of mysterious figures who continued to fly the planes after the RAF pilots had been killed. And memories of the power of angels in the previous generation were still fresh. An uncle told me how the explorer Sir Ernest Shackleton reported that on a return journey across the Antarctic wastes he and his companions were aware of 'one more' who travelled with them. My grandfather, who kept polished First War shell-cases on his mantelshelf, talked of the army of white figures that held off the Germans at

286

Ypres; and tales still proliferated of the Angels of Mons, a legend of shining presences that had started with a fictitious account in the London *Evening News*, only to be confirmed by countless soldiers.

And looming hugely beyond these twentieth-century legends was the dynamic of the war of Christ and the angels against the mighty host of Satan. The received cosmology and history of these superior beings were based on the story that Lucifer and one half of the angel presences had rebelled out of pride against God and had been cast out of heaven, whence Satan fell 'like lightning'. Or in the words of Milton:

> *headlong flaming from th'ethereal sky,*
> *With hideous ruin and combustion.*

In this alternative cosmology the good and the evil angels are ranged against each other, with Christ and his lieutenant and standard-bearer Michael at the head of one army, and Lucifer at the head of the other, locked in combat over the fate of each individual soul. This is the relentless battle between the Powers of Light and Darkness, the background struggle for each human soul, which, as T. S. Eliot puts it, 'shivers and flutters between Heaven-gate and Hell-gate'.

Nowadays some Scripture scholars tell us that the notion of Satan leading a hostile army against Christ and human souls is due to a fatal misreading of a phrase in St Paul, and the misinterpretation of the Greek word 'archai' as 'hostile superhuman powers' rather than 'human rulers'.

All the same, the idea of the almost equal nature of the struggle between heaven and hell, and hence the drama that surrounds the uncertainty of its outcome, has had a profound influence on Judaeo-Christian and Islamic cultures. Eschatological legends and literary masterpieces like *Paradise*

Lost are one thing; applying them to the world of human politics and history is another. It is widely believed in evangelical Christian circles that the Second World War is only to be understood in terms of a suspension of the reign of Christ the King which allowed Satan freedom, through the medium of Hitler, to range about the world for the ruin of souls and the torture and physical destruction of millions. This notion lurks beneath the secular view of Hitler as a dark, superhuman power for evil who prevailed with his followers for a period before the reinstatement of the Light. Insistence on a mythic reading of history leaves little scope for understanding the human mechanisms and failings, the widespread human responsibility for the causes of the Second World War. Variations on such readings of history are shared by Muslim fundamentalists who see the antagonisms between the Middle East and the West in terms of Holy Wars, Jihads, of Allah and the faithful against Satan and the infidels.

So angels were soldiers. Or messengers and intermediaries. Or invisible ministers. Augustine of Hippo explains that the mission of angels as spokespersons belongs specifically to the Old Testament, and not at all to the new dispensation. The God of the Jews seldom spoke directly to humankind, hence the need for angels. In the New Testament the Lord speaks for himself, and in time the Virgin Mary became the principal mediatrix, precluding the need of angels. She bridges the Old and the New Testaments, being the last to receive an angelic announcement. The new role of the angels, the New Testament role, is to act as ministers to Christ, and thereby to us all. As Gregory of Nazianus, a fourth-century Church Father, puts it: 'Ministrants of God's will, strong with both inborn and imparted strength, traversing all space, readily present to all at any place through their zeal for ministry and the agility of their nature ... different individuals of them embracing different parts of the world, or appointed over different districts of the universe . . .'

Very like the notion of pagan gods, although there is from the very outset an absence in these Christian other-world spirits of erotic desire. Not surprisingly the notion of angelic qualities, thus described, was to provide a powerful impetus for the early Christian ideals of celibacy, monasticism and priestly ministry.

But who is Michael? What mythic attributions surrounded the pathetic little Renaissance statue in this dank grotto in Gargano, the last official site of his appearance to humankind on earth?

Michael is a super-angel who bestrides the legend of heavenly aggression and the ideal of heavenly and earthly ministry. His name means 'Who is like God'; Palestine and the synagogue were, in Jewish tradition, his special care.

As we have fallen through sin into the power of Satan, Michael's role is to continue the fight for our deliverance. According to Catholic tradition all our guardian angels are subordinate to him. But he ministers not only to humankind but, in a special way, to God himself. He presides over the worship of adoration rendered to the most High, for he offers to God the prayers of the saints, symbolized by the incense whose smoke rises towards heaven.

Like the ancient Egyptian god Anubis (from whom he possibly descends as from a previous incarnation), he was widely depicted in the Middle Ages as holding scales of justice, and Christians prayed to him that he should introduce them to heaven after death. According to Egyptian mythology, Anubis weighed the human heart against the weight of a feather: only the lightest of hearts would float into paradise. Michael carries on that dread task.

Looking about the gloomy, neglected cave at the top of that

remote mountain in Italy, it was difficult to believe that this had once been the greatest shrine in Christendom to his mighty spirit.

Has Michael had his day? It would seem not. According to the twelfth chapter of Daniel, Michael's most magnificent and crucial role is yet to come. He, it seems, will preside over the End Time, the Final Doom, the Apocalypse:

At that time Michael will arise – the great Prince, defender of your people. That will be a time of great distress, unparalleled since nations first came into existence. When that time comes, your own people will be spared – all those whose names are found written in the Book. Of those who are sleeping in the Land of Dust, many will awaken, some to everlasting life, some to shame and everlasting disgrace. Those who are wise will shine as brightly as the expanse of the heavens, and those who have instructed many in uprightness, as bright as stars for all eternity.

There is a school of scriptural scholars which believes that even now, in the nineties, in the run-up to the third millennium, the dire time is upon us; and that we shall be hearing much of Michael in the years to come.

Could I ever find it in myself to believe in angels again?

There was an occasion when my wife and I took over a rambling apartment in Turin. We thought we had made it child-proof. One Sunday morning as we were sitting in bed drinking coffee, our twelve-month-old boy toddled in with a razor blade trembling on the end of his tongue. I had a curious feeling that he had been steered towards our bed just in time by angelic propulsion.

On another occasion in Zurich I was about to step off a

pavement; I was looking, I thought, in the right direction and began to move out, when something told me to freeze: at that moment a tram-car, horrifyingly silent, swept past from the opposite direction an inch from my nose.

We all have those moments, and it's enough to make one think. But angels with wings! John Henry Newman was convinced that one could only believe in what one can imagine. I could just about imagine the idea of angels as the thoughts of the creator. But the confused history of the angelic hosts involves such a ragbag of legends, sex-changes, fairy-tales and obnoxious myths, such a jumble of meanings and allegories, that I'd sooner leave them alone.

All the same, the words echo through a Christian's life: ' . . . and he shall bear thee up, lest thou dash thy foot against a stone'.

42   The Flying Monk

Driving south through Apulia, it struck me as strange that angels were invariably depicted with wings when it was widely attested by trustworthy witnesses that some favoured human beings had flown without them.

The thought was provoked by signs to Grottaglie, a scruffy provincial district that lies both sides of rusty railway tracks between Brindisi and Taranto. There is nothing nowadays to show for the extraordinary life and antics of the 'flying monk' who once lived there, except the existence of some rare and curious hagiographies that a canon in the Duomo of Taranto lent me to satisfy my curiosity.

From the very outset of my journey I had been pursuing rumours and reports of levitation associated with holiness; all the leads had come to nothing. Somehow levitation is an extremely elusive phenomenon. But those interested in such matters seemed to agree that the most well-attested and astounding instance of the prodigy on reliable record is the case of the flying monk of Copertino. I had first come across Joseph of Copertino in a chapter on levitation in Father Thurston's *Physical Phenomena of Mysticism*. The discussion was intriguing, for it seemed to me that this, of all prodigies, supported the contention of paranormal activity. I was prepared to accept that small metal objects defied gravity through what some people call telekinesis; of moving, rising tables in séance conditions I was less certain. But for a human body to float unaided was something yet again. Even a small exhibition would indicate the presence of a considerable mystery. As Father Thurston sensibly commented, 'So far as regards the law of gravitation in itself, it does not greatly matter whether an ecstatic is raised above the ground three inches or thirty feet, and we have as much reason to be impressed if such an incident happens once as if it happened fifty times.'

The problem was capturing a subject in the act – without the possibility of hypnosis, illusion or fraud; no easy matter in the twentieth century, it seemed. In a list of 'levitating' saints, Father Thurston makes mention of at least fifty, from Andrew Salus in the ninth century to J. B. Cottolengo in 1842. Would I be prepared to accept the affidavits of reliable witnesses who were confident that they had observed scores of instances of such a phenomenon in the case of a single person?

Joseph of Copertino (modern Grottaglie), born in 1603, presents us with a major challenge. Nothing I had previously read about him in Father Thurston, nor in the most recent edition of Butler's *Lives of the Saints*, prepared me for the details reported in the eighteenth-century Italian hagiographies published after Joseph's canonization. I refer principally to the *Vita di S. Giuseppe di Copertino sacerdote professo dell'Ordine de' Minori Conventuali di S. Francesco*, published in Florence in 1768.

Joseph was brought up near Taranto in a land of large skies, clear southern light and the distant prospect of the shimmering Ionian sea. This is the country of the *villanella* and the *tarantella*, the wild leaping dance that was believed to be the only antidote to the bite of the European wolf-spider, the tarantula. He grew up in the repressive post-Tredentine era of the counter-Reformation, when traditional local dances of all kinds were officially thwarted by diocesan law. Yet who can say what profane acrobatic frustrations seethed within young Joseph, to erupt unchecked in the context of his religious life?

His parents were destitute, and he was born (like St Francis of Assisi, and, naturally, his Saviour) in a stable. His childhood was miserable, over-disciplined and prone to painful disease. At the age of seven he developed an abscess that became gangrenous and spread in the form of ulcers, so that he had to be treated with 'iron and fire'. For four years he was plagued by this sickness until he was cured miraculously by the application of some oil from the lamp of the Virgin of Galatone.

He grew up an absent-minded youth and was considered an imbecile, incapable even 'of discriminating between brown bread and white', it was said. He acquired the nickname of *Bocaperta* – 'gaping mouth'. He dropped anything that he carried, especially anything breakable. He was given to sudden tantrums; and yet he was equally capable of long trances and deeply religious expressions of piety and self-discipline.

After failing to acquire any sort of schooling or trade he entered the Franciscans, and despite difficulties with his studies was ordained priest in 1628. By dint of a miracle, so it was reckoned, he managed to learn by heart the only question he was asked in his faculty examination. He was by all accounts virtually illiterate, but his religious life was to become a succession of amazing ecstasies, miracles and prodigies, probably unparalleled – according to Thurston – in the life of any other saint in the history of Christendom.

He multiplied bread and wine, drove out devils, healed the lame and the blind and even quelled storms and tornadoes. He enjoyed the charism of continuous prophecy, and could literally sniff out evil and witchcraft from a great distance. In his ecstasies it was noticed that hosts of flies would enter his mouth and rest on his open eyes without his seeming to notice. Like St Francis he had a special way with animals, and referred to himself as *asinello* – the little ass.

As he matured he was described as 'tall, with fresh complexion, large-boned and athletic . . . tough, strong and capable of withstanding excessive pain . . . His beard was long and thick, his shining eyes were constantly raised to heaven.' His superiors confined him in remote friaries around Italy, but wherever he went his fame quickly followed. His self-denials were extravagant even for that era of harsh discipline and reform. He wore a hair-shirt, deprived himself of bread and meat and sprinkled bitter substances, known as death powders, on his meagre diet of herbs and roots. Others who tried these powders fell violently ill. He slept on bare boards in a robe that he changed seldom in a lifetime. All the same, it was said that every convent he inhabited was filled with a heavenly odour. Like Catherine of Sienna, he sometimes ate leaves filled with pus produced by lepers' sores. Twice a week he beat himself so severely that thirty years after his death the walls of his cell were still caked with blood. In between times a single impure or vain thought would prompt him to scourge himself with skewered needles and lumps of metal that gouged his flesh until the blood flowed and he would collapse in a faint. He also persuaded others to flog him till he was senseless. When his clothes were removed one day under the rules of obedience, it was discovered that he had attached a quantity of chains and lumps of iron to his bare skin. He was, in the words of the witnesses, 'one great open sore'.

But the prodigy that made him famous was the exercise of his *ratto*, an astounding leap or flight through the air accompanied by blood-curdling shrieks and cries. According to the official eighteenth-century *Vita*, containing affidavits taken under oath, some seventy separate flights were observed during his lifetime. It is noteworthy, moreover, that Prosper Lambertini, the future Benedict XV, who was Devil's Advocate in Joseph's cause for canonization, delivered himself of the following verdict in his disquisition on sainthood, *De Servorum dei Beatificatione*:

> Whilst I discharged the office of Promoter of the Faith the cause of the Venerable Servant of God, Joseph of Copertino, came up for discussion in the Congregation of Sacred Rites, which after my retirement was brought to a favourable conclusion, and in this eye-witnesses of unchallengeable integrity gave evidence of the famous upliftings from the ground and prolonged flights of the aforesaid Servant of God when rapt in ecstasy.

An early, somewhat modest example occurred shortly after his ordination when shepherds came to the church to play music: 'When they began to play their instruments, he started to dance in the nave like David before the ark. Then he sighed and with a cry flew up like a bird above the main altar, a height of over six feet, and embraced the tabernacle with his arms.' His biographer comments that the 'prodigiousness of this spectacle filled the pious shepherds with holy terror'.

As the years passed the feats became more complicated, more astounding. One involved a curious combination of flying and paranormal lightness of bodily weight: 'He flew up into an olive tree where he remained in a kneeling posture for the space of half an hour. A marvellous thing it was to see the branch which sustained him swaying lightly, as though a bird had alighted upon it.'

On another occasion he performed a flight combined with an extraordinary feat of weight-lifting, when a Calvary was being erected at Grottaglie: 'Two crosses were already in position, but ten persons together could not lift the third, which was about 36 feet high and very heavy. On seeing this, Joseph flew about 70 yards from the door of the friary to the cross, lifted it as easily as if it were a straw, and placed it in the hole prepared for it.'

Joseph would also sweep others along on his flights. Once, while the monks were at prayer, he sailed over to the father guardian, and, 'grabbing him by the hand, he raised him from the ground by supernatural force, and with a joyful cry dragged him along, spinning him round and round in a violent dance; the priest being moved by Joseph, and Joseph by God.' Another time he snatched a sick man by the hair and flew into the air, drawing the man with him; on reaching the ground the man found that he had been cured of a 'severe nervous malady'. Once he threw a lamb into the air and took flight after it to the height of the trees, where he 'remained kneeling in an ecstasy with extended arms for more than two hours'.

In the course of his life Joseph was to perform astounding *ratti* in various parts of Italy – Copertino, Fossombrone, Naples, Rome and Assisi. These flights occurred as much in the presence of the sophisticated and educated as of the credulous and ignorant. He counted among his admirers Prince Casimir of Poland, Prince Leopold of Tuscany, the Duke of Bouillon, Isabella of Austria, the Infant Maria of Savoy and various cardinals. The Duke of Brunswick was instantly converted from Protestantism on witnessing one of his flights.

The *Vita*, again, describes a typical exhibition. While the Lord High Admiral of Castile, Ambassador of Spain at the Vatican, was passing through Assisi in the year 1645, the father guardian at the Franciscan monastery commanded Joseph to descend from the room into the church, where the admiral's lady was waiting for him. 'As he entered the church and gazed on the statue above the altar, he threw himself into a flight of twelve paces, passing over the heads of the congregation. After staying there some time he flew back over them with his familiar cry, and returned immediately to his cell. The Admiral was stunned, his wife fainted and the spectators were filled with holy awe.'

But his most impressive flight, perhaps, occurred at Fossombrone, where 'detaching himself in swiftest manner from the altar with a roar like thunder, he went, like lightning, gyrating hither and thither about the chapel, and with such force that he made all the cells of the dormitory shake, so that the monks rushed out in fear, crying, "Earthquake! Earthquake!"'

After an extraordinary life of wanderings, alternating with periods of virtual confinement in enclosed monasteries, he was eventually sent to Osimo, where he suffered his final illness. When the surgeon came to bleed him, he observed that Joseph was raised almost a whole 'palm' in the air. A fly had alighted in the middle of the pupil of Joseph's eye, and the surgeon tried to chase it away, to no avail.

This same surgeon certified that after the saint's death on 10 August 1663, Joseph's heart and ventricles were dry – 'devoid of any blood, indeed the heart itself was dry and desiccated'. As the hagiographer commented, this was 'not through the natural burning of a fever, but through the supernatural flame of Divine Love'. After his death the miracles associated with him continued for a century as consistently as they had done during his lifetime.

He was canonized one hundred years later, in 1767. His life and amazing prodigies were thus unabashedly proclaimed during the first full flush of European scepticism and empiricism.

So what are we to make of these extraordinary claims, these

'miracles' witnessed by so many people over a period of almost forty years? One thing seems certain: his style of flight bears little resemblance to the much-vaunted yet seldom-witnessed cross-legged levitations of Eastern yogis. Nor was it dependent on the sort of low-lit, illusory effects that obtained when D. D. Home, in the presence of witnesses, was said to have floated out of a third-floor window in London in 1868. Joseph's feats were performed before large numbers of educated witnesses, indoors and out, and in the searching light of day.

Could Joseph of Copertino's witnesses have been, in any sense, hypnotized? The description of his flight from *behind* the distinguished visitors at Assisi in 1645 seems to preclude such a possibility. And yet, a sense of illusion combined with an extraordinary acrobatic athleticism might provide a rational explanation for the phenomena. We are told that he had unusual strength and that he was amazingly uninhibited; his *ratto*, like the currently fashionable cinematic performances of Ninja martial arts, was always preceded by a loud cry, denoting huge and sudden effort. Is it not possible that he had developed fierce leaps and jumps well within the capacities of a modern ballet dancer, or a high-jumper, but which seemed praeternatural in his own era, and especially in the context of a church, or a monastery orchard? His flights and spinning dances, his noisy gyrations, are reminiscent of the lads of Illfurt and the girls at Garabandal, suggesting the possibility of almost pathological bursts of energy; yet, as I suggested earlier, such feats seem normal nowadays to the exponents of break-dancing techniques.

Reading the testimonies of the details of Joseph's life, I wondered, too, whether his behaviour might be linked with his habit of indulging in long fasts alternating with unusual foods and additives. Ever since I arrived in Italy I had been carrying around with me an absorbing book called *Il Pane Selvaggio* (published in England as *The Bread of Dreams*), by the controversial Italian historian, Piero Camporesi.

Camporesi, whose work has acquired something of a cult status in Italy, believed that there was a link between the use of seeds and herbs in times of famine and the incidence of altered mental states, trances and convulsive dancing. Camporesi was convinced that many of these alternative substances were hallucinogenic and explained the extraordinary powers of many of the wandering jugglers, acrobats and tricksters who traversed the country during this period. By the same token he believed that the relationship between fasting and ascetic diets might shed some light on the tales of visionary experiences, the spiritual crises and physical phenomena of mysticism associated with many saints of this and other earlier periods.

Camporesi's central argument, however, was concerned with the use of alternatives to wheat in the making of bread in rural Italy during the seventeenth century, and the curious divide between white-bread eaters and dark-bread eaters, the latter known throughout Italy as *matta panes* (bread-crazies). The significance of the description of Joseph as one who did not discriminate between dark bread and white bread made sense against this background, as did the account of his peculiar diet of herbs and roots and the death powder that made others ill but upon which he thrived.

But what were these substances, and how, precisely, would they have affected him? The hagiographers give no clue; but Camporesi's free-wheeling exposition puts Joseph's diet and behaviour into a rather more intelligible context than that of routine religious asceticism. Among the flour substitutes for wheat-bread, he lists water brambles, acorns, turnips, dog grass, lupins, hazelnuts, sorb-apples, pumpkins, elm leaves, broad beans, various pulses, millet, panic grass, rye, barley, vetch, sorghum and a variety of 'tasty roots'. 'Among the most common and popular foodstuffs,' writes Camporesi, 'was ... a bread disguised and flavoured, and in addition spiced with coriander seeds, anise, cumin, sesame seed, and all the possible delectable additives available in the "vegetable kingdom" ... even the flour of hemp seeds.'

Then there was 'darnel', a wild grass that formed the basis of what Italians called 'dazed bread'. According to a seventeenth-century apothecary quoted by Camporesi, bread made in this way gave rise to 'every pernicious adventure possible'; the 'evil darnel' causes people 'to beat their heads against walls'.

Ergot, a fungus that grows on cereal crops (and is nowadays the basis of the modern drug lysergic acid diethylamide, or LSD), was probably responsible for the motor crises and neuroses of St Vitus's Dance. Little wonder that the seventeenth-century poet Giulio Cesare Croce could write what Camporesi terms a 'not unfamiliar sample of his generation's dreams':

Almost every day I dream I am flying ...
Last night I sailed through the air,
And on top of a high mountain I was captured,
And was put inside a cloth sack.

I have even dreamed that storks
Carried me to some dark cave
And buried me along with the carrion.

Sometimes I have been lifted up
And carried inside a well, and the well became
A lantern, and myself a burning taper ...

In a telling peroration on the combined effects of protein and vitamin deficiency, Camporesi evokes some of the leading characteristics of common diseases in seventeenth-century Italy: poor wretches, 'tormented by shingles, subjected to sudden attacks of convulsions and epilepsy, the deliria of fevers, the festering of wounds, ulcers which ate away at the tissues, unrelenting gangrene and disgusting scrofula, the crazed patterns of "St Vitus's dance" and other choreographic epidemics', all of which are reminiscent of the symptoms of Joseph of Copertino, to which we might add self-inflicted punishments, fastings and vigils. Is it surprising that he took screaming leaps and thought that he was flying?

The Church, mercifully, no longer holds up the likes of Joseph as a model of heroic sanctity, so a reductive interpretation of his life is of little consequence to the modern faithful. On the other hand, he is cited by people of all faiths, and none, even to this day, as evidence of the possibility of levitation. My own guess – in the light of Camporesi – is that he never flew, nor did he levitate; in the surrealistic settings of sanctuaries and monastery gardens, his immense reputation for sanctity and asceticism raised expectations of prodigies that were fulfilled by his noisy, energetic acrobatics. There is nothing so very unusual about leaping a height of six feet, nor a distance of twelve paces: it seldom happens in a church, however, accompanied by a scream. As for sitting on light branches, or lifting heavy weights – this is the stock-in-trade of activities on the margins of the paranormal, but it is not hard evidence of levitation as such. On the other hand, there is little doubt that Joseph himself, intoxicated, half-starved and yet amazingly athletic, was quite convinced that he was capable of taking to the air.

But perhaps Father Thurston should be allowed a last word on the question of flying and angels, which is where we came in. At the end of his discussion on levitation, he says this:

The Flying Monk

Assuming, then, that we have reasonable ground for crediting the fact of levitation, there remains the question of its possible explanation. Theologians for the most part offer the rough and ready solution that in the case of holy people it is a manifestation of divine power, effected perhaps through the ministry of angels; but that in such cases as those of Simon Magus, sorcerers, and spiritualistic mediums, it is the work of the devil. Without venturing to reject this explanation outright, I found certain difficulties, too complex to summarize here, which suggest that it would be wise to suspend our judgement.

With which I heartily concur.

43 The Weeping Statue of Syracuse

It had been a year of jumping, shaking, winking, bleeding, weeping statues. Ever since my encounter with the stigmatic effigy of the child Jesus in the Bronx, I had been noting parallels across the world.

At Denia near Alicante in Spain, a bust of Christ crowned with thorns wept tears the colour of blood for ten days on end in the home of one Antonia Alvarez, and in the presence of assembled villagers. In Granada, Spain, an estimated 130,000 people flocked to the Basilica of Saint John of God; four streaks of blood-red tears had appeared overnight on the plaster face and the liquid had also seeped into a handkerchief that had miraculously materialized in the statue's hand.

At Sezze in the province of Latina between Rome and Naples, the faces of both the Virgin and Christ were seen to weep tears and blood in the local church. At Caltanisetta in central Sicily villagers witnessed a red-coloured liquid several inches long issuing from a ceramic statuette of the Virgin in the possession of a local woman.

At Ballinspittle in Ireland, a wayside statue of the Virgin rocked to and fro. Up to 10,000 pilgrims were gathered each day for a month from every part of the country. And the prodigy seemed to be catching. In the neighbouring parish of Courtmachsherry the Virgin's statue swung so vigorously one lunch-time that the parish priest had to hold on to it for more than an hour. In Asdee, County Kerry a group of children claimed to have seen a statue of the Virgin open its eyes and move its hands. And in Castleblaney in County Monaghan clergy were appealing to the faithful not to give credence to paranormal phenomena after several hundred people attended an all-night vigil at the Church of All Saints, where a statue of the Virgin appeared to have shifted its location. Throughout the summer, sightings of moving statues had been claimed in fifteen of the Irish Republic's twenty-six counties.

In the Church of the Holy Trinity in Ambridge, Pittsburgh, USA the Franciscan pastor along with at least one hundred parishioners declared that the eyes of a life-sized statue of the crucified Christ closed during a prayer meeting. 'I am still in shock!' said the artist who had recently redecorated the eyes with acrylic paint.

In Akita, Japan, Bishop John Shojiro Ito was rejoicing at the news that Rome had officially ratified the miracle of a weeping wooden statue of the Virgin in a convent of nuns. Over a period of six years some 500 Christians and non-Christians had reported the phenomenon in 101 separate incidents. The eye-witnesses included the mayor, Keiji Takada, who is a Buddhist.

I was pondering the significance of these prodigies when I arrived in Syracuse in Sicily to visit the Shrine of Our Lady of the Tears, perhaps the most acclaimed weeping Virgin in modern times, and, until the Akita decision, the only phenomenon of its sort approved by a local bishop.

The old quarter of this ancient sea-port is separated by a bridge from the mainland; the locals refer to it as the 'island'. It is a warren of narrow streets and flights of steps, with sudden piazzas lined with orange trees, and glimpses of the sea at every corner. Syracuse was once the pivot of eastern and western sea-lanes, where pagan pieties merged with early

Christianity. The decaying Duomo with its Baroque additions was once a temple to Athena, and there are ancient catacombs alongside sacred caves and ruins of a Greek theatre; a fountain in a chasm below the sea-wall is said to be the transformed nymph Arethusa, chastely bubbling for all eternity so as to escape the unwelcome attentions of Alpheus, who himself was transmogrified into a river.

Nowadays the economy of the region is dependent on the petrochemical plants that straddle the coastline north of the town, although not so long ago, in the immediate post-war period, poverty seemed endemic and the Italian Communist Party was fiercely contesting the power of the Mafia, the Church and the Christian Democrats.

It was in 1953, during a period of austerity and political strife, that a recently married young woman, Antonina Giusto, aged twenty, witnessed a curious phenomenon in her bedroom that was to stimulate an upsurge of piety in the region. Above the matrimonial bed she had hung a plaque of the Virgin made of glass, ceramic and plaster – nothing special, a trifle sentimental and of no artistic or commercial value. On the morning of 29 August Antonina was lying in bed after her husband had gone to work; she had been suffering from pregnancy toxaemia, with episodes of blindness. She looked up at the plaque above her and saw that the face of the Virgin was suffused with tears.

She called her sister-in-law, then her aunt, and within an hour crowds were gathering outside the house. By the time Angelo Giusto, her husband, returned from work the town was in uproar and police were patrolling the street. According to hundreds of sworn testimonies, the plaque wept profusely. People queued all day to wipe away the tears with cotton-wool and handkerchiefs; the quantity of liquid was prodigious and inexplicable. They put the plaque in a box, and then into a drawer; they took it out and it continued to weep. It wept by day and by night. Thousands came and went in the bedroom, soaking cotton-wool and handkerchiefs in the liquid, tasting it with their fingers and declaring that it was indeed 'salty', just like human tears. The plaque was paraded in the main square of the town in the glare of the midday sun and it wept without ceasing. Priests and monsignori turned up, and eventually the bishop. On the fourth day of the prodigy scientists were summoned by the Episcopal Curia of Syracuse. Immediately after they had taken their samples the weeping stopped abruptly and has never resumed.

I heard this tale from the mouth of the shrine's director, a rotund, sweating gentleman called Signor Carmelo Maconda, as he sat in his office next to the vast concrete basilica that, at a cost of $32 million, is still being built twenty-six years after the event.

He leant across his desk and handed me a paper. 'You should know,' he said, mopping his brow, 'the full details of what the doctors think.'

The document was signed by a team of officials, including six medical doctors, a chemist and a professor of pathology, along with police officers and two lieutenant-colonels from the local garrison. It told how these gentlemen had squeezed into the narrow bedroom of the young couple to gather a decent quantity of the liquid on 1 September 1953.

The young wife kept the object covered with a cloth in a locked drawer. The plaque was clearly wet in many places on the face and bust and the scientists had to struggle in competition with hysterical devotees to collect a cubic centimetre of the liquid in a glass tube.

The document concluded:

An examination with a magnifying-glass of the inside

corners of the eyes did not show up any pore or irregularity in the surface of the enamel. The part of the plaque apparently made of maiolica was taken off the black glass that supported it, and it was noticed the image was made of a layer of chalk of about 1–2 centimetres thick, painted with different colours on the outside and left uncoloured on the inside, where there was an irregular white surface that at the moment of the examination was completely dry.

After I had digested this information Signor Maconda now handed over the details of the scientific analysis. First they wanted to see whether the two elements from which the picture was made were present in the 'miraculous' tears; then the scientists compared the plaque's liquid with the real tears of an adult and of a child. Real tears, according to these Italian experts, contain sodium chloride, plus very small particles of protein or analogous substances formed of carbon, hydrogen, oxygen and nitrogen. 'In the Virgin's "tears",' they said, 'we noticed the presence of sodium and chlorine and also some black amorphous nodules.' The same elements were found in the tears taken from the adult and the child present. No trace was found of the substances from which the plaque was made, indicating that the liquid had not come from inside the object.

In conclusion, they asserted that the alkalinity and the composition of the weeping plaque indicated that the liquid was of analogous composition to 'human lachrymal secretion'. This final affirmation was signed by Drs Michele Cassola, Francesco Cotzia, Leopoldo La Rosa and Maria Marletta, on 9 September 1953.

Signor Maconda now took me on a tour of the unfinished basilica, which was being completed with the financial assistance of the local province. We clambered over duck-boards, up ladders and along gangways supported by scaffolding; there were piles of sand and cement and girders, but all was silent and deserted. The works had come to a standstill.

If it is ever completed, the immense basilica, designed to take 20,000 pilgrims at a time, will look like a giant witch's hat. There are to be twenty-two chapels in the crypt; there will be reception areas, car parks, and hostels to house tens of thousands of pilgrims at a time. And yet, there is some doubt as to whether the shrine will ever again attract a significant number of pilgrims. The cult of Our Lady of the Tears, while not exactly dead, is suffering from proliferating rival cults throughout Italy and elsewhere.

After viewing the miraculous plaque, which struck me as cheap and sentimental, we ended up in an office where a team of nuns was sitting at tables making up relic cards for distribution around the world. Each card showed the image of the original plaque and contained a tiny piece of cotton displayed within a see-through envelope, above which was written: 'This has been rubbed on the miraculous image.'

Signor Maconda now introduced me to a wizened man who turned out to be Antonina's husband, Angelo, who was responsible in some way for handling the relic and running errands. With considerable ceremony he withdrew the silver-and-gold reliquary from a safe, holding it by the hand-grip with a white cloth. In the centre of this elaborate monstrance was a phial in which one could see a small portion of limpid liquid, faintly blue in colour.

Angelo looked worn and distracted. I asked him how he felt about the miracle after all these years. Did he have any regrets? Had he been happy?

His brow was furrowed and he shook slightly. He had blood-shot eyes and a smoker's cough.

'Well,' he muttered, 'the problem is that everybody said I

was a Communist. But that wasn't true. They also said we weren't married – but that wasn't true either. Of course we were married!'

'What do you think of the relic?' the director asked me, as if to forestall further conversation with Angelo. I realized that I had been staring at the relic glumly, as if waiting for something to happen. The sight of the phial, which few people ever saw at close quarters, did nothing for me. Signor Maconda was looking at me curiously. 'It's not getting through to you, is it?' he murmured.

'I'm afraid not.'

With this, he clapped a hand on my shoulder and said: 'Come with me: I'm going to show you something else!'

Outside in the car park was an ancient Lancia. Signor Maconda ordered me into the front passenger seat and we lurched off with screeching tyres out into the traffic of Syracuse.

After a fifteen-minute drive we pulled up outside an unkempt modern public building on the outskirts of the town.

Signor Maconda marched up a sweeping marble staircase, gesturing me to follow. At the top he ushered me through some swing doors into a convention hall where there was a film screen in front of a stage. Two young people were sitting at the far end talking.

He clapped his hands. 'The film!' he shouted. 'Now we show the film.' Turning to me he said, 'Listen, Mister, I am going to show you something that not even the cardinals and the bishops see. This film is very old and in bad condition. But because you are a writer . . .'

After some delay in the projection room above, the lights went down and an ancient black-and-white home-movie flickered into life on the screen. There was some pious music and an urgent commentary; scenes of Syracuse, forty years ago, still war-damaged, poverty-stricken. The young couple, Antonina and Angelo, were introduced, smiling, standing in the doorway of their house; then the famous plaque, at this stage dry-eyed.

The story was being told with some embellishments, including the antagonism of the Communists to the local Church; then, suddenly, we were out in the main square. The plaque was placed on a black-velvet catafalque, raised above the heads of a vast crowd so that it could be seen by all. The camera zoomed in on Mary's face, and there were the tears clearly to be seen, welling in the eyes of the plaque and rolling down its cheeks.

Now the camera panned to the crowd, showing the faces of the people: there was wonder, devotion, joy; a sort of common expression of dazed happiness. Next the camera showed a street off the square; sick and elderly men and women were attempting to hasten with painful steps towards the gathering crowds.

Once again the camera focused on the plaque and the rolling tears, and I began to understand the importance of the immediacy of a living prodigy of this sort: the sense of presence, the importance of the moment. No basilica, no silvered reliquary, no dabs of cotton-wool could substitute for the special atmosphere of a miracle in progress. The faces of the crowds were truly pathetic, gripped with a sort of common stamp of possession.

I heard a snuffle; I looked at my three companions. They were all shedding tears. And I must confess that it was as much as I could do to keep back my own.

Before leaving Syracuse I walked into the offices of the Communist Party off the main square. There were four men wearing dark-blue open-necked shirts sitting beneath a poster of

Gramsci. One had a black shaggy beard; he invited me to speak.

I explained that I had come to visit the Shrine of the Tears. I said I was wondering what the impact of the miracle had been on the fortunes of the Communists in the town.

'Do you think the miracle was an anti-Communist plot?' I asked.

Black-beard shrugged: 'It was a lot of nonsense,' he said.

He looked at the others and said something in dialect; at which they burst into laughter. The man gurgled a little. 'I was saying that the miracle happened in August, and it's bloody hot here: even the statues sweat.

'Look, Signore,' he went on, 'I could think of a lot of psychological or sociological reasons for the miracle, but no, it wasn't a plot.'

At this point the others started talking and laughing, swapping private jokes.

Black-beard talked over them. 'There were rumours at the time of Communists trying to undermine the miracle, but the truth is that there is no distinction between Catholicism and Communism, especially in the south. The distinction is between Communists and capitalists, and that cuts through religion as well. We have a saying in this part of the country: "The Communists carry the Virgin on their backs" – you know, at the processions – "and the capitalists carry the Devil."

'In *somma*,' he said, 'what can one say? The Virgin started to produce drops of water and some scientists said that they were real tears. So now they're going to produce that horrible monstrosity of a basilica, like an ice-cream cone. It's no concern of this Party office.'

With this he shook my hand, and the others leant over and followed suit.

The Weeping Statue of Syracuse

*

As I drove back north towards Messina and the ferry to Reggio di Calabria I found myself meditating on the possible meaning of the language of tears of the Virgin of Syracuse.

All the principal apparitions that I had studied on my journey had featured the sorrowing Virgin – Medjugorje, Garabandal, Hrushiw – and I was aware she was a convention of Marian visions over hundreds of years, as well as a subject of countless icons in the East. The idea of weeping Mary ultimately derived from the 'Stabat Mater' – Mary at the foot of the Cross, Mary in the Pietà, the moment at which the Mother of God and the Passion and death of Christ come together in a single image. Mary's tears express the sorrow of the human race for the death of Christ; but they are also a symbol of mediation, for what son can refuse the tears of a mother?

And the religious metaphor runs even deeper. When I was a boy I remember the collects in the Mass *pro petitione lachrymarum*, asking God for the gift of tears out of the hardness of our hearts, just as, in Ezekiel, he drew from the desert rock a fountain of living water for his thirsty people. I remembered, too, the outstanding example of the charism of tears displayed by the medieval mystic Margery Kempe of Lynn, who wept so copiously and noisily that one priest of her acquaintance banished her to the crypt of the church during his sermons.

Margery had consulted another mystic, Juliana of Norwich, about the matter of weeping, who advised her that when God visits a creature with tears of compunction, devotion and compassion, one ought to believe that the Holy Spirit is present in the soul. Juliana added that no evil spirit could grant the gift of tears, for, according to St Jerome, 'tears torment more the devil than do the pains of hell'.

The tears of Syracuse had left me mystified, and a little humbled. My suspicion that the phenomenon was merely a

313

hoax, perpetrated to confound the Communists and to attract tourism to the region, was probably wide of the mark. I did not set much store by the scientific data, nor did I rule out the possibility of freak condensation, but I felt that as long as I concentrated on authenticity, rather than the meaning of the cult itself, I was missing the point.

While watching the film of the miracle in action, I had felt moved and touched, almost on the point of understanding. Yet I was tempted to wonder whether the wider theme of all this secreting, bleeding, lactating, liquefying, weeping and sweating, so widespread in Mediterranean folk-religion, might not signify some very simple and obvious psychological mechanism.

I was headed for Naples and the most famous phenomenon of secretion of them all: the liquefaction of the blood of St Januarius in the cathedral, which I planned to witness on the saint's feast day. Would this encounter yield a profound enlightenment of a psychological nature?

The question of a psychological explanation was tantalizing in view of the fact that the Neapolitan liquefaction phenomenon has given rise to perhaps the most intriguing 'Freudian slip' of them all. Travelling northwards through Italy on a train one summer, Freud found himself sitting opposite a young Jew; they fell into conversation. At a certain point the young man attempted to quote a line from the *Aeneid*, about Dido committing the next generation to vengeance. But a single word eluded him.

Freud supplied the forgotten word, which was *aliquis* – '*Exoriare aliquis nostris ex ossibus ultor*'.

Clearly aware of Freud's work, the young man asked for an explanation as to why he should have forgotten that specific word, and an impromptu free-association session followed.

The young man betrayed an association between *aliquis*

and 'liquefy' – probably as a result of phonetic similarity – and then went on to link *'aliquis'* and 'relics', no doubt because of the Neapolitan context and the dried-up blood of St Januarius which liquefies on the saint's day. Still free-associating, the young man remembered a story about Garibaldi, who had once grown threatening in the cathedral when the blood relic failed to liquefy, and this in turn reminded him of something else – which he had no wish to talk about.

At this point Freud put his finger on the problem: the young man had been having an affair with a woman, and she had missed her period. Now all was clear: the failure of the liquefaction of the blood of St Januarius had reminded him of the failure of a menstrual blood flow, which in turn had provoked an unconscious anxiety, which had blocked his ability to remember the word *aliquis* with its liquefying connotations.

44   A Miracle in Naples

Where in the world can one observe a physical miracle made manifest at an appointed hour, except in Naples, when the blood of the martyr St Januarius liquefies before thousands of its citizens on his feast day?

St Januarius is believed to have been thrown to the bears and decapitated in the amphitheatre of Pozzuoli during the Diocletian persecution of 305. According to legend a certain Eusebia scooped up the martyr's blood from the dirt and placed it in a sealed *ampolla* such as contained embalming ointment; this blood relic then accompanied the rest of his remains on a tour of the crypts of Campania – to Capodimonte, to Benevento, to Monte Virgine, and who knows where else – before being translated to its final resting place in the *tesoro* of Naples Cathedral in 1497. The earliest documented report of the miracle, however, is suspiciously late: 1389, during a period of unparalleled relic fakery.

But Naples boasts not only the liquefaction of the blood of St Januarius: it has been blessed with no less than sixteen other liquefaction miracles – including the milk of the Virgin Mary (in the Church of St Louis), the blood of St Alfonsus Ligouri (collected by an enterprising dentist) and no less than two liquefying heads of John the Baptist. Is it something in the air of the Bay of Naples? Or was some mixture accidentally (or not so accidentally) discovered which hardens when enclosed in the dark, but liquefies when exposed to warmth and light? How else should we explain the incidence of so many liquefaction prodigies within a ten-mile radius of this city, the majority of them appearing in the late sixteenth century?

Whatever the case, when the dried blood of St Januarius is placed close to his skull and bone relics on his feast day, it is said to liquefy, *senza dubbio*. What is more, tradition has it that if the blood remains dry in these circumstances, dire consequences for the people of Naples may ensue: earthquake, revolution, outbreaks of cholera, the eruption of Mt Vesuvius, the death of the archbishop ... A band of women, known as the *zie di San Gennaro* – literally the 'aunts of St Januarius' – take up their position before the altar steps; if it looks as if the relic may fail to do its stuff they scream insults at the saint in unrestrained dialect.

I passed through Naples on the eve of the saint's feast, 18 September. And so it was that after a disturbed night in a hotel near the station (some ten youngsters were sleeping in cardboard boxes beneath my window) I walked to the Via del Duomo through streets clogged with mounds of uncollected refuse. In the shadow of the cathedral crowds had gathered, amongst whom mingled bands of child gypsies, transvestite male prostitutes, vague-eyed down-at-heel conscripts and phalanxes of ill-dressed, undernourished, hard-faced teenagers.

What dire consequence, one wondered, could be visited upon this city, more dire than what it had already suffered? The marauding hooded bands of Camorra bandits, the unemployment, the black-market, the sweat-shop labour, the protection rackets, the drugs, the homeless tens of thousands, the North African migrant problem, the violence (some 130 murders a year), the water shortage, the hunger, the polluted air. And yet a walk across this city to the cathedral on the feast day of its favourite saint revealed that Neapolitans were anything but defeated.

A monsignor in the Vatican had furnished me with a letter of introduction, which I duly presented at nine o'clock at the door of the cavernous sacristy whence issued, mysteriously, a delicious smell of coffee and sweetmeats. A fussy young priest led me to the sanctuary through the packed congregation to join a privileged group of dignitaries within a roped-off section bordered by banks of orange gladioli. There were a dozen coquettish Neapolitan ladies fashionably dressed in large hats, and as many males – local politicos and *padroni* it seemed – in pale-blue suits and dark glasses. One of the women was praying the rosary with deep fervour while her companion, who had a sinister bulge in his jacket, was scanning the stock-market listings in the *Messaggero*. I took my place among them and sat in wait for the ritualized miracle, listening to the approach of drum-beats like thunder in the air.

At length the congregation burst into applause as a file of altar boys and ecclesiastics began to make its way up the nave to the accompaniment of two or three steel bands, at odds with each other and with the full-throttled organ. Banners and flags and gonfalons and cloth-of-gold umbrellas were held aloft at all angles; loutish, unshaven seminarians in grubby dog-collars carried smoking candles and glittering incense thuribles. There were monks, friars, canons, monsignori, sword-bearing carabinieri in cockaded hats and high boots, brilliantined fops in tails and decorated sashes and gun-toting policemen. Following up the rear was the Cardinal Archbishop of Naples, Monsignor Giordano, a humble little man in glasses who looked as if he'd rather have been elsewhere; then the bearers with the blood reliquary and the silver bust of St Januarius, adorned with a cloth-of-gold cope and mitre. The saint's skull, I understood, lay beneath the silver mask.

Standing out from among the prelates was an immensely tall arch-priest with a long craggy face the colour of parchment. He was strutting about, casting complacent looks from side to side, his aquiline nose at an imperious angle. As he approached the altar some of the men in dark glasses sprang forward and kissed his out-thrust ringed hand.

When the members of the procession were ensconced in the choir stalls, and the bust and the blood phial had been placed on their stands on the left side of the altar, the cardinal came forward to a lectern to begin his sermon. At this point a line of women in black dresses closed in on the rails below; these were the formidable *zie di San Gennaro*, and they looked in no mood to be messed with.

The cardinal began to speak in a small, tired voice. I guessed that he was not a Neapolitan, nor even a southerner. And within a few minutes it seemed abundantly clear that he did not care too much for miracles of the sort he was about to preside over here. Incredibly, he was lecturing the five or six thousand faithful in the church on the need to believe without seeing.

And as he continued it became clear that he was not carrying his congregation with him, and especially not the prelates and priests on the altar. The complacent-looking fellow with the hook nose was chatting and chortling in pleasant vein with two elderly canons who sat on either side of him. One or two of the younger priests were yawning extravagantly and looking at their watches, while the master of ceremonies, whose surplice contained enough lace to make a bridal train, was assiduously picking his nose.

When the sermon, *finalmente*, came to a conclusion, a gasp of anticipation rushed through the vast cathedral like a passing express train. Now to the important business. The miracle!

The cardinal took hold of the blood reliquary and held it

up while the priests began to intone a litany to the saints. Two phials were contained within the reliquary: one was empty and seemed to contain no more than a few dust stains; the other, which was slightly larger, being about four inches high and four inches across, contained the 'blood', a solid mass of black stuff that filled half the phial.

When the litany had finished the cardinal turned the reliquary around several times, but the substance within remained a solid and immovable lump. A credo followed the litany; then the rosary; then another litany. And every so often the cardinal would turn the monstrance around and around. To no avail.

Things were getting a little tense down at the altar rails. The *zie* were looking fidgety; there was a discernible note of hysteria in their responses and supplications. The complacent prelate came forward and whispered something in the cardinal's ear, whereupon His Eminence began to blow hard on the glass phial, as if he were trying to breathe life into a dying fire. The moment was reminiscent of another supposed miracle, although one widely deemed of dubious authenticity, namely the spontaneous kindling of the holy fire in the Greek Orthodox rite at the Church of the Holy Sepulchre in Jerusalem.

Suddenly the cardinal stopped blowing. He blinked once or twice, then his face was suffused with intense relief. Something was happening. Hook-nose came forward and inspected the phial closely; he was smiling, his complacency now knew no bounds. He summoned a decorated fop in scarlet sash and tails, who took out an enormous white handkerchief and waved it aloft.

With this the cathedral shook to the rafters with cheers and shouts. The blood of St Januarius had once again liquefied. The city would not, after all, fall to pieces. The city was safe for at least another year!

A Miracle in Naples

The cardinal was turning the reliquary this way and that. He came forward to the pen where the dignitaries were standing and showed the phial to each of us in turn. As he thrust it towards my face, he managed to clout me on the nose with it.

The solid, dry-looking lump was now shiny and viscous; the edges had turned dark brown; fine grainy specks were suspended in muddy liquid; the mass inside the phial was swimming about like a lump of lamb's liver.

What did I feel at that moment? The organ was surging and the bells of the cathedral were pealing; I was immensely impressed, for the original mass had seemed as dry, as solid, as a piece of stone. I was thinking, 'Wow!' And yet, the prodigy failed to exert the slightest sense of moral or spiritual power for me personally; at least, not at that moment. At the very second that the evidence of the miracle was presented incontrovertibly before my eyes, I could only wonder whether I was observing an exhibition of magic, a clever material trick – coloured beeswax? honey? – developed by some smart alec in the fourteenth century and surviving to the present day. And what if I *were* witnessing a marvellous manifestation of God's intervention? The significance, as far as I was concerned, had less to do with God's mercy, his action in the world, than with procurable and primitive emotions of superstition, propitiation, manipulation.

Was the congregation inhibited by such scruples? Not a bit of it. The crowd was ecstatic, roaring, threatening to take the roof off the Duomo. Some serious-looking foreigners, Swiss, Scandinavians, Germans perhaps, were peering forward with puzzled looks, much as I had done, as if they were examining some baffling chemistry experiment. Others were reacting to the unbridled jubilance with a faintly disdainful, Protestant air.

But we foreigners were missing the point! The whole point,

it occurred to me suddenly, was surely the sense of resurrection, triumph, re-awakening, in those cheers. And the noise was now stupendous. It was as if the city's darling, Diego Maradona, had scored the winning goal against Juventus in the Supercup. Except that it was the city itself – along with its ancient, its *local* pieties – that had somehow scored, resurrected, overcome its perennial miseries, its disadvantages, its demoralization. The spontaneous combustion of Easter fire; the arrival of spring rain; the flow of milk and honey . . . The blending of Christian and pre-Christian sacramentals and emblems, each and all seemed to blossom and ignite in the culmination of this extraordinary ritual. And seen in this light, it mattered not a jot whether the phenomenon was authentic or fake.

Even as I entertained these thoughts, the phial of the saint had been placed back on its stand on the side of the altar; the members of the congregation were embracing and kissing each other, turning their backs – so soon – on the relics, and making for the wide-open doors and the sun-lit city streets beyond; meanwhile the prelates and priests and altar servers were charging down the nave in a motley scramble, hastening, I imagined, towards the treat of nougat and doughnuts and sweet black coffee that awaited them in the sacristy.

PART SIX

Powers of Darkness

45   Archbishop Milingo

On my return to Rome I spent some time in the library of
the Venerable English College reading around the liquefaction phenomenon. I discovered that my own reaction had
been typical of non-Neapolitans for hundreds of years. Writing
in 1785 a Spanish prelate, one Abate Don Juan Andres, commented on the 'discordant shrieking' of the 'common people',
and the 'contemptuous amusement of the foreigners'. 'In no
single instant,' he continued, 'could I perceive anything of that
devout and respectful impression of awe which ought, one
would think, to be the natural effect of a miracle . . . a manifestation of the divine omnipotence in overriding the laws of
nature.'

The view seemed to support my contention that the mere
fact of an inexplicable prodigy carried no power to change
people's hearts and lives, to move them morally or spiritually;
and yet there was evidently a huge cultural gap, both in what
might be considered a spiritual stimulus and an appropriate
reaction, between northerners and Italian southerners. The
miracle of Naples belonged to the people who lived there.
Maybe, I reflected, a little cynically, God has another miracle
for the likes of us northerners!

Working through scattered materials on Neapolitan devo-
tions one evening, I came across a report by a Jesuit priest
called Father Putignani on the liquefaction of the 'milk of the

Mother of God'. Writing in 1725, Father Putignani described the venerated substance as 'fine grain, whitish in colour, like dried-up milk but rather of hard texture, until the vigil is reached of Our Lady's Assumption into heaven. For on that day in a solemn procession of the Fathers it is carried from its shrine to the High Altar, and at that same hour it liquefies. The veneration of it is attended with much pomp, nor is one day sufficient to content the devotion of the people in regard to this prodigy of the Mother of God. The celebration is continued for a whole octave.'

Suddenly I was filled with disgust at the description of the obnoxious ritual. I shut the book with a bang. I felt that I had reached the end of a cycle in my quest, and I had no wish to go any further with such prodigies. Even if a liquefaction, or a lactation, or a shedding of tears, was reliably reported to be occurring in the next room, I would not have taken three steps to observe it. I left the library and went back to my room.

That night I found it hard to relax. I felt that I had reached an impasse; I had no idea how I was going to proceed. Going over the various phenomena I had seen, and people I had met, in Yugoslavia, Ireland, Spain, the United States, Canada, Italy, nothing had truly impressed me purely for its paranormal or inexplicable quality. What was more, I was now quite convinced that if I were to be hit on the head by a miracle, as I nearly had been in Naples, it would make not the slightest difference to me.

The mystery of the original dream remained, but the more I travelled and the more I saw, the less I was convinced by the simplistic notion of supernatural intervention with which I had started out. The strongest impression seemed to have come from the journey itself – the search, a sense of hunger, of dissatisfaction, and the feeling that something would eventually be resolved. But what? And where would I go next?

When I at last fell asleep I had a vivid dream. I was in an unfamiliar, dismal church attending Mass. A prelate was dispensing Communion and I found myself standing back from the congregation, unable to receive the sacrament because I was not in a state of grace. After the last person had left the altar steps the priest came forward and presented the host to me. I lowered my head and shut my mouth tight, refusing to take the host. With this he pushed the host viciously into the side of my face, shouting, 'Take it! Take it!'

At last I gave in and opened my mouth, almost with a sense of relief at the prospect of reconciliation, but at that moment I realized that the bread was not the body of Christ: it was the body and spirit of the Devil, and I woke in terror with a shout that must have roused everybody on my corridor.

As I lay in the darkness wondering about the significance of the dream, I knew that I had yet to address a path of my journey that I had avoided confronting ever since the beginning. I now acknowledged that for all my years of agnosticism, which included, of course, a confident rejection of a personal focus of Evil, I was nevertheless afraid of coming into contact with anything to do with demonology or possession. Yet I felt that I was obliged to take stock of the Christian claims for the reality of the powers of darkness before I could say that I had brought my journey to a conclusion. But how should I do this? Where should I begin?

Ever since my childhood experience of the 'Evil Eternity' I had maintained a healthy unease about the Satanic, despite Dr Fielding's explanations. And I had remembered all my life a remark made by one of my seminary professors: 'You start by dabbling in demonology, and in the end demonology dabbles with you!'

The precise focus of my fears as a boy was to do with the casual, vindictive way in which the Devil was said to choose his victims. We were once given a retreat at St Wilfred's by a cadaverous-looking Jesuit who told the story of a seminarian in Rome who was suddenly seized by the Devil. 'The youth in his frenzy laid his hand on the oak panel of the refectory,' said the priest,' and immediately a perfect burn-mark of his hand appeared on the wood.

'If you do not believe this story,' he added, 'the burn-mark is there for all to see to this day.'

That night we quaked in our beds.

And here, more than thirty years on, I was back in a seminary, lying awake in the early hours mulling over Catholic teaching on the Devil.

Traditional Catholic teaching holds that the Evil One is not merely a notion of negation, he is an effective agent, a living, spiritual being, perverted and perverting, a mysterious and terrible reality. It is contrary to the teaching of the Bible and the Church to refuse to accept the existence of Satan, or to dismiss him as a pseudo-reality, a convenient fantasy for the unknown cause of suffering, violence and misfortune in the world.

Satan is described by Christ as 'the Father of Lies', the 'murderer from the very beginning'. Satan launches insidious attacks on humankind. Not all sins are directly attributable to diabolical action, but a lack of moral strictness exposes souls to the influence of what Paul calls the *'mysterium iniquitatis'*, 'the mystery of evil' and the risk of damnation.

Christian demons are the fallen angels who under Satan seek to drag human souls into a state of rebellion against God (thus forcing us to identify with their own situation). In this struggle the point of death is all decisive, for the doomed souls will be dragged at that moment into eternal loss:

Shipwreck'd, he kindles on the coast

False fires, that others may be lost.

But what had this mythic stuff to do with the alleged realities of Satanism, possession and exorcism?

The next morning at breakfast I brought up the subject with a college member of the staff, who promptly suggested that as far as contemporary phenomena were concerned the case of Archbishop Emanuel Milingo deserved careful consideration and investigation.

Milingo, who now lived in Rome in an apartment owned by the Vatican, had been accused of witchcraft by his fellow bishops in Zambia, where he had been head of the hierarchy since 1969. He was summoned to see the Pope in 1982 and allegedly confined in the Augustinian monastery close to the Vatican City, where he was obliged to undergo various inquisitions and psychological tests. Despite these humiliations he remained loyal to the Church and his priesthood. Relieved of his diocese he had been given a job at the Vatican Commission for Tourism and Immigrants, which he used as a base to continue his controversial mission involving the casting out of devils and the castigation of Freemasons.

Assuming that it would be difficult to approach him through official channels I called my friend David Willey, the BBC's correspondent in Rome, and he provided me with the archbishop's home address and directions.

His Grace's apartment was situated in a palazzo immediately opposite the Porta Sant' Anna, the entrance to the business sector of the Vatican City. Without an appointment I set off to attempt to meet the archbishop one afternoon in mid-siesta when most prelates could be expected to be at home.

Inside the lobby of his apartment there was a queue of

young black men and women sitting as if in a doctor's surgery. There was an impression of lassitude, of deep resignation.

A door opened and a girl in African costume emerged carrying a plate of fried sausages and bacon; she disappeared through another door further down the corridor. Distantly I could hear the sound of a ranting, high-pitched voice through closed doors.

Another girl appeared wearing the same costume; seeing that I had nowhere to sit she ushered me into a spacious parlour with comfortable modern sofas and armchairs. On the walls were various African artefacts: leopard-skin shields, clubs, sticks with hairy mops; they were hung alongside pictures of the Pope, the Sacred Heart, the Madonna and Child. A straw fetish shared the sideboard with a plastic statue of the Virgin Mary. Beautiful black girls came and went. One of them put a plate of steaming vegetables on the table and left it there to get cold.

I waited for an hour. The hour stretched to two. Outside I could hear the people in the corridor chatting as if they belonged out there permanently. At last I fell asleep.

I woke to the sight of a wide black glistening face peering down at me. There was a flash of purple, a gleam of gold and amethyst. It was Archbishop Emanuel Milingo.

'Have you an appointment?' he cried in a high-pitched, strangulated voice.

'Of course,' I lied.

I saw that he held in his hand a copy of the Jerusalem edition of the Bible.

'Who are you? British? British royalty?' He laughed shrilly. 'I have no time.'

He seemed about to withdraw when I said, 'I came to ask you about Satan, your Grace.'

The archbishop pulled forward an easy chair and sat down

so close to me that he was practically in my lap. He gave off a heady stench of incense and musk. Holding me by the arm he cried out, 'O Holy Michael Archangel, defend us in the day of battle! Be our safeguard against the wickedness and snares of the Devil!' As he spoke his lips seemed to explode with energy, showering me with a not-so-fine rain of spittle.

'That prayer,' he now whispered huskily, 'was written by the good Pope Leo XIII, one hundred years ago. He promulgated that it should be read in all churches throughout the world at the end of every Mass. And why? In the year 1890 Christ Our Saviour appeared to Pope Leo and told him that he had given Satan to the world for exactly one hundred years.' The story was, I reflected, the same as that propounded by the monk with the goatee beard at Medjugorje.

The archbishop's eyes stretched wide. 'We are now in the last days of Satan's reign, and he is working overtime through his agents to complete the takeover of the world. His agents are nothing less than the Freemasons who have penetrated to the very heart of Christ's Church. It is the task of the Freemasons to lull Christians, especially priests, into believing that the Devil and his demons don't exist. Satan plays with priests like toys when they don't believe in him.

'After the last war bright young Freemasons were placed in seminaries around the world. These agents of Satan were waiting for their time to come. That time was the Second Vatican Council. Many of these brilliant men were by now the leading experts who advised the Council Fathers. And what did they do? They had the rite of exorcism taken out of the sacrament of baptism; they eliminated exorcist from the orders leading to the priesthood; they banned the prayer to Michael the Archangel; they took the Devil out of the Catechism. They left Christ's Church defenceless against the wiles of the Devil. Above all they succeeded in making Christians think that *the*

Devil does not exist! The Freemason Antichrists became priests for this purpose. They aim to take religious power throughout the world, just as they have taken economic and political power.' The archbishop was crying out in an incantatory, piping voice, his lips blowing out the words with an explosion of musky breath and saliva.

I interrupted him to say, 'Archbishop, are people influenced or possessed by Satan himself, or by numbers of devils?'

'By both! I have delivered a young girl of twenty-five devils, including Satan himself!' he bellowed. 'Twenty-five! The hospital could do nothing for her. So they brought her to me, this sixteen-year-old girl. Her body was as stiff and dry as a stick and she could not talk. I called the parents and some relatives and we gathered around her. Her mother began to speak to the spirits. It was terrifying! The spirit-voice came out of the girl, a different voice from the girl's. Her body was frozen, no evidence of blood circulation. The voice said, "Go and bring her elder sister, then we shall discuss matters." This sister was eighty miles away, and so we summoned her.

'The background to this case was that both these sisters had decided to become nuns. The spirits were revenging themselves on both girls by disturbing them. When the other sister arrived we discovered all this. Then I exorcised her; but as the spirits left they said that they would wait for her at home and re-enter her; and this is precisely what happened on several occasions. Sometimes she fell at the door of her parents' home just as she was about to go into the house. These were very difficult devils. I tried everything. I even left her all night in the church before the exposed Blessed Sacrament. I felt that my powers had been exhausted.

'One day in the chapel I managed to speak to the spirits and by the authority of Christ Our Lord I ordered them to answer the questions: How many are you? What are your names?

Why do you not obey the Lord? They answered that there were now only three remaining: Satan; the grandmother, or an evil spirit taking the name of the grandmother; and a nameless spirit.

'Satan then told us that the girl was a pledge. The spirits had healed her mother of a mysterious illness. In her misery she took an oath that if Satan healed her she would give him her daughter for seven years. Satan said that it would not be possible for them to leave her for another five years. But we used the authority of the Lord to destroy this pact, and the girl was healed.'

'People say that you are practising witchcraft,' I said. 'Is there any truth in this?'

'Why do they say that I am making false doctrines? I do nothing but teach by the Scriptures. Christ spent his entire mission casting out devils. And now they say that the Devil doesn't exist!

'Why – don't – they – read – the – Scriptures? Read St Paul to the Ephesians – "Put on the full armour of God so as to be able to resist the devil's tactics. For it is not against human enemies that we have to struggle, but against the principalities and the ruling forces who are masters of the darkness in this world, the spirits of evil in the heavens."

'Then St Peter: "Keep sober and alert, because your enemy the Devil is on the prowl like a roaring lion, looking for someone to devour . . ." The Devil plays with the unguarded like toys! Remember Acts 19, the seven sons of Sceva, the Jewish exorcists. The evil spirit said: "Jesus I recognize, and Paul I know, but who are you?" and the man with the evil spirit hurled himself at them and overpowered first one and then another, and handled them so violently that they fled from that house stripped of clothing and badly mauled.

'Read Apocalypse 12, about Our Blessed Lady and the

Dragon, and the war that broke out in heaven and how Michael with his angels attacked the dragon, and the dragon fought back with his angels, but they were defeated and driven out of heaven. It is for this reason that when the Devil was disappointed he came to the earth to fight the generations of Jesus and he tortures and destroys them.

'Now Satanism is at its strongest throughout the world. These are the years of the Devil. Black Masses, and blaspheming God, and Judas priests. Before he died Pope Paul VI knew what he had done. He knew it! He had let Satan free within the Church. He said he could smell the stench of smoke around the sanctuary. He said the truth!

'I was in Holland two weeks ago!' The archbishop was now shouting and spitting again. 'I was praying in Amsterdam from seven in the morning to half-past two, and the priests were falling like corpses before me. The Devil congratulated me for calling him a liar. A witch came to me and said, "How dare you!" I received a letter from the Devil telling me that I should never dare to speak to the demons like that. It said the devils are more powerful than me and they'll be watching for their chance. But this isn't true, you see.'

As the archbishop continued to rant in my face I suddenly felt myself coming over faint. I was terrified to the core. I felt as if I were losing control, that I was somehow ready to surrender myself to this chanting, ranting prelate. I rose and started backing out of the room, and he followed, still ranting and banging his well-thumbed Bible.

'Come to my service! Come to my service! At the Ergiffe Hotel, out on the by-pass.'

I stumbled out of the front door and, abandoning the idea of waiting for the lift, leapt down the marble staircase three steps at a time, still pursued by his strange smells and echoing incantations. 'Come to my service . . .'

46   Evelyn Waugh's Demons

A rchbishop Milingo's 'service', I gathered on inquiry, was nothing less than a session of exorcism conducted in the conference hall of a hotel on the Rome autostrada. I had every intention of attending this spectacle at the next opportunity, although I felt that I was in need of some preparation by discussion and reading.

That very evening I was to receive some unexpected guidance. I had arranged to have ᵈ nner in a restaurant on the Campo de Fiori with a Jesuit historian, Father Philip Caraman, who was doing research in Rome for a new biography of Ignatius Loyola. In his time Father Caraman had been the personal confessor of a circle of famous literary figures in England, including Graham Greene, Evelyn Waugh and Edith Sitwell, and had been much in demand for more than half a century as a wise and scholarly spiritual director. At almost eighty Father Caraman was the very picture of the Jesuit of mythology. Emaciated, with skin like ancient parchment, his dark, intelligent eyes scrutinized me through heavy horn-rimmed spectacles.

After listening to my story about Milingo, he began to snuffle and heave his shoulders with hilarity.

'One has to be extremely cautious,' he said eventually. 'Evelyn Waugh once thought he was possessed by demons and asked me to exorcise him.' Toying with his wine glass, Father Caraman leaned back and launched into his story.

In January 1954 Evelyn Waugh had travelled alone by ship to Ceylon. He was attempting to throw off a bout of depressive illness. In the course of the voyage he was disturbed by the sound of voices which he thought at first to be the result of defective ventilation pipes in the vessel. Eventually he became convinced that the entire crew and passengers were plotting against him. He believed that someone on board had been murdered and buried at sea; he tried to send radiograms back to England, but he discovered evidence, so he thought, that these messages were being distributed among the passengers. The voices in his cabin plagued him by day and by night and he suspected that the BBC was somehow involved in the plot. In a letter home from Cairo he described the plotters as a party of 'existentialists' who were practising a form of long-range telepathy to persecute him.

As soon as he reached Colombo Waugh took a plane back to England and on arriving in London installed himself at the Hyde Park Hotel and sent for his wife, Laura.

Father Caraman, who was living at Farm Street at that time, was invited to join the Waughs for dinner at the hotel. Laura met him in the lobby and hustled him straight into the dining room. Waugh leant across the table and said, 'I have invited you to dinner here this evening, Father, because it is imperative that you exorcise me! I am possessed by devils, and they are telling me that you have the priestly power to put them to flight.'

'I thought this was one of Evelyn's elaborate practical jokes,' went on Father Caraman, 'but he so persisted with his demands for exorcism that I began to wonder whether he was not in earnest. He left the table for a few minutes to go to the lavatory, and only then did I gather from Laura how serious matters were. When Evelyn came back I told him that I had no objection to exorcising his presumed demons, but that I would like first as a matter of precaution to get a doctor to take a look at him. I had a friend called Dr Eric Strauss who was one of the top psychiatrists of the day and a specialist at the Maudsley Hospital. He was also a Catholic and certainly would not have dismissed out of hand the notion of demonic possession. I called him straightaway and found him at his flat in Wimpole Street.

'Dr Strauss joined us by the time we had withdrawn for coffee and he immediately asked Evelyn some very direct questions, avoiding all but purely medical matters. Evelyn answered in a very humble, child-like manner. When Strauss asked for details of his medication, Evelyn described his habitual sleeping-draught, which was a potent cocktail of alcohol and barbiturates.

'At length Strauss got out a pad and pen and said, "Instead of taking your usual draught tonight I want you take a dose of something else to help you sleep. Perhaps Mrs Waugh could fetch it from the all-night chemist at Piccadilly Circus."

'As things turned out Strauss had pinpointed the problem, which was alcohol and barbiturate poisoning. I later discovered that Evelyn's voices had disappeared by the following morning. There was no more mention of demons or exorcism.' For the rest of his life Waugh apparently remained free of persecutory voices.

It was on Dr Strauss's suggestion, according to Father Caraman, that Waugh eventually recorded his experiences in *The Ordeal of Gilbert Pinfold*, but all references to demons and exorcism were entirely expunged in the novel.

In the conversation that followed Father Caraman seemed to be of the opinion that in the ancient world possession by demons was a common description of a very wide range of illnesses. Hence the emphasis on exorcism in the New Testament. While not ruling out entirely the idea of possession, it was important to approach the question, both in Scripture and in subsequent times, with great caution.

'Discernment is enormously important,' he went on, 'not only in the matter of ascertaining the presence of supernatural phenomena, but in attempting to distinguish whether these derive from the good or the bad.'

St Ignatius, he said, had been prone to voices, ecstasies and revelations, but was convinced that such promptings could as well come from his own imagination as from God or indeed the Devil.

'Ignatius insisted that the grace of discernment is aided by man's activity, especially his prudence and learning,' said Father Caraman. 'You should read Ignatius on the "Rules for the Discernment of Spirits", which you'll find set out in his *Spiritual Exercises*.'

Back in the English College that evening I found a copy of the *Exercises* in the library. This famous treatise, which I had not dipped into since my youth, is the key to the spiritual life of all Jesuits; it is short, dry and formulaic, not unlike a military drill book. The spiritual life is seen as a battleground, in which one is called to follow either the standard of Christ or the standard of Satan. For all its brevity and slavish adherence to categorizing, the *Exercises* can become an imaginative stimulus in the hands of a skilled spiritual director or preacher:

'Smell the indescribable fragrance, and taste the boundless sweetness of the divinity . . . Touch by kissing and clinging to the places where those persons walk or sit . . . Hear in the imagination the shrieks and groans and the blasphemous shouts . . . smell in the imagination the fumes of sulphur and stench of filth . . .'

Ignatius's imagination, during prayer and while saying Mass, frequently ran riot. He saw demons as black dogs and glittering snakes' eyes, the Trinity as a burning ball of fire, the Godhead as a powerful flash of lightning, the Virgin Mary as a lady bathed in white light. There were voices and lights and heavenly music. He often found it difficult to distinguish the products of his imagination from supernatural encounters, and he was further assailed by scruples as to possible supernatural origins: were they from God, or from the Devil?

Ignatius's method of discrimination set out in the chapter entitled 'Rules for the Discernment of Spirits' proceeds from an obvious distinction between 'spiritual consolation' and 'spiritual desolation'. It is a development of the idea – 'by their fruits you shall know them'. Good spirits fill us with tranquillity and peace and happiness; bad spirits leave us ultimately disturbed, agitated and unhappy. The problem is, however, that the evil spirit may begin by appearing in the guise of a good spirit. 'It belongs to the bad angel,' says Ignatius, 'transfiguring himself into an angel of light, to enter with the devout soul, and to come out his own way; that is to say, to begin by inspiring good and holy thoughts in conformity with dispositions of the just soul, and afterwards gradually to endeavour to gain his end, by drawing the soul into his secret snares and perverse intentions.'

The evil spirit is like a 'military chief' who examines the 'citadel' for its weak points; he is like a 'false lover' who wishes to hide his true desires from a woman's 'honest father' or 'honest husband'. Less flattering to women, Ignatius likens the evil spirit to a 'woman, inasmuch as he is weak in spite of himself, but strong in will; for as it is in the nature of a woman, quarrelling with a man, to lose courage and to take to flight when he shows himself undaunted ... If the man begin to take flight and to lose courage, the rage, the spite and the ferocity of the woman become very great, and altogether without bounds.'

It is clear that for long periods of his life Ignatius longed to find incontestable evidence of the supernatural, and was at pains to develop a system of verification. Leafing through J. C. Aveling's excellent study *The Jesuits*, I learnt that Ignatius was so desperate at times to establish direct communication with the supernatural that he even tried to test whether God was contacting him by a code. At one time he carefully noted the passages in the Mass when he felt ineffable feelings coming on.

Yet I gathered that in his cooler moments Ignatius wondered whether many of his apparitions, voices and visitations might not be the result of illness, eye-strain or merely an overheated imagination. 'To the end,' wrote Aveling, 'he remained quite undecided whether his visions and sensations were a spiritual help or a hindrance.' Authentic or otherwise, it appears that he granted that 'sensible' phenomena might be an aid to beginners in the spiritual life, but that 'progressives' should wean themselves from all interest in or encouragement of voices, visions and extraordinary feelings.

If Ignatius was, as Father Caraman had assured me, an expert in the matter of discernment of good and evil spirits it struck me that he had ended his life, nevertheless, little wiser than the rest of us.

47   Casting out Devils

I took a taxi to Archbishop Milingo's Mass at the Ergiffe Hotel on the Rome by-pass. I had already gathered from a Vatican contact that the archbishop was obliged to conduct his services in a hotel because he had been forbidden the use of any church in the diocese of Rome. It was not simply that the Pope did not approve of what went on at these services; Milingo could not find a single parish priest in a city of a thousand parish churches that would allow him to celebrate his unusual Mass.

The sun had set and the service had already started by the time I arrived. With some difficulty I pushed my way into the crowded hall, in order to observe the makeshift altar.

Milingo was dressed in a red silk vestment; there were six priests in white robes on either side of him. All seven celebrants were spreading their arms forward in a hieratic gesture, as if warding off evil. Many of the congregation had also adopted the same gesture.

It was an early stage in the Mass, he had not reached the Gospel, but the room, which held about 600 people, was already stifling and permeated by a heady, musky stench that I had noticed in Milingo's presence in his apartment. The secular atmosphere of the venue and the absence of all the familiar emblems and sacramentals of a Roman church lent an atmosphere of illegality and strangeness to the proceedings.

341

There was a preponderance of Italians in the congregation, most of them women; there were just a few black faces. The devotees looked for the most part like manual workers; many of the younger women were dressed in jeans; some of them had taken their shoes off. There was a mood of nervous tension, and people looked wild-eyed with expectation. It was as if each person were wondering whether the proceedings would evoke an evil spirit from the depths of his or her own soul.

Having met Milingo face to face I have to confess that I was wondering about myself. Not that I gave much credence to the belief in possession by demons; but I was convinced that Milingo had considerable powers, perhaps of hypnotism, and I wondered whether I should have enough strength to withstand his ability to evoke unwelcome, hysterical emotions.

The homily was short; Milingo spoke in rapid but poor Italian, his voice shrill, insistent. He spoke about Christ's healing ministry, about the demons of ill-health, about Christ casting out demons. There was more than a hint of paranoia in his drift: he spoke of his enemies; he ranted about the evils of the Church of the Spirits – although I was uncertain what this meant.

As the Mass resumed, I began to hear odd sounds here and there, not at all the sort of sounds one expected to hear in a congregation at Mass; now somebody would murmur, then there would be a whimper and a little cry. People looked petrified. Why, I asked myself, should people come to these proceedings in order to be scared out of their wits? Was it the same sort of thrill as that which attracted people to horror films like *The Omen*?

After the Communion, which was distributed speedily by the concelebrant priests on the altar, Milingo came forward with a holy-water stoup and sprinkler. The people were pressing forward. He told them that when they had been touched by the water some people would begin to tremble and cry out, but they were not to be afraid. At the very mention of the word fear – *paura* – the congregation seemed to stir with a renewed sense of terror. Then he began to sprinkle about him on all sides with the holy water.

The shock of the first series of shrieks was so awe-inspiring that it took me a few seconds to regain my breath. A young woman, just five yards from me, had gone into a paroxysm of screaming; her eyes had risen so that only the whites were visible, and she collapsed into the arms of those about her. The room had become hot and airless; I guessed the temperature might be as high as 100° Fahrenheit.

Milingo was being brought to the woman. He had his hands stretched out and he was praying in a strange tongue; the sweat was rolling from his face. But within a space of five or six seconds, shrieks were coming from several different parts of the room, and one or two people had passed out and fallen to the floor. The priests were praying on the altar, some of them with their eyes shut tight, others in a distracted, terror-stricken manner; members of the congregation were weeping and offering supplications in a babble of voices; Milingo was going from one screaming person to the next, talking rapidly and shrilly in a language that I could not understand; he seemed to be expending extraordinary energy.

Just when it appeared that the seizures and paroxysms had reached their height I saw a middle-aged woman go down, writhing and shaking in a quite obscene fashion. She seemed to be having an orgasm before our eyes. But even as I looked away a young man went down on the floor almost in front of me and began to paw and scrape the floor and bark and whine like a dog.

Meanwhile Milingo seemed to have had success with one of his exorcisms. A woman had got back to her feet and was looking about her sheepishly; her friends were clapping and cheering and praising God. Milingo was standing over each afflicted person one by one, and, as far as I could tell, he was entreating the demons to depart. From time to time he seemed to enter into a trance. One by one the demons were obliging.

I pushed my way to the doors of the conference hall and took a deep breath of fresh air. I had no desire to witness another moment of the session.

As I was driven back to Rome by taxi I noticed, as did the driver, that the whole of the interior of the vehicle was permeated with the strange musky stench that I had noticed in Milingo's apartment and in the conference hall. It was on my hands and in my clothes.

Milingo had frightened me once again, not so much with an impression of evil as with a threat of loss of control. I had a sense of foreboding, having witnessed the intrusion of pagan rites into the Mass. I was reminded of the discomfort I had experienced in my dream in Dubrovnik in which I had seen prelates cavorting in the sanctuary; and I reflected wryly that some sort of vestigial feeling for the integrity of the Church had survived in my nature.

At the same time, it reinforced my view that Milingo's cosmology of demons encouraged a dualistic, a fundamentalist, approach to the world. If every misfortune in life, from a lost purse to the measles, can be put down to the presence and activity of demons, there was little room for alternative interpretations of the world's ills. It also struck me that public exorcisms and sprinklings with holy water only served to strengthen the idea that fear and the powers of darkness hold the centre stage of life, rather than the love and mercy of God.

48   *The Exorcist*

On the evening of the following day I made my way to a Jesuit community house in Via dei Penitenzieri, to talk with an expert on the subject of exorcism and possession.

A scholarly-looking man with silver hair met me at the porter's lodge. He wished to remain anonymous, so I shall call him Father Stephen. He was dressed in black and I guessed that he was in his sixties. He looked highly intelligent and alert; but he moved slowly, as if in delicate health.

He led me upstairs to a spacious room, bleak and bereft of creature comforts. There was a desk near the windows, which had been thrown wide open to the raw autumnal evening air. There was a black crucifix on the wall and an icon of Our Lady of Pity. The only cheerful feature was a bookcase filled with scholarly editions. His breviary lay open on the table.

The priest was mild-mannered and quietly spoken. He asked me to sit down opposite him. He had agreed to answer my questions in a formal interview, but he warned me that he might not be able to talk about specific cases or persons.

He started by saying that there had been a renewed interest in possession and exorcism, partly as a result of a resurgence of Pentecostalism in the Churches. 'People are rediscovering the long neglected gifts of the Holy Spirit. They are fascinated by the idea of being able to exercise the charism of discernment of good and evil spirits; but most of them are out of their depth and they are hooked on the idea of the power that's involved.'

'But is Satan a reality, as a person?' I asked.

'Yes,' said the priest quietly. 'St Ignatius calls him "the enemy of human nature". Scripture presents him as a personal being, without a body, but with intelligence and freedom. But we mustn't make the mistake of thinking of him as someone capable of confronting God as an equal.'

'But don't the majority of Christians in the twentieth century play down the idea of Satan?' I said. 'People don't really believe in him any more than they believe in Santa Claus.' Even as I said it, I was conscious of being crass.

The priest was gazing patiently into his lap. 'It would be a great mistake to dismiss Satan,' he murmured. 'You should remember that Christ encountered him in the wilderness at the very beginning of his public life. We find it easy to accept the presence of evil in the world. We see it all around us. Evil phenomena are not entirely the work of Satan. There is the sense of natural evil we find everywhere in nature – genetic handicaps, cancer, droughts, earthquakes, pain – these are privations of good which are part of the mystery of God's creation. We recognize as Christians that nature is fallen, and we human beings have shared in that fall. But there is also the evil that is caused by deliberate acts of will, by individuals and groups of individuals. Satan was the first to establish injustice in creation, by his pride and disobedience, and we humans are similarly capable of evil by free and responsible acts of wickedness. Personal, responsible evil is an inward closing of our will against God, like a closed fist. It is saying no to God.'

'But do we ever sense Satan's presence? How do we tell whether Satan is actually present, in possession of a human being?' I asked.

The priest was leaning forward intently. He was silent for a few moments, as if trying to control my impatience.

'One tends to gather confidence in one's diagnosis in retrospect, where ritual has succeeded after medical means have failed.'

'Tell me about that,' I said.

'There is exorcism, of course, and then there is deliverance. In exorcism we address the Devil in person so as to force him to leave a situation or release a person who is in his power. Exorcism often involves a direct address of Satan or an evil spirit, and the exorcist may even attempt to encourage the Devil to reveal his identity. In the rite of deliverance on the other hand we call upon Christ or God to order the Devil to depart. Deliverance is much more common; and although the presence of a priest is not necessarily required, it is better that it should be done with the knowledge of the local bishop and in the presence of a priest. Exorcism is very rare indeed, and ideally should involve two exorcists working together at the specific request of the bishop. There are certain dangers for exorcists.' As if by way of an afterthought he added: '. . . and also for those who are engaged in deliverance.'

'Is there a danger that an exorcist can become possessed himself?'

The priest smiled. 'You don't catch the Devil in the same way as you catch flu,' he said. 'Possession is a state of affairs that develops in stages, and a person's will is involved. The possessed person has invited the evil spirit in. You have to distinguish between temptation, which can amount to an obsession with demonic interference, and demonic oppression, which often comes in the form of dreams. In both these latter cases a person should still be capable of praying on his own behalf for deliverance. But possession is different; this state is brought about by that person's deliberate courting of the powers of darkness, and the common circumstance in which this happens is membership of or contact with Satanist groups.'

'Can you describe, Father, some of the common characteristics of possession?'

'I have to repeat the reservations I made earlier,' he said evenly. 'Any of the symptoms of oppression or possession may just as well be the result of psychosis, depression or auto-suggestion, but the symptoms are cumulative. They would include a hatred of the sacred – including holy objects, or reading matter, prayers and even the mere presence of Christians. Constant fear, paranoia, restlessness, lying, foul language and obscene and murderous thoughts. Possessed people often give way to cursing, violence, unbridled lust. They cannot go into church without vomiting and laughing and jeering out loud. They are prone to frightening grimaces, cramps and wasting of the body; raving, screaming, unnatural voices, the speaking of unknown languages, the display of incredible strength and rage in the presence of an exorcist; clairvoyance, psychic and poltergeist activity in the immediate vicinity; visions of abhorrent and threatening figures. When all these things come together in a unique circumstance, and when medical help has repeatedly failed, we would be advised to consider deliverance, and then exorcism.'

'From what you say, Father, the practice of Satanism is to be taken seriously.'

'It's a bit like drugs,' said the priest. 'You start by experimenting, and in the end it controls you.'

'Do you think,' I asked, 'that Archbishop Milingo is dabbling with powers that are dangerous?'

'I can't comment on an individual case,' said the priest abruptly, 'but I can say this: I've witnessed the archbishop dealing successfully with a very difficult case of presumed possession. And now we really must end this conversation.'

Before I left the priest handed me a prayer-card. 'Keep this by you,' he said. 'It's known as the breastplate of St Patrick.'

The Exorcist

As I stood to go, he took me by the forearms and to my astonishment began to recite the prayer over me. As he did so my blood ran cold:

> *Christ be with me, Christ within me,*
> *Christ behind me, Christ before me,*
> *Christ beside me, Christ to win me,*
> *Christ to comfort and restore me.*
> *Christ beneath me, Christ above me,*
> *Christ in quiet, Christ in danger,*
> *Christ in hearts of all that love me,*
> *Christ in mouth of friend and stranger.*

49   Satanism and the New Age

Before leaving Rome I had arranged to meet with a young man back in London who had suffered from oppression, and had been helped and rehabilitated by deliverance prayers.

Before this encounter, and on my arrival in England, I took the opportunity of reviewing a quantity of research material I had gathered on the vexed subject of modern Satanic cults. Rumours of Satanic activity seemed to be proliferating throughout the United States, Britain and many parts of western Europe, and yet there were disputes over the exact nature of the abuses that were involved. Allegations by social workers that Satanists used young girls as 'brood mares' to acquire foetuses for ritual sacrifice, and that children had been sexually abused and even murdered, were being challenged both by the police and by the press in a number of countries. What was the nature and the extent of this spread of Satanism? Was it merely an excuse for deviant sex? Or did it contain a sinister demonic content? And what did that mean?

The current rise in Satanism appears to have developed on the periphery of the hippie, flower-power movements of the late sixties and early seventies. Mind-expanding drug usage, the free-love ethic, the quest for alternative lifestyles, extensively promoted in the popular music culture, preceded a significant shift towards experience-based pseudo-religion and intuitive philosophies of life. There was a renewed interest in

Eastern religions, spiritualism and guru-centred cults, accompanied by a rediscovery of the occult, witchcraft, astrology, 'channeling' and voodoo. Everything and anything – including the darker regions of belief – seemed to provide a possible idea or theme in the quest for do-it-yourself rituals and alternative religions. And the quest, like the promotion and commerce of popular music, was marked by an ethos of consumer choice; people were shopping around, procuring and discarding their latest cult fads, just like any other commodity in the pop-culture.

By the mid-seventies these proliferating expressions of religious counter-culture were increasingly associated with the loose alliance of spiritual quests known as New Ageism. New Ageism is a focus for the view that human beings are approaching another stage of evolution by discovering alternative powers within themselves, within the planet and cosmos. New Ageism seeks to heal the perceived social malaise of modern life, the drastic effects of Western civilization, by promoting a rebirth into a new stage of power, consciousness and control over one's destiny.

New Ageists believe that the planet Earth moves through the zodiac every 26,000 years; our entry into Aquarius, the New Age, started in the 1960s. Humanity is returning to nature, and we have the opportunity to become autonomous individuals in a decentralized society, stewards of our own resources and heirs to riches and powers far beyond our present state. In the coming civilization we shall inherit beauty, love, creativity beyond our wildest dreams, provided that we can learn to stand firmly centred between the Earthly Mother and the Heavenly Father. Meditation is crucial; our prayers are answered by the celestial figures, the teaching presences of the universe, as well by God – the total living force of the universe.

A central concept of the movement is holism, the notion that mind, body and spirit, all the systems of the planet and cosmos, must be seen as a whole, seen in terms of multi-relationships. In this sense the insights and efficacies of Eastern philosophies, alternative technologies and healing arts, are deemed superior to most reductionist Western science and medicine.

Dogma is frowned upon. The movement finds room within its ambit for such diverse convictions as belief in UFOs, visitors from outer space, Gaia science, astrological speculations and ESP. Healers, prophets and seers abound, as do their methods of operation, which range from immersion in rebirth capsules to the application of crystals: one directory that came into my hands listed no less than 4,000 resident healers in Britain alone. And the myriad movements incorporate and overlap with enthusiasm for ecology, self-sufficiency, herbalism, vegetarianism and the quaffing of distilled water.

The New Ageists regard Christ as merely another 'evolved master', along with Krishna, Muhammad, Buddha and other gurus and major and minor prophets of the various world religions. Moreover, by the discovery of the divine spark within us, we can ourselves become prophets, or create our own gods and goddesses. In this general drift, Christianity has not been condemned as such, but relativized as one of many means to achieve the promise of a wholly new approach to spiritual consciousness and practice. Some New Ageists have forged alliances between their overall philosophy and traditional faith; thus the North American witch, known as Starhawk, has been experimenting in Spiral Dances with the Dominican priest Father Matthew Fox. Fox expounds the importance of ancient earth spirituality, which he would like to incorporate into Creation spirituality liturgy. At the same time, some feminist groups have found philosophical and ritualistic sustenance in a re-examination of ancient Mother God religions and benign witchcraft.

Against this background of widespread fragmentation of mainline religious systems, the appearance of Satanic cultism is hardly surprising. The ethos of choice and privatization, the tendency to dabble and experiment, naturally led to a peripheral interest in the darker side of the spectrum of spiritual possibilities. The quest for a means to control the powers of light naturally found a corresponding tendency in the opposite direction. The quest for wholeness, peace, beauty, sensitivity, joy has found a corresponding, if minority, desire to celebrate evil, violence, ugliness, coarseness and hatred. The splintering of religious authority, the process of voluntarism, relativism and pluralism-run-riot, made it inevitable that Satan would be on offer in the supermarket of cultic options. Groups have tended to flourish and die away with the bewildering and prolific rapidity of childhood games, making it difficult to study the phenomenon with any degree of accuracy or detail.

In many cases the experiments have been no more (or less) harmful than the effect of films such as *Rosemary's Baby*, *The Exorcist*, *The Omen*, the novels of Dennis Wheatley, or student Hallowe'en japes. Overt expressions of Satanism in the late sixties and early seventies seemed in most cases as frivolous as they were ephemeral. A Church of Satan was founded on the west coast of America by one Anton Szandor LaVey in 1966, which was to spawn in turn a splinter group known as the Temple of Seth. These sects studied and disseminated a so-called Satanic Bible, an anthology of occult mumbo-jumbo and permissive platitudes. LaVey and his followers proclaimed the cult of the ancient Egyptian god Seth, associated with creative and sexual freedom. Satan, the devotees insisted, was a much maligned, much misunderstood spiritual entity.

Yet during this same period there was at least a hint of

more sinister influences at work. Charles Manson's millennialistic 'family' cult, which culminated in a series of multiple killings, including Sharon Tate, in 1969, was influenced by a local neo-Nazi Satanic organizition known as the Ordo Temple. Many of the characteristics of charismatic cults were discovered in Manson's relationships with his devotees as inversions of traditional norms of spiritual values. Self-sacrifice, obedience, austerity, discipline, surrender to a higher power, the rejection of 'negative feedback' of society, parents and prevailing culture, culminated not in spiritual growth but in hatred, violence, paranoia, destruction and murder. The Manson killings, the Moors Murders in England, the fifteen serial killings committed by Dennis Nilsen in London between 1979 and 1983, the mass suicides of nearly 1,000 devotees at 'Jonestown' in Guyana, were stark reminders of the dark potential of do-it-yourself ritualism in a permissive society.

But does this add up to a thriving, dangerous, worldwide system of Satanic abuse? One of the principal problems of assessing the nature and the danger of criminal Satanic practice is the absence of firm evidence of the sort that would get through a court of law. The Christian Exorcism Study Group based in the Marylebone Road in London has built up a composite picture of occultism and Satanism in Britain and other parts of the world. Whenever priests or parish workers are alerted to Satanic practices in the locality, they are asked to provide the study group with details.

Recruitment, they say, often begins at university, and even at school, among the sexually deviant, the lonely and those with a propensity or fascination for the weird, the terrifying and the gothic. The softer occult-interest groups, like palmistry, tantric yoga and astrology, are also targets for recruitment, as are covens for white witchcraft. Drug pushers gravitate towards Satanic groups because of the obvious opportunities they afford. Secrecy is of the essence and the path from early introduction to full initiation into the hardcore practices is apparently conducted with elaborate caution. If some of the practices are indeed abhorrent and involve drugs, paedophilia and techniques of mind-manipulation, it is not surprising that Satanist ringleaders wish to keep their activities secret. Initiation ceremonies are said to be sexually compromising, and can lead to blackmail when members attempt to leave a group.

Yet what is it that these various independent groups believe in common? According to the Christian Exorcism Study Group, Satanists hold that the Creator God has withdrawn from his world and does not intervene in its affairs. Satan is the true Son of God and is locked in a struggle with Christ for control of the world; the outcome of the contest is uncertain.

Satan has his sacred days when Sirius is behind the sun, when it rises or sets, reaches its highest point in the sky or is at its lowest declination under the horizon. Sirius is thus the 'sun behind the sun', which is deemed to be one of the great 'mysteries' of Satan's power. These astrological motions correspond with Satanic feast days, which occur on the eves of some of the most important Christian feasts: Imbolc, Beltan (Walpurgis night), 1 August and Samhain are the eves of the Christian feasts of Candlemas, St Philip and St James, Lammas and Hallowmass (All Saints). Beltane and Samhain are usually occasions for the celebration of Black Masses.

My own research, derived from sources in Britain, Holland, Italy and the United States, indicated that many Satanist groups are principally fascinated with blasphemy and sacrilege for its own sake. And it is for this reason that the alleged rites are based on an inversion of Christian prayer and liturgy, and a deliberate distortion of Christian beliefs. Stimulus for ideas for ritual, which are constantly revised, is derived from sources such as the *Malleus Maleficarum*, the seventeenth-century Inquisitional handbook by the Dominican Fathers, Kramer and Sprenger, and the *Compendium Maleficarum* by Francesco Maria Guazzo. Repeated translations and reprintings of such books have ensured the continued spread of interest in, and experimentation with, ideas and rituals that are described in their pages. Descriptions of the supposed beliefs and practices of seventeenth-century witches thus find their echoes in alleged reports of the more excessive current Satanic rituals. In the *Compendium*, for example, in a chapter entitled 'A Summary in a Few Words of All the Crimes of Witches', we find the following indictment passed in Avignon in 1582 against accused witches:

> You did swear homage and obedience to his [Satan's] behests upon a circle (the symbol of Divinity) traced upon the earth (which is God's footstool); and each of you bound herself to tread under foot the Image of the Lord and the Cross ... You did kindle a foul fire and after many rejoicings, dancings, eating and drinking, and lewd games in honour of your president Beelzebub the Prince of Devils in the shape and appearance of a deformed goat, you did worship him in deed and word as very God and did approach him on bended knees as suppliants and offered him lighted candles of pitch; and (fie for shame!) with greatest reverence you did kiss with sacrilegious mouth his most foul and beastly posterior; and did call upon him under the name of the true God and invoke his help; and did beg him to avenge you upon all who had offended you or denied your requests; and, taught by him, you did wreak your spite in spells and charms against both men and beasts, and did murder many new-born children ... and your own children, many

of them with your own knowledge and consent, you did with those magic spells suffocate, pierce, and kill, and finally you dug them up secretly by night from the cemetery ... And most hateful of all, at the bidding of the aforesaid Serpent thrust from Paradise, you did keep in your mouths the most Holy Sacrament of the Eucharist received by you in the sacred Church of God, and did execrably spit it out.

The details are familiar, but to what extent are the modern variants fact or fantasy? In a prominent case of child abuse this century, more than a hundred children from sixty-three families were alleged to have been subjected to sadistic sexual abuse associated with Satanic ritual at Pekela in Holland in 1987. The events came to light when a local doctor examined a four-year-old boy suffering from anal bleeding without apparent cause. Further investigation led to allegations that a wide circle of Satanic ritual had routinely involved children in horrifying sexual abuse. The doctor, Frederich Jonker, said: 'The children spoke of being in church, of having to lie down on a table naked ... They also mentioned the presence of babies ... of them being "strapped up in candles", of having to cut the babies loose, and of having to cut crosses in their backs. There was also a baby put in a plastic bag. They spoke of a black baby which they were forced to hit with sticks, but they told us that this wasn't bad because black babies don't have hearts or blood anyway. We asked them, "Was the black baby a doll then?" The children told us that dolls don't cry or crawl.' According to Jonker the children were obliged to kill animals with shovels and forced to watch the 'execution' of a cat with a chain-saw.

The police conducted a year-long investigation in Pekela, and there was a number of arrests, but due to lack of hard evidence there were no convictions. The press in Holland eventually dismissed the allegations as mass hysteria; yet stories of a similiar nature have continued to come in from various parts of the world. Organizations in London such as the National Society for the Prevention of Cruelty to Children, the National Children's Home, Childline and Male Survivors' Training Unit have all reported recent case-histories of child abuse linked with Satanic ritual in various parts of Britain and especially in the north-east and the East Midlands: eight-year-olds involved in the killing of babies; the use of girls as 'brood mares'; boys being abused in the anal passage with live snakes; buggery and abuse with crucifixes and animals; children being subjected to drug abuse. Yet despite extensive police investigations no conclusive evidence has been produced to bring charges, and academic and media sceptics continue to associate the accusations with a lack of objectivity and the tendency to seek confirmation of a prejudice rather than the truth.

The tension between the sceptics and the convinced is all the more intriguing in the light of historical research in the 1970s into the witch hunts of the seventeenth century. Norman Cohn's *Europe's Inner Demons* (1975) conclusively demonstrated that witchcraft and Satanism existed purely in the minds of the inquisitors who were seeking it out. He claims that he has not found a single case of alleged witchcraft or sorcery in which the documents are not tainted. The so-called witnesses were the victims of the fanciful projections of Church officials. And beneath the urge to engage in mass witch-hunts Cohn speculates that the phenemonon of Satanism was 'seen as an incarnation of apostasy, a living proof of the power wielded by the Devil in his battle against the Christian God': the collective obsession with witches, he suggests, arose out of a need for scapegoats on the part of those who had an unconscious urge to apostasize during a period of widespread scepticism in Europe.

Do modern social workers represent a priestly ethos of unproven Freudian, Kleinian and other hypothetical beliefs, increasingly under attack by officialdom that seeks forensic verification as the acid test of propositions about human behaviour? Is child abuse, and now child abuse with Satanic associations, a projected collective fantasy? A new witch hunt?

For my own part, I was inclined to remember the life and example of the seventeenth-century Jesuit, Father Friederich von Spee. In 1627 the Bishop of Würzburg appointed Spee as confessor to those condemned to the stake during a period when tens of thousands were dying as a result of the witch trials. Spee attempted to console more than 260 victims of these pogroms; the majority of them were women, and many were girls aged under ten years. Sickened by all that he had seen and heard, Spee wrote a book, without leave from his superiors, which he published anonymously in Latin in 1631 as *Cautio Criminalis seu de Processibus contra Sagas Liber*. The book exposed the injustice, the false confessions, the brutal stupidity of trial by ordeal, the wickedness, the insanity of the witch-craze. It was the act of a brave man, certainly comparable to the courage of those isolated Germans who attempted to speak out about Nazi atrocities from the inside. He was, of course, dismissed, and he ended his days in exile writing mournful nature poetry.

But one of the great ironies of the *Cautio* is that despite its sanity and deep humanity nobody has bothered to translate it or to provide us with a scholarly modern edition of the work. In the meantime the bloodthirsty fantasies of the *Malleus Maleficarum* continue to go through countless reprintings in dozens of languages.

It seems that in our own times both social workers and charismatic Christians set much store by processes of 'discernment'. In the secular sphere the use of the much-discredited anal-dilation test has been claimed as an infallible symptom of child abuse. Charismatic Christians, meanwhile, are in the habit of diagnosing demonic possession when they encounter what they deem to be a horror of Christian symbols. But there is no guarantee that the discerners of this age are any more accurate than those of former ages, when the victims ended up roasting on a bonfire.

50 Oppressed

Philip Tudor lived in a cramped council flat high above the Elephant and Castle district of south London. He met me as I came out of the lift on the eleventh floor. He was, I guessed, in his mid-thirties, tall and broad in the shoulder. He wore his hair almost shoulder length at the back, but he was balding at the front, which gave his head a dome-like, intellectual appearance. He was dressed in black corduroys and a black sweater, and it was quite obvious that he was wearing make-up, which gave his long, oval face a pallid, effeminate look. He could have been an off-duty ballet-dancer.

He offered me some Scotch out of a quarter bottle and when I declined he poured himself a third of a tumbler and topped the glass up to the brim with water.

'I'm trying to get off this,' he said, 'but I prefer controlled drinking to complete abstinence; it's not very realistic – complete abstinence, I mean.'

There were several crucifixes on the walls, a holy-water stoup and a print of Millais' painting, *Christ the Light of the World.*

He sat opposite me in a battered armchair, leaning forward, glass in one hand, a smoking cigarette in the other. He was shaking slightly, as if he were cold.

'You've heard of phrases like "his hair stood on end",' he said, 'or, "he jumped out of his skin", or, my "blood froze". I can tell you that when you get mixed up with Satanism those phrases become a literal reality. But it's not what people think.

'Let me tell you the whole thing from the beginning . . . I'm going to be frank with you, and you're going to be shocked, but people have got understand what they have to be afraid of.' He paused a moment as if to gather his thoughts.

'Three years or so ago,' he began, 'I joined an amateur theatre group; I can't tell you where – it wasn't around here. I don't want any more hassle from them. The bloke that ran the thing, let's call him Michael H., was a very forceful type; people tended to get involved with him. He was bisexual and seemed to be able to pull blokes or girls just as it suited him. I admit that I was quite attracted to him myself. If you haven't guessed already, I'm gay.

'Michael H. had a strong presence and a very quick tongue. He made me feel inadequate – yet the more he put people down the more they got infatuated with him. He had terrific self-confidence, appeal. I'm not sure what his background was; he gave the impression he'd dropped out from something . . . medicine or law. He was well-educated; he knew a lot of people and he was on the fringes of the art world.

'We did some quite good things, a bit high-brow and gloomy – *Huis Clos*, *Dr Faustus*, *The Seagull*. I never got a part in a play, but we used to do improvisation sessions, method acting and so on, most weeks in the evenings. The improvisations used to get hairy; he liked to experiment with power situations, like when somebody's taken prisoner or made a victim. He wanted to bring latent aggression and fear out of people.

'I realized that he had an inner circle and it irritated me that I didn't belong to the favoured few. He would come and have a drink with some of us occasionally, as if he were doing us a favour, but he was always rather cool socially, and sort of knowing – as if he had you taped.

'Then one day, out of the blue, he rang me in a friendly way and asked if I'd like to take part in a sort of theatre workshop; he said it was hush-hush and involved some experimental work. "I think it might appeal to you," he said. I was flattered, and I agreed to go along; in fact I was fetched by car and driven with several other members of the group to a house somewhere in Byfleet.

'As soon as I arrived I guessed what was going to happen. There were twelve of us, including myself and Michael H. It was a large room at the back of the house and a table had been set up to look like an altar; we were asked to take our clothes off and put on long blue robes. At first I thought it was rather pathetic, a bit of a cliché, like Hellfire Club stuff, or *The Omen* or something. But when we got started I realized that the whole point of it was to give vent to a stream of blasphemy. The idea was to outdo each other . . . take it to the ultimate extreme.

'By upbringing I am Church of England, but I hadn't been to church for years and I wasn't particularly interested in religion. But somehow you retain a basic feeling of reverence for it. Michael H. told us that the point of the exercise was to release ourselves from the stranglehold of subconscious ties, to make ourselves free and thereby powerful.

'He would begin to recite a prayer – asking us to repeat it reverently with him; then he would suddenly say something obscene and make us repeat it. At one point two or three of the group started to giggle, but each time this happened he stopped and made us do it again. He kept saying, "Come on! Don't send it up! Don't send it up! Enter into it!"

'The next stage was the ritual. There was a chalice filled with wine on the altar and some Communion breads, and after saying reverent prayers like a priest he spat into the chalice and started cursing. Then somebody turned the light out so that there was only one candle, and everything started to degenerate.

'In the end there were people copulating, or at least they were going through the motions – like realistic improvising. Then one of them started masturbating for real and came all over the altar; people were making obscene gestures with the chalice and the crucifix, and Michael H. was urging everybody on with a stream of filth, getting everyone worked up. In the middle of all this he got one of the girls to lie on the altar and started fondling her, then he took one of the Communion breads and pushed it up her vagina, saying, "Fuck Christ! Fuck Christ!" It sounds pathetic, a bit comic, just to talk about now, but at the same time it started to make me feel really weird. I was taking pleasure in the blasphemy. But he still hadn't reached the really scary part.

'Towards the end he put his arm around me and looked into my eyes. He said to me, "How would you like to make a pact with the Devil, Philip?" Then he kept coaxing me to ask out loud for the Devil to take possession of me. He kept on and on and on; he wouldn't let me go. The others were all joining in. In the end I gave way, and said what he wanted me to say . . .' At this point Philip was pressing the whisky glass to his head; his shoulders were heaving slightly and the tears were rolling down his face.

'He said to me, "Philip, if you want to see the Devil, just look into the corner of the room." I was petrified, and I didn't want to look, but he just kept coaxing me, saying, "Come on, Philip, don't be frightened. He's over there and he wants you to look at him." All the others were standing round me and saying, "Come on, Philip, come on . . ." In the end I looked into the corner . . . and I saw this thing, I don't know how it got there, it looked as real as anything else in the room; it looked like a sort of monstrous filthy crow, it was as big as a man standing up, and the longer I looked at it the clearer it became. It was *horrendous*, its wings were covered in shit and slime, and when it opened its beak a huge bloody penis came out and it made this dreadful retching sound . . .

'I ended up in complete hysterics, screaming my head off. I don't know how it ended, or how I got home. I suppose they took me. Anyway, I eventually got to bed and fell asleep and I woke up at about four o'clock in a state of unbelievable terror. It's difficult to describe; it was as if from moment to moment I was about to be swallowed up in a sickening total abyss, annihilation. I was into a level of fear I'd never encountered before. I never thought such fear was possible. I felt as if the bird was at my shoulder. It was as if the ground kept disappearing from under me. Somehow we all take our security for granted, but once you've had the experience of losing it nothing is the same again. My mind seemed to be invaded by an endless stream of filth and obscenity and disgust that had nothing to do with my will-power. It was like being controlled. I was so frightened I thought I was going to have a heart attack. Then at about five in the morning the phone rang and it was Michael H. He just said to me one thing. He said, "Hallo, Philip, are you enjoying the feeling?" Then he started to laugh, and I could hear some other people laughing with him. Then he shouted, "Say hallo to Satan for me!" and slammed the phone down.

'The following days and weeks were a nightmare of purest hell. I felt as if my personality wasn't my own, I felt outside of myself in some way. My head was filled with involuntary obscene ideas like an echo chamber, and I had a constant battle with myself not to scream out obscenities in public. The strangest thing of all was that I couldn't stand the sight of a flower, or anything nice or beautiful, or the sound of pleasant music . . . And it seemed that whenever I was getting a bit of a grip on myself Michael H. would ring and it would start all over again. The frightening thing was that he seemed to know exactly what I was feeling; it was as if I were completely in his control and that he had a malignant power over me.

'I never went to the drama club again, and I stopped going to work. I went to the doctor, but somehow I couldn't tell him or anybody else the whole story, partly because I was frightened of Michael. The doctor gave me some pills, which didn't touch me, in fact they seemed to make things worse. When I wasn't thinking of vile ways in which I could kill people, especially little children, I was thinking of killing myself – all day long. I'd be walking along the street and all the time I'd be thinking, "I'll throw myself under the next bus!" It was a constant struggle not to actually do it.

'In the end I confided in a friend of mine, who told somebody else who was a keen member of a local church. It turned out to be the worst thing I could have done. This person came round one evening. She was a young woman with a really crazy look in her eye; she asked me lots of questions and I could see that she was getting more and more worked up. She kept saying, "Yes, I know ... yes, I know ... I know all about this ..." Then she went off saying that she'd be back later.

'When she returned she had about eight people with her including two really strong blokes. They charged into the apartment and took over the place, taking pictures off the wall and moving furniture. Next they put me down on the floor and started reciting prayers and chants and throwing water all over me. They kept shouting out, commanding the devil inside me to identify himself, and holding crucifixes in front of my face and slapping me. Eventually I started to struggle and they began pummelling and punching me and kicking me. When they left I was drenched to the skin and black-and-blue all over. But they didn't do the slightest bit of good.

'They came back quite a number of times and I was convinced for a time that I really was possessed, which only made matters worse.

'One night I was so restless that I couldn't stay in the house. I thought I'd go and throw myself under a train. I wandered all over south-east London looking for a bridge to throw myself from. You've got to laugh, I suppose ... There just weren't any trains running. I kept bumping into all these weird down-and-outs, winos and people sleeping rough; they're up all night these people, talking weird stuff. I walked with this old girl for about two hours and she didn't stop talking. And I kept thinking, "This is how I've ended up!"

'In the early morning she disappeared and I was by myself walking along a road. I was passing a church with the priest house next to it. The door of the house opened and a young priest came out and started walking across towards the church, I suppose he was going to say early-morning Mass or something. I just ran straight up to him and asked him to help me. It turned out to be the best thing that could have happened. He took me back into the house. He was a very gentle person; he sat me down and coaxed the story out of me.

'We must have sat together for two or three hours; I was in a terrible state, shaking and crying, and he just kept saying the Lord's Prayer over and over again, especially the part that goes "but deliver us from evil". He put a little silver chain with a cross around my neck and he took me to see a doctor, who gave me some sleeping pills.

'I saw a lot of the priest after that and he became a friend. He helped me to get grounded again, and to realize that I'd been under the psychological domination of Michael, not the Devil. I believe in the power of evil, I've experienced it and it's terrible; and I believe that I've been helped by Christianity, but I don't believe in demons and all that stuff. The sort of thing I experienced is much more frightening than any demon.'

I have only recorded here the barest outline of Philip Tudor's story. There were many other things he told me about the improvised ritual and his reactions to it that cannot be printed. When Philip had finished we shook hands and he extracted from me a promise that I would not divulge his real name.

As we said goodbye, he said, 'I'll never understand why they do it, that's one of the most frightening things, the sheer pointlessness of it. I was lucky to escape. The idea that they're doing this to children is appalling.'

As I reflected in the following days on Philip Tudor's story and the widespread rumours of Satanic child abuse it struck me that it would be tragic to rule out the possibility of such deadly activities for the simple reason that there was an absence of tangible evidence. How would Philip Tudor, an intelligent adult, have proved anything against his tormentors? His experiences were real, and yet there was nothing to show except his fear. And it appears to be the same with mounting numbers of children who have been subjected, by their own accounts, to extremes of Satanic terror. Nobody would want to argue that convictions should be brought on the evidence of the children's stories alone. Yet there is a danger in the chorus of scepticism and mockery aimed at these children and their social workers.

The predicament is somewhat analogous to the gulf that separates benign religious experience and normal criteria of empirical verification. Just as we find it difficult to measure holiness, the power of prayer or a sense of spiritual presence, so scientific, forensic evidence is largely useless when it comes to matters of psychological influence, mental cruelty, oppression and evil intent; absence of evidence does not mean that such things are not real, it simply means that it is difficult to nail the alleged culprits.

What convinced me, in the end, that these children and their social workers deserve careful consideration was the effect of my encounter with Philip Tudor. For several days I found myself haunted by his story, and strangely undermined in myself; I understood something of what he had felt; I empathized with his experience to the point of entering into it, and I was frightened. In consequence I felt compassion for both the child victims of these alleged attacks, and for those who are attempting to care for them – they, too, will have been more deeply affected than we can ever understand.

I also learnt the value, the importance, of being *grounded*, and something of the power of religious sacramentals and prayer in achieving this. Yet how was one to regard the efficacy of tangible Catholic sacramentals – crucifixes, holy water, holy medals – without slipping into the dangers of procurable, exploitable religion, the religion of fetishes and magic?

At the time that I met Philip Tudor I came across an intriguing letter in the *British Journal of Psychiatry* by Frances Marks and Ian Groves of the Department of Child Psychiatry at the London Hospital in Whitechapel. These doctors had made a study of Muslim Bangladeshi patients in East London, who believed themselves to be suffering forms of oppression as a result of sorcery. The mullahs recommended amulets containing verses from the Koran, to be worn round the neck or arm, or holy water, or holy mustard oil over which Koranic verses have been read. Not surprisingly, among Muslim Bangladeshis an indication of oppression, or possession, is a disinclination for learning or listening to the Koran.

Muslim fundamentalists may well overstep the bounds of

common sense and balance, just as Christian evangelical fundamentalists do; yet there is no reason to doubt that the use of Islamic sacramentals in conjunction with Western medicine brings definite psychological and spiritual benefits to such patients. There is no cause-and-effect magic power within any specific set of objects themselves; the power resides within the wider context of associations, and has to do with an acknowledgement of what they represent.

It is humbling for sophisticated sceptics to accept the effect of these small objects, normally dismissed as items of superstition. In the days that followed my meeting with Philip Tudor I shared something of what I believe he had suffered. One night as I lay in the small hours unable to sleep I was grateful for the presence of Briege's small Celtic cross on the bedside table.

51 Gift of Tears

I had brought my travels to an end, but I could point to no specific, objective phenomenon that demonstrated supernatural intervention that contravened the laws of nature, and I was convinced that if I were to journey 'ten thousand days and nights', till, like John Donne's rider, age snowed 'white hairs' on me, I should still bring back nothing in the way of proof.

The mystery of my dream persisted, and a sense of having been led; but this remained a private, subjective riddle, which continued to tantalize without promise of conclusion or meaning.

I tried to turn my mind to other things; to prepare myself for a return to journalism and publishing, but I was restless, hungry, in a way that I could not describe. I could not say that I had found God, nor that I had been encouraged to believe in him again; yet I had been making, for the first time in my life, some complex distinctions between religion's dark and benign faces; I had begun to cherish the grounding of religious belief. My regard for those who could believe and practise a non-judgemental respect had developed almost to the point of envy.

One day I found an echo of the peculiar quality of my mood while attending the funeral of a friend who had remained a loyal and pious Christian to the very end. At an early point in the service they sang a Psalm that I had not heard for thirty years:

> As a deer yearns
>   for running streams,
> so I yearn
>   for you, my God.
>
> I thirst for God,
>   the living God;
> when shall I go to see
>   the face of God?

I could not subscribe to the full meaning of the words and yet I experienced a consciousness of dependence, an acknowledgement of the existence of a creator on the horizon of my life and consciousness.

Not long after this I accepted an invitation to go to Dublin to see Briege McKenna once more. I flew to Ireland in a state of confusion.

On the evening of my arrival at All Hallows, Barbara, the retreat administrator, came to fetch me after supper and took me to Briege.

She was waiting in a ground-floor parlour at the back of the building. There were a dozen armchairs set in a circle, as if for a conference. She did not get up when I entered the room; she asked me to come and sit next to her.

She looked tired; there was a weary edge to her voice. She chatted amiably for a while, telling me about a recent trip to Nigeria. I could not take my eyes off the marked gap in her front teeth that gave her face a sort of street-urchin appearance when she smiled. I was wondering, once again (unworthy thought!), what she would do if she fell in love with one of her priests. But she unnerved me by suddenly stopping and looking at me curiously.

I said, almost without thinking, 'How do you get through life – loving Christ, a figment of history?'

Even as I said it, I hated the superficial question and I braced myself for a pious answer. I should, by now, have known her better. She merely laughed.

Then she said gently, 'The only way any of us are going to discover God's love in life is through the love of human beings. Christ's love comes through you and me as loving people.'

We were silent for a while; I was looking out towards the playing fields and the lines of horse-chestnut trees on the perimeter.

Suddenly she leaned forward and, before I could utter a word or resist, she took my hand and said, 'Just before we go, John, I'd like to say a prayer with you.'

To my embarrassment she immediately began to pray out loud, in short impromptu sentences, as if she were seeking guidance as she went along. I had seen evangelicals praying in this way on American television. There were occasional pauses for a breathless 'praise you Jesus . . . Praise you . . .' She was thanking God for the opportunity to talk with me, praising Jesus, asking for guidance and grace. I was seized with a mixture of outrage and curiosity. I wanted to tear my hand away and tell her to stop, but fascination kept me rooted to the chair. Every so often she paused again, as if inviting me to praise Jesus.

I could not. I would not.

She stopped suddenly. I stole a look at her face; her eyes were shut tight with concentration and her lips were pursed. She seemed to hold on to me tighter, with both hands. Then she said, 'I see an image, John. You are sitting in a chapel.

You are all by yourself, in complete solitude. On the chair next to you is a Bible. You pick it up and open on a certain page. I see that page open.'

I had heard this tone of voice before – the fortune-teller gazing into the palm of the credulous client. I wanted to giggle, and yet I was consumed with curiosity as to what she was going to say next.

Her eyes were still shut tight. Her concentration seemed immense, her face almost in pain. 'I can see the heading of the Book of Wisdom, Chapter Nine,' she said. 'I feel that the Lord has a special word for you in Wisdom, Chapter Nine.'

She was finished. She seemed to jump up out of her seat. She was smiling and pulling me to my feet as well. 'God bless you, John,' she said, 'and now let me kiss you.'

With this she gave me a tight hug and kissed me on both cheeks.

As I left her at the door, I said, 'Sister, what's in this Wisdom, Chapter Nine?'

'I've no idea,' she replied. 'I don't ever recollect reading it.'

A snack of biscuits and tea was provided for the retreatant priests at ten o'clock. I escaped the jovial clerical throng and went out of the grounds in search of a pub.

The Cat and the Fiddle on the Drumcondra Road welcomed me into its roaring bosom with an hour to closing time. I was standing sipping a glass of Guinness, trying to put my thoughts in order, when I felt a finger on my shoulder. I turned to find a stocky little man with pale, thinning hair and spectacles. I recognized him as one of the priests from All Hallows.

'You've escaped too,' he said, toasting me with his glass.

We sat ourselves down in a corner.

'So what do you make of Briege, Father?' he said.

He was surprised to discover that I was not a priest.

'She's great, but a bit manipulative,' I said.

'Rubbish!' said the priest. 'If you had an inkling of the problems she's sorting out among those priests you wouldn't say that.'

'So?'

'There are a lot of priests go off the rails; for some of them she's the only answer. Take me. I'm a chaplain in the Irish Army: my milieu is the NCOs' mess, not a nun's apron-strings. I was out in Beirut, being shelled. Some of our youngsters copped it. There's not an ounce of sentimentality in me, I can tell you. That woman put a finger on a deep-rooted problem I've had for ten years. She shocked the life out of me. She knew the effect she had, she's been keeping an eye on me. Several times she's looked across at me, and just the eye contact is enough.'

'Do you believe that she has special powers?' I asked.

'I do,' said the priest.

'But why *her*?'

'I don't know.'

'And how does it work?'

'I don't know,' said the priest. 'It's a mystery. And I'll tell you another thing . . .' He was looking me directly in the eye. 'Your coming here is no idle coincidence in your life; when you get mixed up with Briege it's for a reason.' The priest could see that he had embarrassed me. He guffawed to himself and took a draught of his stout.

He looked around the pub as if searching for a change of focus. Then he said, 'Briege can be a bit of holy terror, you know. When she was a novice she got hold of one of these fox furs that women used to wear – from the wardrobe of abandoned clothes from when they entered the convent. She ran this thing under the tap and put it at the bottom of the bed of the Mother Superior. They heard the screams all over Newry . . .'

*

I woke with a start and saw by my watch that it was two in the morning. I had fallen asleep on the bed after returning from the pub, and I was still fully dressed.

I felt restless, hungry. I wondered if I might find some biscuits in the room where the priests had gathered for their night collation. On tiptoe I went down the granite staircase to the ground floor, but everything had been cleared away in the common room and there wasn't a crumb to be found.

On the way back I stopped at the oratory door. It was open and a light was still on. I went in and sat down in sight of the Blessed Sacrament tabernacle.

I must have sat there for thirty minutes in the stillness of the night, thinking about faith and its relationship to evidence. Could faith be acquired by a sceptic who had merely been granted a small shred of evidence? Or did faith only feed on faith?

Sitting there gazing at the flickering sanctuary lamp, I began to wonder again whether it was possible to pray without faith. Did it make sense for an agnostic to seek guidance and help from God? Surely it was no more unreasonable, I thought, than the act of someone adrift at night on the ocean, who cries for help or fires a signal that may never be seen. What was the prayer of the agnostic, if it wasn't a cry for help?

Just at that point I noticed a Bible on the chair next to me, and I remembered Sister Briege's 'vision' that afternoon. 'I see you sitting in solitude in a chapel,' she had said. I picked it up and turned to Wisdom, Chapter Nine. It began with the passage:

God of our ancestors, Lord of mercy,
who by your word has made the universe . . .
grant me Wisdom, consort of your throne,

and do not reject me from the number of your children,
For I am your servant, son of your serving maid,
a feeble man, with little time to live,
with small understanding of justice and the laws . . .
What human being indeed can know the intentions of
God? . . .
It is hard enough to work out what is on earth,
laborious to know what lies within our reach;
who, then, can discover what is in the heavens?
And who could ever have known your will, had you not
given Wisdom?
who has learned thy counsel, unless
you sent your holy Spirit from above?

Had I been made especially susceptible by my mood, by an
indefinable sense of hunger and restlessness? Or was it one or
two drinks too many in the Cat and the Fiddle on the Drumcondra Road? Whatever the case, in the solitude and silence of the
oratory the words opened my mind and my heart; and the
phrase 'do not reject me from the number of your children'
echoed the yearnings I had felt when face to face with the
rejected religion of my childhood and youth in my American
dream. I wanted to believe this, and I was moved to tears by
the force of the appropriateness of the words I had read.

I lost all sense of time, until the tall windows captured the
first pale light of day. I felt that I had found an acceptable
prayer to pray, and in the silence and stillness of this moment
I was even prepared to believe it possible that my tears were a
token of the 'loving-kindness of the heart of our God', who
gives 'light to those in darkness'.

52   Journey's End

People who knew I had undertaken a journey in search of the supernatural made visible would ask, 'Have you come across *anything* that was absolutely inexplicable?' My first reaction was to say no, as I have said in the previous chapter.

That answer is not strictly true.

I have to admit, although it embarrasses me to do so, that I was baffled to the point of mystification by just one phenomenon: namely the tears of the Virgin of Syracuse. After looking at the evidence with some care I simply could not find an explanation as to how it might have happened. What is more, I was impressed by the fact that a similar phenomenon had occurred in Japan over a period of several years and, even as I write, there are reports of an identical phenomenon in New York City.

My reluctance to admit that I was impressed by this event stemmed from my unhappiness about the implications. For it seemed to me a crude, unaesthetic exhibition, and to focus merely on the lack of explanation was to put the phenomenon within the ambit of magic, and at the mercy of some scientific explanation in the future.

And what would be the purpose of such a miracle? To demonstrate the power, the legitimacy of the cult that laid claim to it? What if I heard of a Hindu or a Buddhist statue that wept, would I immediately accept that it lent credibility to

Hinduism or Buddhism? I rather think that I would not. In fact, I would tend to be annoyed at the idea that somebody should attempt to offer evidence for a creed or philosophy of the supernatural in this way.

There is, of course, a secondary question, one which addresses the meaning of the phenomenon: what is the significance of the Virgin's tears in traditional Mariology? Yet the symbolism of the sorrowing Virgin – in Michelangelo's *Pietà*, for example – has far more impact, it seems to me, as a product of religious and artistic imagination than as a magic trick on a plastic plaque; so why should the Virgin, or God, or any other supernatural being, take time out of eternity to create an effect that is more successfully achieved by human hands and heart? The obvious, and unsatisfactory, answer brings us back to the suggestion that it would be a display of power, an item of evidence.

As my journey progressed I became increasingly bored by the idea of *physical* prodigies: the gold Medjugorje rosaries, the liquefaction of blood in Naples, the jumping of Virgin statues. A token of my disgust with such miracles was my disinclination to walk even a few yards to witness such a thing. Crossing Europe on my way back from Italy I had stopped in Nevers in France and found myself deliberately deciding against visiting the incorrupt body of St Bernadette which, apparently, is there in the cathedral for all to see. The idea of such an exhibit seemed repellent and irrelevant.

By the time I had reached Syracuse I had undergone a change. I believe that I had begun to discern more clearly the difference between the apprehension of mystery on the one hand, and crude magic masquerading as supernatural evidence on the other. And this development in discernment had much to do with a stealthily growing conviction that I no longer had need of evidence.

*

After leaving Dublin, where, ironically, I had experienced that taste of tears, I was conscious of no great spiritual conversion. I had prayed, in the fashion of a shipwrecked mariner calling out for help on a dark sea – just in case. But I felt nothing. If anything I felt a sense of dryness, of cynicism even, at the exercise I had put myself through: the journalist in search of God – and in search of one or two good stories to boot on the way.

But the futility of the quest was even more apparent to me than those possible layers of self-seeking and self-deceit with which I had exploited my quest for faith. It reminded me of a priest friend who had a dream in which the members of a religious community were searching for God, in cupboards, in drawers, under the stairs, on the undersides of their plates. And yet, regardless of my explicit and my hidden motives, I realized that something had happened.

One morning after returning to England I drove up to the West Midlands to visit my old junior seminary. What led me there I have no idea, any more than I had an inkling what I should find there.

As I drove down the quiet country lane the building and its church looked much the same, but when I parked the car at the back of the buildings I began to see the extent of the calamity that had befallen the place. The refectory, the lecture rooms, the libraries and the cloisters had been looted, vandalized, devastated. The gardens, once beautifully tended, were swathed in bindweed; the little cemetery at the head of the valley was completely overgrown. Father Faber's retreat had been demolished by a falling tree, and the church was locked up. St Wilfred's, which had survived 200 years, educating so many generations of priests, was a ruined shell.

Standing in the main courtyard I looked up to see written in crudely painted letters an item of graffiti: *'This place is a shit hole!'* Indeed. The abomination of the desolation.

It struck me at that moment that I was beginning to understand an inner truth that I had been trying to articulate with difficulty for so many months. As a boy at St Wilfred's I had once listened during Easter week to a Franciscan retreat leader, talking of the strict vocation to the contemplative life in the silence and austerity of a Carthusian monastery. Afterwards I had walked in these same gardens thinking how heroic, how unattainable an ideal that was. How I longed for the courage to love God that much! And now, thirty years or so later, I was only just beginning to understand that the desert wilderness of spirituality is not to be found exclusively in those convents and houses of prayer where men and women dedicate themselves, externally, to the service of God. The desert may lie at the very heart of a person's life, in the depths of one's being.

Many people who have turned away from religion – even with a sense of hatred, rejecting all its idiosyncratic externals – to embrace scepticism, agnosticism, even militant atheism, are perhaps as much in the desert, in the 'dark night of the soul', as any contemplative. What we are fleeing, perhaps, is not God at all, but the false or the inadequate representations of him which hinder any possibility of ever making progress in coming to recognize him or reach out for him. What we are rejecting, even hating, is not God, but the 'trash and tinsel' that passes for him.

And thus it is that 'Hatred of God may bring the soul to God'.

As I walked through the devastated, deserted gardens of St Wilfred's, my younger self seemed to come to meet me: without reproach or condemnation on his part, and without remorse or self-recrimination on mine.

EPILOGUE

The Religious Imagination

Consider the striking preliminary vision in The Revelation to John:

> I saw . . . one, like a Son of man, dressed in a long robe tied at the waist with a belt of gold. His head and his hair were white with the whiteness of wool, like snow, his eyes like a burning flame, his feet like burnished bronze when it has been refined in a furnace, and his voice like the sound of the ocean. In his right hand he was holding seven stars, out of his mouth came a sharp sword, double-edged, and his face was like the sun shining with all its force.

To attempt to read the passage literally, applying strictly concrete or rigidly allegorical meanings, would severely diminish its power and significance. The polarities of snow and fire, rushing waters and roaring furnace, the majesty of the sun and stars contrasting with the tactile tensions of brass and wool, combined in the single image of a being both youthful and ancient, human and divine, are the discourse of poetry.

John brings to his writing the history of his own reading of Scripture, and his skill as a poet; and we, the readers, are invited to respond with an appropriate receptivity. We are aware that he is selecting, shaping, fusing images and allusions

383

to create an imaginative effect. He is inspired, but he is by no means recording a series of dictated instructions; his inspiration is that of the poet: captivated, yet free.

In drawing together Scripture and poetry in this way, I want to prepare the ground for suggesting, in conclusion, that a crucial key to understanding the nature of popular or folk mysticism involves an acknowledgement of the power of the imagination. I want to argue that through a deeper understanding of the nature of imagination, both artistic and religious, we may reclaim a wide range of religious experience from scientific debunking and religious fundamentalism.

This is by no means to propose that such mystical experience is purely subjective. It is a plea, rather, to elevate religious imagination above superficial fantasy and make-believe on the one hand, and fundamentalist magic on the other. It is no easy matter to distinguish fantasy from imagination, for the meanings are subject to alteration from era to era, but an essential distinction involves separating disinterested originality and creativity from shallow, vicarious figments of hallucination and ego-centred daydreaming.

Coleridge describes imagination as a shaping power, that 'dissolves, diffuses, dissipates in order to recreate', extending our consciousness by providing a new unity to our perceptions; it is an 'echo' of the imagination of God himself in his 'eternal creation'.

This is an extraordinarily radical notion; for he is suggesting that we can perceive God's action in the world through language, images, nature and human relationships. He is saying that God is to be apprehended not as an object competing for our attention with other objects in, or outside, the world, but wherever the imagination expresses itself in the opening up of the human heart. In this way, says Coleridge, it is possible to discover 'transcendence' in 'the incidents and situations of common life'.

Coleridge's favourite image of transcendence in nature ('counterfeit infinity', he sometimes called it) was the waterfall or the fountain: 'What a sight it is . . . the wheels, that circumvolve in it – the leaping up and plunging forward of that infinity of pearls and glass bulbs – the continual *change* of the *Matter*, the perpetual *Sameness* of the *Form* – it is an awful Image and Shadow of God and the world.'

This notion of the meeting of the finite and infinite in a single image prepares us for the idea of a symbol as something that, in Coleridge's words, 'partakes of the reality which it renders intelligible', as something that shares in the power, the mystery, the presence even, of what it represents.

Symbolism in this sense is not so much true or false, accurate or inaccurate, nor is it amenable to any of the measurements we would expect to bring to material phenomena. Symbols are weak or strong, depending on the extent to which they participate in the reality they exemplify.

At the same time, symbolism yields not to probing and measurement, but to sensitivity, tact and acquiescence; as Jacques Maritain puts it, we should 'listen to the interiority . . . to the poetic sense, be open to what it conveys, let ourselves be attracted by the magnetic ring . . . and this requires a sort of previous, tentative *consent*'. For the theologian Karl Rahner, this tentative consent is a 'pre-apprehensive openness in a person's nature to the mystery of being'.

It is clear that imagination, symbolism, in this sense, plays a crucial role in many forms of religious practice and experience: in the reading of Scripture, in prayer, in acts of faith, in liturgy; and in the highest mystical states, as widely endorsed by contemplatives such as John of the Cross, Teresa of Avila and Ignatius Loyola.

Epilogue

In the milieu of popular mysticism, however, there is a tendency to ignore the role of the imagination and to emphasize literalism. And yet, in the context of a Marian apparition, a prophecy, a miracle of healing, we surely should be prepared to interpret the externalization of the phenomena – the reported images, the iconography, the narrative and theatrical elements – as forms of interior and transcendental truth rather than as concrete descriptions. The intention should be to understand, as we would understand a poem or a piece of music, rather than to explain and control.

The Medjugorje and Garabandal apparitions are, as we have seen, unfolding stories in the context of the folk religion of Mediterranean communities. They are about the motherhood of God, the caring presence of her mediation, her assent to God exemplified in the Gospel of Luke. To the extent that apparitions symbolize Mary's promised availability, they offer the promise of her living participation in the narrative of the children who see and address her. Such apparitions could be said to be the language, the theatre, the liturgy of folk mysticism, the authentic imaginative perceptions of people steeped in traditions of local spirituality.

But fundamentalists will ask: what of the *reality* of Mary's presence? Is she really present in a spatio-temporal sense? And if she is not, how are we to distinguish genuine apparitions from make-believe?

This kind of questioning betrays, I believe, a lack of trust in the authenticity of the religious imagination of the child seers, as well as a lack of confidence in the discernment of those pilgrims who have made their journeys and experienced what they believe to be a sense of God's amnesty and mercy. This is not to evade the central question; for at the heart of mystical experience, poetic or religious, there seems to lie a deeply felt impression of real presence that goes beyond superficial literalness.

Thomas Merton once entered into correspondence with Aldous Huxley on the question of genuine and pseudo-mysticism. Merton wrote:

> What I would call a *supernatural and mystical* experience ... has in its very essence some note of a direct spiritual *contact of two liberties*, a kind of flash or spark which ignites an intuition ... plus something much more which I can only describe as 'personal', in which God is known not as an 'object' or as 'Him up there' or 'Him in everything' nor as 'the All' but as – the biblical expression – I AM, or simply AM ... this is not the kind of intuition that smacks of anything procurable because it is a presence of a Person and *depends on the liberty of that Person.*

The Medjugorje apparitions, as with those of Lourdes, Fatima and Garabandal, focus on the person of Mary, who in Catholic belief is the Mother of God. It seems to me that the notion of a child perceiving Mary's presence (which is rooted, in Catholic understanding, in God's presence) as a 'contact of two liberties' is equally valid. And to interpret the narrative and theatre of her visitations as symbolic rather than literal (in a procurable, spatio-temporal, concrete sense) is to enhance that presence rather than to diminish it.

The argument, I am convinced, can be extended across a great many experiential phenomena that have been covered in this book, including visions, divine healing, religious dreams, stigmata, prophecy, even, alas, in a negative and antagonistic sense, oppression and encounters with the so-called powers of darkness.

Such experiences and aptitudes are properly characterized as 'private revelation', in that they convey no infallible message from the supernatural to society at large (beyond an endorsement, or revaluation, of religion's traditional truths); yet neither can they be said to be purely subjective or fanciful.

Who are these seers, these stigmatics, the healers and

religious dreamers? They are special people, artists of the popular religious imagination, endowed with a more than usual sensitivity to the rhythms and archetypes of the transcendental, who are capable of perceiving a sense of the presence and love of God in vivid images and even physical symptoms.

To this end they may apprehend, exert a mastery over, unconscious archetypes (in a Jungian sense) and the physical workings of the body's autonomic and neuronal systems. They are not magicians, nor do they exert power in a dualistic realm of matter versus spirit; they inhabit our world of flesh and blood and people and human relationships, and work through them.

The principal opposition to such a view will come not from scientists, nor even from theologians, but from the religious fundamentalists who seek to subject supernatural encounters to management, exclusive ownership and manipulation. For the fundamentalist, the religious imagination is too inclusive, too open to religious pluralism, too liberal, too available to rival denominations and religions, and even to agnostics and atheists.

The awakening of religious imagination does indeed open the transcendental to all, for it is surely part of what it means to be fully human. It may come in various guises and in various degrees: through love; through poetry, music, art; through nature; through compassion for those who suffer or who are in need; through Scripture, prayer and ritual.

For some, like myself (and I must confess to being humbled by the admission), it may take an encounter with folk mysticism to kindle, or rekindle, the jaded religious imagination. The allure of such phenomena can be treacherous, for it can lead to narcissistic interiority, to the temptation of power and manipulation. For my own part, these wanderings in the milieu of popular mysticism led not to the discovery of evidence for the supernatural but to the conviction that I could no longer bask in confident unbelief.

Index

Italic references indicate illustrations

Index

Index

Index

Index

Index

Index